Related Books of Interest

Enterprise Master Data Management
An SOA Approach to Managing Core Information

By Allen Dreibelbis, Eberhard Hechler, Ivan Milman, Martin Oberhofer, Paul Van Run, and Dan Wolfson
ISBN: 0-13-236625-8

The Only Complete Technical Primer for MDM Planners, Architects, and Implementers

Enterprise Master Data Management provides an authoritative, vendor-independent MDM technical reference for practitioners: architects, technical analysts, consultants, solution designers, and senior IT decision makers. Written by the IBM® data management innovators who are pioneering MDM, this book systematically introduces MDM's key concepts and technical themes, explains its business case, and illuminates how it interrelates with and enables SOA.

Drawing on their experience with cutting-edge projects, the authors introduce MDM patterns, blueprints, solutions, and best practices published nowhere else—everything you need to establish a consistent, manageable set of master data, and use it for competitive advantage.

The Business of IT
How to Improve Service and Lower Costs

By Robert Ryan and Tim Raducha-Grace
ISBN: 0-13-700061-8

Drive More Business Value from IT…and Bridge the Gap Between IT and Business Leadership

IT organizations have achieved outstanding technological maturity, but many have been slower to adopt world-class business practices. This book provides IT and business executives with methods to achieve greater business discipline throughout IT, collaborate more effectively, sharpen focus on the customer, and drive greater value from IT investment. Drawing on their experience consulting with leading IT organizations, Robert Ryan and Tim Raducha-Grace help IT leaders make sense of alternative ways to improve IT service and lower cost, including ITIL, IT financial management, balanced scorecards, and business cases. You'll learn how to choose the best approaches to improve IT business practices for your environment and use these practices to improve service quality, reduce costs, and drive top-line revenue growth.

D0179530

Related Books of Interest

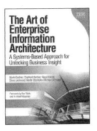

The Art of Enterprise Information Architecture
A Systems-Based Approach for Unlocking Business Insight

By Mario Godinez, Eberhard Hechler, Klaus Koenig, Steve Lockwood, Martin Oberhofer, and Michael Schroeck
ISBN: 0-13-703571-3

Architecture for the Intelligent Enterprise: Powerful New Ways to Maximize the Real-time Value of Information

Tomorrow's winning "Intelligent Enterprises" will bring together far more diverse sources of data, analyze it in more powerful ways, and deliver immediate insight to decision-makers throughout the organization. Today, however, most companies fail to apply the information they already have, while struggling with the complexity and costs of their existing information environments.

In this book, a team of IBM's leading information management experts guide you on a journey that will take you from where you are today toward becoming an "Intelligent Enterprise."

The New Era of Enterprise Business Intelligence:
Using Analytics to Achieve a Global Competitive Advantage

By Mike Biere
ISBN: 0-13-707542-1

A Complete Blueprint for Maximizing the Value of Business Intelligence in the Enterprise

The typical enterprise recognizes the immense potential of business intelligence (BI) and its impact upon many facets within the organization—but it's not easy to transform BI's potential into real business value. Top BI expert Mike Biere presents a complete blueprint for creating winning BI strategies and infrastructure, and systematically maximizing the value of information throughout the enterprise.

This product-independent guide brings together start-to-finish guidance and practical checklists for every senior IT executive, planner, strategist, implementer, and the actual business users themselves.

Listen to the author's podcast at:
ibmpressbooks.com/podcasts

Visit ibmpressbooks.com
for all product information

Related Books of Interest

Mining the Talk
Unlocking the Business Value in Unstructured Information

By Scott Spangler and Jeffrey Kreulen
ISBN: 0-13-233953-6

Leverage Unstructured Data to Become More Competitive, Responsive, and Innovative

In *Mining the Talk*, two leading-edge IBM researchers introduce a revolutionary new approach to unlocking the business value hidden in virtually any form of unstructured data–from word processing documents to websites, emails to instant messages.

The authors review the business drivers that have made unstructured data so important–and explain why conventional methods for working with it are inadequate. Then, writing for business professionals–not just data mining specialists– they walk step-by-step through exploring your unstructured data, understanding it, and analyzing it effectively.

Understanding DB2 9 Security
Bond, See, Wong, Chan
ISBN: 0-13-134590-7

DB2 9 for Linux, UNIX, and Windows
DBA Guide, Reference, and Exam Prep, 6th Edition
Baklarz, Zikopoulos
ISBN: 0-13-185514-X

Viral Data in SOA
An Enterprise Pandemic
Fishman
ISBN: 0-13-700180-0

IBM Cognos 10 Report Studio
Practical Examples
Draskovic, Johnson
ISBN-10: 0-13-265675-2

Data Integration Blueprint and Modeling
Techniques for a Scalable and Sustainable Architecture
Giordano
ISBN-10: 0-13-708493-5

Decision Management Systems

Dave -

Enjoy !

Palo Alto 2011

Decision Management Systems

Systems

A Practical Guide to Using Business Rules and Predictive Analytics

James Taylor

IBM Press
Pearson plc
Upper Saddle River, NJ • Boston • Indianapolis • San Francisco
New York • Toronto • Montreal • London • Munich • Paris • Madrid
Cape Town • Sydney • Tokyo • Singapore • Mexico City
ibmpressbooks.com

IBM Press Program Managers: Steven M. Stansel, Ellice Uffer
Cover design: IBM Corporation
Associate Publisher: Dave Dusthimer
Marketing Manager: Stephane Nakib
Executive Editor: Mary Beth Ray
Senior Development Editor: Kimberley Debus
Managing Editor: Kristy Hart
Designer: Alan Clements
Technical Editors: Claye Greene, Don Griest
Project Editor: Jovana San Nicolas-Shirley
Indexer: Lisa Stumpf
Compositor: Gloria Schurick
Proofreader: Seth Kerney
Manufacturing Buyer: Dan Uhrig

Published by Pearson plc

Publishing as IBM Press

IBM Press offers excellent discounts on this book when ordered in quantity for bulk purchases or special sales, which may include electronic versions and/or custom covers and content particular to your business, training goals, marketing focus, and branding interests. For more information, please contact

U. S. Corporate and Government Sales
1-800-382-3419
corpsales@pearsontechgroup.com

For sales outside the U. S., please contact

International Sales
international@pearson.com

ISBN-13: 978-0-13-288438-9
ISBN-10: 0-13-288438-0

Text printed in the United States on recycled paper at R.R. Donnelley in Crawfordsville, Indiana.
First printing October 2011

For Meri, even though it's not poetry

For my parents

And for my boys, again

Contents

Foreword by Deepak Advani

Over the last couple of decades, businesses gained a competitive advantage by automating business processes. New companies and ecosystems were born around ERP, SCM, and CRM. We are at a point where automation is no longer a competitive advantage. The next wave of differentiation will come through decision optimization. And at the heart of decision optimization is a smart decision system, a topic that James Taylor does an outstanding job of explaining in this book.

As James explains, a smart decision system encapsulates business rules, predictive models, and optimization. Business rules codify the best practices and human knowledge that a business builds up over time. Predictive models use statistics and mathematical algorithms to recommend the best action at any given time. Optimization, through constraint-based programming or mathematical programming techniques originally applied to operations research, delivers the best outcome. It is the combination of all three disciplines that enables organizations to optimize decisions. What used to be called artificial intelligence became predictive and advanced analytical techniques and are now Decision Management Systems, which are increasingly populating business processes and making adopters competitive.

As James describes in the book, a Decision Management System optimizes decisions not only for knowledge workers, but for all workers. This enables a call center representative to make the best offer to reduce customer churn, a claims processing worker to maximize fraud detection, and a loan officer to reduce risk while maximizing return. And it's not just decisions made by people— a Decision Management System can enable your e-commerce site to present the next best offer, traffic control systems to automatically make adjustments to reduce congestion, and so on. Well-designed Decision Management Systems keep track of decisions taken and outcomes achieved, then have the ability to make or recommend automatic mid-course corrections to improve outcomes over time. Decision Management Systems provide competitive differentiation through every critical business processes, at each decision point, leading to optimized outcomes.

I'm convinced that Decision Management Systems have the ability to deliver significant competitive advantage to businesses, governments and institutions. James does a thorough job of explaining the business value and the design elements of Decision Management Systems that are the enablers of a formidable business transformation.

Deepak Advani

Vice President, Business Analytics Products & SPSS, IBM

Foreword by Pierre Haren

In the past 30 years, the evolution of computer science can be described as a constant effort to "reify," a long march to transform all activities into "digital things." We started with the structuring of data and the advent of relational database systems, which led to the ascension of Oracle; then with the reification of processes, with the Enterprise Resource Planning software wave leading to the emergence of SAP, and later of I2 for Supply Chain Management and Siebel Systems for Customer Relationship Management.

We moved on to the Business Process Management wave, which now enables the description of most service activities into well-defined sequences of processes weaving human-based processes with computer-based processes. This BPM emergence sets the stage for the next reification wave: that of decisions.

And this is what this book by James Taylor is about: how we can transform the fleeting process of decisions into digital things that we can describe, store, evaluate, compare, automate, and modify at the speed required by modern business.

The rate of change of everything is the global variable, that has changed most over the last 30 years. Relational databases postulated the value of slow-changing table structures. Enterprise Resource Planning systems embedded best-of-breed processes into rather inflexible software architectures. However, nowadays, most decisions live in a very fast-changing environment due to new regulations, frequent catastrophic events, business model changes, and intensely competitive landscapes. This book describes how these decisions can be extracted, represented, and manipulated automatically in an AAA-rated environment: Agile, Analytic, and Adaptive.

The long successful industrial experience of the author and his supporting contributors, and the diversity of their background, has enabled them to merge the points of view of business rules experts with predictive analytics specialists and operations research practitioners. This variety of expert opinions on decisions and their reification has produced a very rich book sprinkled with real-life examples as well as battle-tested advice on how to define, implement, deploy, measure, and improve Decision Management Systems, and how to integrate them in the human fabric of any organization.

The next area in the continuous integration of humans and computers in our modern world will be decisions. All decision-making managers—that is, every manager—should use this book to get ahead of the competition and better serve their customers.

Pierre Haren
VP ILOG, IBM

Preface

Decision Management Systems are my business and one of my passions. I have spent most of the last decade working on them. Four years ago I wrote *Smart (Enough) Systems* with Neil Raden, in which we laid the groundwork for talking about Decision Management Systems. I have spent the time since then working with clients and technology vendors to refine the approach. I have read a lot of books on business rules, data mining, predictive analytics, and other technologies. I have had a chance to work with lots of great people with deep knowledge about the technologies involved. And I have been fortunate to work with many clients as they build and use Decision Management Systems. This book is the result.

The book is aimed at those at the intersection of business and technology: executives who take an interest in technology and who use it to drive innovation and better business results, and technologists who want to use technology to transform the business of their organization. You may work for a company that has already built a Decision Management System, perhaps even many of them. More likely you work for an organization that has yet to do so. This book will show you how to build Decision Management Systems, give you tips and best practices from those who have gone before, and help you make the case for these powerful systems.

I wrote the book the way I talk to my clients, trying to put on the page what I say and do when I am working with them. As a result, the book follows the same path that most organizations do.

It begins by setting a context and showing what is possible. By showing what others have done and discussing the Decision Management Systems that other organizations have built, the book draws out what is different about Decision Management Systems. By establishing that these systems are agile, analytic, and adaptive, it shows how these differences allow Decision Management Systems to be used to transform organizations in critical ways.

The core of the book describes the principles that guide the development of Decision Management Systems and lays out a proven framework for building them. It shows you how to find suitable decisions and develop the understanding of those decisions that will let you automate them effectively. It walks through how to use business rules, predictive analytics and optimization technology to build service-oriented components to automate these decisions. And it explains why monitoring and continuous improvement are so important to Decision Management Systems, and describes the processes and technology you need to ensure your Decision Management Systems perform for the long haul.

The book concludes with a set of people, process, and technology enablers that can help you succeed. The end result is a book that gives you the practical advice you need to build different kind of information systems—Decision Management Systems.

James Taylor
Palo Alto, California
james@decisionmanagementsolutions.com

Approach

The objective of this book is to give the reader practical advice on why and how to develop Decision Management Systems. These systems are agile, analytic, and adaptive—and they fundamentally change the way organizations operate. The book does not get into the details of every stage—it would have to be many times its length to do so—but focuses instead on the critical, practical issues of these systems.

If you are not sure about the value proposition of Decision Management Systems, or have never come across them before, read Part I—Chapters 1-4. These chapters will introduce Decision Management Systems, and give you a sense of their importance to your organization. If you are already sure that you want to build Decision Management Systems, skip straight to Chapter 5 and read Part II—the core "how-to" part of the book. Don't forget that first part, though—you will want to use it when building your business case!

If you are about to embark on building a Decision Management System, check out the people, process, and technology enablers in Part III, Chapters 8-10, if you haven't already.

How This Book Is Organized

This book is organized into three parts.

- **Part I: The Case for Decision Management Systems**

  The first four chapters make the case for Decision Management Systems—why they are different and how they can transform a 21st century organization.

  - **Chapter 1, "Decision Management Systems Are Different":** This chapter uses real examples of Decision Management Systems to show how they are agile, analytic, and adaptive.

  - **Chapter 2, "Your business is your systems":** This chapter tackles the question of manual decision-making, showing how modern organizations cannot be better than their systems.

  - **Chapter 3, "Decision Management Systems Transform Businesses":** This chapter shows that Decision Management Systems are not just different from traditional systems – they represent opportunities for true business transformation.

- **Chapter 4, "Principles of Decision Management Systems"**: By now you should understand the power of Decision Management Systems. This chapter outlines the key guiding principles for building them.

- **Part II: Building Decision Management Systems**

Chapters 5 through 7 are the meat of the book, outlining how to develop and sustain Decision Management Systems in your organization.

  - **Chapter 5, "Discover and Model Decisions"**: This chapter shows how to describe, understand, and model the critical repeatable decisions that will be at the heart of the Decision Management Systems you need.

  - **Chapter 6, "Design and Implement Decision Services"**: This chapter focuses on using the core technologies of business rules, predictive analytics, and optimization to build service-oriented decision-making components.

  - **Chapter 7, "Monitor and Improve Decisions"**: This chapter wraps up the how-to chapters, focusing on how to ensure that your Decision Management Systems learn and continuously improve.

- **Part III: Enablers for Decision Management Systems**

The final part collects people, process, and technology enablers that can help you be successful.

  - **Chapter 8, "People Enablers"**: This chapter outlines some key people enablers for building Decision Management Systems.

  - **Chapter 9, "Process Enablers"**: This chapter continues with process-centric enablers, ways to change your approach that will help you succeed.

  - **Chapter 10, "Technology Enablers"**: This chapter wraps up the enablers with descriptions of the core technologies you need to employ to build Decision Management Systems.

- **Epilogue**
- **Bibliography**

Acknowledgments

First and foremost I would like to acknowledge the support of IBM. Deepak Advani and Pierre Haren were enthusiastic supporters of the book as soon as I proposed it. Mychelle Mollot, Brian Safron, and Erick Brethenoux helped close the deal with IBM Press and get the whole process kicked off. Many others were incredibly helpful during the production of this book.

In particular, two IBM employees helped throughout the process. They supported me through the process, shared their thoughts and suggestions, helped me find other IBM experts in a number of areas, and made extensive direct contributions:

Erick Brethenoux—Executive Program Director, Predictive Analytics & Decision Management Strategy, IBM.

Erick's responsibilities within IBM include mergers and acquisitions, strategic planning, predictive analytics corporate messaging, and future scenarios analysis. He also plays a major role in the industry analyst activities and various operational missions within the company. Erick was a VP of Corporate Development at SPSS, the predictive analytics company that IBM acquired in 2009. Prior to SPSS, Erick was VP of Software Equity Research at Lazard Frères, New York, and Research Director of Advanced Technologies at the Gartner Group. Erick has published extensively in the domains of artificial intelligence systems, system sciences, applied mathematics, complex systems, and cybernetics. He has held various academic positions at the University of Delaware and the Polytechnic School of Africa in Gabon.

Jean Pommier—Distinguished Engineer & CTO, IBM

Jean is a Distinguished Engineer and CTO in the IBM WebSphere Services organization and is in charge of Service Engineering (implementation methods, best practices, and consulting offerings). Prior to joining IBM in 2008, he was ILOG's VP of Methodology. Jean joined ILOG upon its creation in 1987 in R&D, moving into consulting and then management in 1990. From 2003 to 2006, Jean led Worldwide Professional Services for ILOG; prior to that he headed worldwide consulting and U.S. sales operations for ILOG's largest division. Jean has contributed to more than 400 successful customer implementations of Decision Management Systems.

In addition, a number of IBM employees put their expertise to work helping me with specific sections. Many of them had to respond incredibly quickly so I could meet publishing deadlines and I could not have gotten the book done on time without them:

- Jerome Boyer—Senior Technical Staff Member, BPM & BRM Implementation & Methodology
- Dr. Asit Dan—SOA/BPM and Information Agenda Alignment, Chief Architect
- Sarah Dunworth—Advisory Product Manager
- Michael McRoberts—SPSS Chief Architect
- Dr. Greger Ottoson—Product Management, Business Process & Decision Management
- Vijay Pandiarajan—Product Marketing Manager, WebSphere Decision Management
- David Pugh—Senior Manager, Product Management, Business Analytics (SPSS)
- Bruno Trimouille—Program Director, WebSphere Worldwide Industry Marketing

In addition, a number of IBM staff helped me find suitable case study material:

- Dr. Jeremy Bloom—Senior Product Marketing Manager, ILOG Optimization
- Martha Mesa—Client Reference Manager, ILOG and WebSphere
- Caroline Poser—WebSphere Client Reference Manager
- Cheryl Wilson—BRMS Demand Generation Program Planning and Management

Pearson's team was superb as always. Mary Beth Ray, Chris Cleveland, Kimberley Debus, and Jovana Shirley all excelled and made what was a compressed production schedule look easy. Thanks also to Steve Stansel for managing the IBM Press end of the process.

I would also like to acknowledge the work of Dr. Alan Fish in the United Kingdom on decision dependency diagrams. Alan was generous with his time and ideas, and I for one am looking forward to his forthcoming book.

Thanks to you all. Without you the book would be thinner, less accurate, and less complete. Any remaining mistakes are my own.

About the Author

James Taylor is the CEO of Decision Management Solutions, and is the leading expert in how to use business rules and analytic technology to build Decision Management Systems. James is passionate about using Decision Management Systems to help companies improve decision-making and develop an agile, analytic, and adaptive business. He has more than 20 years working with clients in all sectors to identify their highest-value opportunities for advanced analytics, enabling them to reduce fraud, continually manage and assess risk, and maximize customer value with increased flexibility and speed.

In addition to strategy consulting, James has been a keynote speaker at many events for executive audiences, including ComputerWorld's BI & Analytics Perspectives, Gartner Business Process Management Summit, Information Management Europe, Business Intelligence South Africa, The Business Rules Forum, Predictive Analytics World, IBM's Business Analytics Forum, and IBM's CIO Leadership Exchange. James is also a faculty member of the International Institute for Analytics.

In 2007, James wrote *Smart (Enough) Systems: How to Deliver Competitive Advantage by Automating Hidden Decisions* (Prentice Hall) with Neil Raden, and has contributed chapters on Decision Management to multiple books, including *Applying Real-World BPM in an SAP Environment*, *The Decision Model*, *The Business Rules Revolution: Doing Business The Right Way*, and *Business Intelligence Implementation: Issues and Perspectives*. He blogs on Decision Management at www.jtonedm.com and has written dozens of articles on Decision Management Systems for *CRM Magazine*, *Information Management*, *Teradata Magazine*, *The BPM Institute*, *BeyeNetwork*, *InformationWeek*, and TDWI's *BI Journal*.

He was previously a Vice President at Fair Isaac Corporation, spent time at a Silicon Valley startup, worked on PeopleSoft's R&D team, and as a consultant with Ernst and Young. He has spent the last 20 years developing approaches, tools, and platforms that others can use to build more effective information systems.

He lives in Palo Alto, California with his family. When he is not writing about, speaking on or developing Decision Management Systems, he plays board games, acts as a trustee for a local school, and reads military history or science fiction.

I

The Case for Decision Management Systems

The first part of this book uses a group of real customer stories to make the case for a new class of systems—Decision Management Systems.

The organizations described are developing systems that are fundamentally different from what has gone before. These systems are agile, handling changing circumstances and allowing for continuous process improvement. They are also analytic, identifying and eliminating fraud, managing risk and targeting opportunities by analyzing the data these organizations have collected. Finally, they are adaptive, helping these organizations find and manage innovative new approaches to their business.

The context for these systems is one in which your business *is* your systems. The need for instant and 24/7 responsiveness, the changing scale of modern organizations, and the changing ways in which consumers and organizations interact all combine to make the behavior of your systems central to your organization's success. This context means that Decision Management Systems have the power to transform organizations, making those organizations fundamentally different from those without these systems.

This new class of systems has a set of principles that define them, that explain why they are different, and that allow them to have this transformative effect.

I

Decision Management Systems Are Different

Organizations of every size build, buy, and use information systems. For most organizations, information systems store and manipulate the information the organizations need—information about products, customers, suppliers, claims, transactions, payments, employees, sales orders, marketing campaigns, and much more. Almost everyone in the organization uses these systems, and many spend every hour at work interacting with them.

In many ways these systems have changed much in recent decades. The underlying technology has changed, and new systems handle more transactions more quickly than systems did in the past. The user interface of a typical system has improved, with graphical and web-based user interfaces replacing text terminals and greenbar reporting. New programming languages and design approaches have made development of these systems quicker and more reliable. Yet these systems continue to have a set of defining characteristics that have not changed:

- *They stop and wait rather than act:* Most information systems do not act on behalf of the organization or the users of the system. All too often they wait until a human operator comes along to tell them what to do next. At best they might ask, sending a notification that some action is required.

3

- ***They escalate rather than empower:*** *In a similar vein, they often don't allow the day-to-day users of the systems to take action either. Instead they require managers or supervisors to log in and approve actions. The call center representative or first point of contact cannot tell the system to do something but must instead refer customers or transactions to those more senior.*

- ***They report but don't learn:*** *These systems are full of information about customers, transactions, suppliers, employees, and much more. Most systems will allow this information to be reported out, or presented in some format for human consumption. What these systems don't do is learn from the data they contain; they don't improve their behavior based on what has happened in the past.*

- ***They have been built to last, not to change:*** *To be robust and scalable these systems have been built to last. They tend to be hard for non-technical people to understand; they are "opaque," making them hard to change and brittle when they are changed. IT departments act as the bottleneck through which all systems changes must pass, making change slow and expensive.*

Not all systems are like this. Over the last decade, many organizations have seen the value of developing Decision Management Systems. This new class of systems is increasingly in evidence and has a track record of success. Decision Management Systems are different from typical information systems in three ways—they are more agile, more analytic and more adaptive.

Agile

The word "agile" is overused when it comes to information systems. Making systems more agile—easier, quicker and cheaper to change in response to changing needs—is important in rapidly changing industries and circumstances. Many approaches and technologies are promoted as helping organizations become more agile or as helping organizations build information systems that are more agile. Most information systems are still not agile, however, and remain hard and expensive to change.

A Decision Management System is agile because it can be easily changed to respond to changing circumstances. Agility cannot come at the cost of being inefficient or non-compliant, so agile Decision Management Systems are also compliant and able to increase process effectiveness.

Changing Circumstances

One of the world's leading botanical beauty care retailers sells natu-rally-based beauty products to millions of customers through its 1,500 beauty centers and stores worldwide. Tens of millions of transactions a year are the basis for its loyalty program—a key differentiator from other beauty care retailers. This program is based on a constant series of promotions, with two rounds of promotions produced every month, each one comprising 50 items. It also offers special discounts on combina-tions of products when bought at the same time, as well as local promo-tions and other specials.

But the program faced numerous challenges. The company found it could not bring the promotions it wanted to market at the pace it was hoping for. New offers would take several weeks to be deployed by the IT department and had to conform to an overly restricted format. Once new offers were deployed, cashiers in its beauty centers could not keep track of the changing promotional offers. The offers were wide-ranging and often overlapping, with customers eligible for multiple discounts on the same order, further adding complexity. These problems meant that the program was not fulfilling the expectations of either the company or its loyal customers.

The retailer developed a Decision Management System to handle mar-keting promotions and the loyalty program. Using the point-of-sales transaction as well the customer profile and sales history, the system ensures that all applicable customer discounts and loyalty rewards are calculated automatically. Embedded in the point-of-sale terminal itself, the system makes the pricing decision for the cashiers. The same infor-mation is also used to present business- and relationship-maximizing cross-sell offers to the customer during checkout. All the promotions, eligibility rules, and calculations are centrally managed in a business-friendly format, allowing for rapid changes and deployment.

With the new system in place, the company saw a four-fold improve-ment in the time to market for hundreds of promotional offers every month. With more flexibility, the offers could be more creative and heavily personalized to target each customer. Accuracy improved too, with the most loyal customers getting the maximum discount, accu-rately calculated and very timely. Using the current basket of purchases to drive cross-sell offers represented a clear advantage over the fixed offers made by competitors, and the automation of the calculations reduced check-out time, further improving customer service. In some areas where the solution has been implemented the company has seen a 20 percent lift in revenue in one year.

Compliance

Decision Management Systems like this offer agility—an ability to make changes quickly—but the changes have to be the right changes. Particularly when systems must be compliant with external regulations or internal policies, Decision Management Systems can deliver agile compliance. Consider Benecard, a leading provider of prescription benefit programs. Benecard works with an extensive network of pharmacies nationwide and provides prescription drug programs and specialized services to organizations across the public and private sectors.

One of the critical services Benecard provides to its customers (healthcare insurance plans) is the processing and settling of prescription drug claims. How well a claim transaction is handled can affect everything from service commitments and regulatory compliance to a plan's profitability and ability to attract and retain members. As a pharmacy benefits management company, Benecard needs a claims system that supports a complex distribution channel, delivers customized programs, and meets changing market and regulatory demands.

Benecard built a new claims system—a Decision Management System—in a Service Oriented Architecture (SOA). The company improved collaboration between business and IT by allowing senior pharmacist business users to work with a business analyst to define, test, create, and maintain the many rules that determine which claims should be paid. These rules validate member, claim, and clinical data as well as handling segmentation and assignment, adjudication, payment, and settlement. These rules are compliant with regulations that vary from state to state, as well as with federal regulations such as the Health Insurance Portability and Accountability Act (HIPAA).

The new claims system delivered time-to-market gains of more than 70 percent, a reduction in claims processing time and costs by 30% and an increase in pass-through rate of more than 80%. Benecard can roll out new programs and add members faster and demonstrate its compliance thanks to comprehensive audit trails of rules and decisions rendered at any given time.

Process Improvement

Another healthcare company illustrates a common consequence of improved agility—an ability to dramatically improve the effectiveness of business processes. HealthNow New York is the leading healthcare company in western New York. Since 1936, it has been a pioneer in providing quality healthcare services to companies and individuals in the region. With approximately 680,000 insured members, HealthNow New York provides a full spectrum of healthcare services including disease and care management, pharmacy benefit management, and physician and hospital quality incentive plans.

Like many companies of its size, HealthNow had multiple legacy systems and a number of manual and disjointed processes. This was having an impact on its ability to respond quickly to changes in regulatory, internal, and external mandates. Integrating and maintaining these systems was a costly and resource-intensive endeavor. Core processes such as member enrollment were hard-coded, making it difficult to implement policy changes and perform critical tasks in a timely and cost-effective manner. The enrollment process was predominantly paper-intensive with several manual touch-points, thus elevating the risk of errors and delays.

HealthNow built a new member enrollment process using a modern Business Process Management System in an SOA. A Decision Management System was built to automate, optimize, and monitor key business decisions throughout the enrollment process. These key processes included determining eligibility and applicable coverage, easily identifying pending enrollment and exception cases, processing new member application and current member policy changes, enforcing regulatory compliance, disseminating tasks, and triggering notifications as required.

HealthNow demonstrated the benefits of this with a dramatic improvement in agility—it showed time-to-market gains of more than 50%. The company could introduce new behaviors into systems in days rather than weeks or months thanks in part to increased collaboration between the business and IT. The overall process showed a reduction in enrollment time and administrative costs as well as improved end-to-end visibility that resulted in greater clarity, accuracy, and consistency.

Improving Decision Making by Capturing Rapidly Changing Know-How

Decision Management Systems deliver significantly greater agility than traditional systems. This agility is focused on improving decision-making by capturing rapidly changing know-how. The beauty retailer captured the know-how of its marketing team to create an agile loyalty and rewards program. Benecard made sure it stayed up to date with regulations so it could deliver great services for its customers. HealthNow used agility in decision making to radically overhaul its member enrollment process.

Analytic

Analytics is a hot topic and a focus area for investment in many organizations. Much of this investment is targeted at helping business people become more analytical in how they make decisions by giving them visualization and analysis tools. Although many underlying information systems remain unable to use the data they store, new analytic Decision Management Systems are using this data to act analytically on behalf of their users. These Decision Management Systems are analytic in how they target and retain customers, how they manage risk and fraud, and how they focus limited resources where they will be most effective.

Managing Risk

Managing risk is a critical aspect of Decision Management Systems. The first real commercial use of predictive analytics was to manage credit risk by predicting the likelihood that a consumer would miss a payment in the immediate future. The first Decision Management Systems took these predictions and made decisions with them to better manage credit risk. Managing risk—credit risk as well as other risks—remains one of the leading uses of Decision Management Systems. More recently, the use of analytic Decision Management Systems to manage insurance risk has significantly increased.

One leading property and casualty insurance company with more than $20 billion in net premiums earned uses Decision Management Systems to manage risk in business insurance. Business insurance is one of the company's three major business segments and is divided into a number of markets. One of these sells a variety of insurance products to small businesses (those with fewer than 50 employees) and represents just under one quarter of the company's total business insurance volume.

The small business insurance market is competitive, and this company identified several business drivers to gain a competitive advantage. This included getting products to market quickly, more sophisticated and granular pricing, responding to changes quickly, and being easier to do business with.

The previous policy processing system couldn't support automated underwriting and pricing. Only 17% of small commercial policies qualified for straight-through processing, and rules could not be changed quickly. Crucially, the old system was also unable to differentiate between risks, so it priced them all the same. This led the company to become a victim of "adverse selection."

ADVERSE SELECTION

Adverse selection refers to the process by which an insurer that prices in a less granular way than its competitors acquires an unusually high number of "bad" customers. The process works like this: Within a pricing tier, all customers get the same price. Some of these customers are good—they are less risky than the average for the group—and some are bad. If another company offers several price tiers to this same group of customers, the "bad" customers will tend not to switch as their price will be better if they stay, but the good customers will likely get a better price from the competitor. The effect is that a company "selects" more bad risks when its risk pricing is less granular than its competitors.

It now offers a complete, quote-to-issue platform for agents and customers. This has proved itself to be an important element in its go-to-market strategy in the small business segment.

At the core of the new platform is an underwriting Decision Management System. A predictive analytic model—a multivariate pricing model—was used to target pricing based on risk. An initial buildout of models used three years' worth of data and a thorough examination of various "what if" scenarios using a predictive analytic workbench. Every quote is now saved for future analysis so the models can be refined based on results. This new risk model was wrapped with business rules to ensure that the right policies and regulations were applied and that models could drive completely automated underwriting decisions.

The resulting analytic Decision Management System increased the written premium by 50%. Straight-through processing rose to 75% resulting in an increase in overall business flow of 73%. The number of agents quoting increased 19%, the number of quotes per agent increased 26%, and the submission flow increased 50%.

Reducing Fraud

Another key use of predictive analytics is in the reduction and management of fraud. Grupo Bancolombia, Colombia's largest private bank, has more than 6 million customers, US $31 billion in assets, 700 branches, and 2,300 ATMs. The bank provides traditional commercial and retail banking services, including checking and savings accounts, loans and mortgages, investment banking, and brokerage services. As the nation's leading bank, it strives to set the standard for banking practices and regulatory compliance. One critical area for fraud and compliance is detecting and preventing money laundering through its accounts.

After the passage of stricter money laundering reporting requirements for Colombia's banks, Bancolombia needed to develop new approaches to analyzing transaction data. In addition, an acquisition that substantially enlarged the bank revealed serious drawbacks in its old approach. Under its old decentralized system, staff routinely had to analyze 120,000 customers and transactions per year. Despite this huge amount of analysis, only about 400 reports of suspicious operation were filed with the government, and only 57% of those achieved the government's highest quality and thoroughness rating.

Bancolombia mined its transactional data to detect suspicious transactions that may have resulted from money laundering or terrorism financing. The resulting predictive analytic model powered a Decision Management System that flagged customers and transactions as suspicious. This model-driven Decision Management System produced rapid, significant benefits for the bank. It enabled its specialized analysis unit to narrow its focus to smaller, more precise segments. From 120,000 analyses it was able to focus on just 5,000 to 6,000 identified by the system. Despite this twenty-fold reduction, the bank increased the number of suspicious operation reports filed with the government from 400 to 1,200—an increase of 200%. There has also been a substantial improvement in the quality of these reports, with 97% now meeting the highest rating in terms of quality and thoroughness.

An unsought but welcome benefit has been huge productivity savings generated by this new approach. The bank has been able to redeploy nearly all of the more than 1,000 team members who used to do the reviews. The new system only requires 22 people, so the bank has been able to transfer almost 80% of those resources into bringing new business into the bank and improving the bottom line. This ability to move staff from dealing with transactions to focusing on the business as a whole is a typical side effect of analytic Decision Management Systems.

Fraud is also an issue in insurance, where detecting and handling fraudulent claims is critical to overall profitability. Infinity Property & Casualty Corporation, a provider of nonstandard personal automobile insurance with an emphasis on higher-risk drivers, depends on its ability to identify fraudulent claims for sustained profitability. Following the implementation of a pre-configured Decision Management System, it has doubled the accuracy of fraud identification, contributing to a return on investment of 403% per a Nucleus Research study. In addition to increasing the accuracy of fraud identification, the referral time to send those claims to Infinity's Special Investigative Unit has gone from 45–60 days down to 1–3 days, and customer service has been enhanced through fast payment of legitimate claims, contributing to above-average company growth.

This Decision Management System combines predictive analytics with business rules and what-if analysis in a single system. The system allows business users to ensure the best possible outcome by defining and performing what-if simulations and adjusting the parameters for different situations. Business managers can also quickly modify rules, events, and processes and see their changes deployed immediately, giving them the flexibility to make adjustments as business needs change. As a result, claims adjusters and others with in-depth business knowledge can quickly and easily define how risk should be assessed and automate many routine decisions while retaining full control of the claims handling process.

Targeting and Retaining

Analytic Decision Management Systems originally focused on improving risk and fraud decisions. With the potential for a large downside on each decision—undetected fraud or unmanaged risk translates into losses very directly—the value of a Decision Management System is high. This was important when building these systems was expensive, but as the price of developing analytics and Decision Management Systems has come down, their potential in marketing has exploded. Many organizations use analytic Decision Management Systems to target customers and expand their relationship effectively. One such example is Carrefour Group. Carrefour is Europe's #1 grocery retailer, offering brand name and private label products through a wide range of retail formats from hypermarkets to convenience stores.

Grocery chains like Carrefour are in a ceaseless battle for market share and customer loyalty is critical to growth. Building, sustaining, and strengthening customer loyalty drives store designs, product selections and staffing decisions, not to mention revenue and profitability growth. Carrefour realized that loyalty programs, promotions, and coupons could reinforce the value of its brand across all retail formats and create a common customer experience.

Carrefour's vision was of a Decision Management System that would decide what would be a compelling promotional offer based on each consumer's unique purchasing patterns—regardless of where the consumer shopped. These offers would be highly tailored yet integrated with existing loyalty programs. For example, Carrefour might create a campaign for customers that have purchased organic food products, but have yet to try organic health and beauty aids. To target this customer segment, Carrefour wanted a system capable of crafting a sophisticated and focused promotional program and delivering it at the point of sale.

Carrefour was able to use its in-house analytics expertise to understand its customers and their buying behavior. A Decision Management System leveraged these analytic insights to create more effective promotion programs. Marketers can now craft sophisticated promotional programs using these analytics to target particular groups of customers and particular products. They are able to take available promotional tools such as coupons and loyalty program incentives and analytically determine the optimal mix.

The resulting guidance is managed centrally and then propagated out to each of Carrefour's stores, where a process called offer arbitration micro-optimizes these offers on a customer-by-customer basis. Triggered by the customer's purchases and the scanning of the loyalty card during the checkout process, the software determines the optimal offer incentive. These offers are delivered direct to point-of-sale terminals. The fully integrated solution then prints the coupon, issues the discount and updates the customer's loyalty account—all in real time.

The new model for managing promotional campaigns gets Carrefour closer to its customers, gives it greater control, and vastly improves its overall effectiveness. The new system allows Carrefour to develop deep knowledge of its customers. By tracking transaction history, Carrefour can determine not only which products customers buy but also which promotions they are most likely to respond to, who its most profitable customers are, what products they buy now, and what products they would be willing to buy if the incentive was right.

These analytic insights are put to work in more effective promotional campaigns to drive increased revenue. Carrefour's ability to create, monitor, and continuously adapt these programs helps ensure the effectiveness of the programs and means that Carrefour develops an ever-deeper understanding of its customers, building customer loyalty and a stronger Carrefour brand in the process. A shorter campaign planning-to-execution cycle means faster feedback on promotional effectiveness. More detailed feedback to suppliers improves supplier relationships and the overall efficiency of the system reduces marketing costs.

Focusing Resources

Analytics, especially analytics embedded in Decision Management Systems, are effective at managing risk, reducing fraud and maximizing opportunity. Analytics can also focus constrained resources on the right problem, maximizing their value. One of the most vivid examples of this comes in the use of analytics by public safety organizations like the Richmond Police Department.

Not long ago, violent crime in the city of Richmond, VA, was spiraling out of control. In 2004, Richmond was the ninth most dangerous city in the US, according to annual crime rankings published by Morgan Quitno Press. The following year, the city climbed to fifth. Facing a rising crime rate, the Richmond Police Department needed an efficient and cost-effective way to analyze crime data, assess public safety risks, and make intelligent decisions about personnel deployment.

The Department used a predictive analytic workbench to discover hidden relationships in the data and automatically generate crime forecasts. Predicted crime patterns drove proactive decisions to deploy resources to curb crime.

It usually takes years for police officers to gain a deep understanding of a city's crime patterns. A Decision Management System built around predictive analytics software means that even rookie officers can wield veteran-like knowledge. The model effectively does the work that previously required years of experience. It enables the Department to be efficient about how, where, and when to deploy patrol and tactical units and gives inexperienced officers immediate veteran-level insight into fighting crime.

After the Department deployed the solution, Richmond's crime rates began plummeting. Most notably, the homicide rate dropped 32% from 2006 to 2007, and an additional 40% from 2007 to 2008. The city's dangerous city ranking dropped too—all the way from fifth to 99th.

It's not just human resources that can be focused using Decision Management Systems—the use of physical resources can be optimized also. Aéroports de Paris manages the airports for the city of Paris—Paris-Charles de Gaulle, Paris-Orly, and Paris-le Bourget. Every day it must allocate physical resources from gates and parking stands to luggage conveyer belts and check-in counters for 1,500 flights. It needs to prevent congestion in the air and on the ground so that more than 150,000 air travelers can flow smoothly through the airports. Manual decision-making for a problem of this complexity results in under-utilized and poorly allocated resources. It also takes too long—the manual process for allocating flights to gates, for instance, used to take four hours.

Aéroports de Paris built a Decision Management System to handle this complexity. The new system allocates parking stands to flights while considering everything from security and fuel handling to airline preferences and schedules. Once the best solution is found, all the primary ground resources, like buses and gates, are also assigned. The system considers long-term trends too, assuring continuity for airlines so they can become familiar with their assignments.

The system does all this in just minutes. This means the staff has more time to check and fine-tune the results, and more importantly, it can be used to re-plan in the face of the unexpected. Now when equipment breaks down or the weather causes problems, the allocation of resources can be reassessed immediately to ensure the best possible response. Thanks to the system and its more effective allocation of resources, Aéroports de Paris has fewer flight delays, faster times through the airport for passengers and lower operating costs.

Improving Decision-Making by Using Data to Make More Precise, More Targeted Decisions

Decision Management Systems use the data available to them, delivering analytic decisions where traditional systems deliver only reporting. This analytic decision-making puts historical data to work predicting the future. Predicted insurance risk avoids adverse selection and better targets business customers. Group Bancolumbia used its data to predict money laundering and other criminal fraud, while Infinity Insurance identified high risk claims that needed detailed reviews. Carrefour targeted loyalty customers based on everything it knew about them, while the Richmond Police Department and Aéroports de Paris put constrained resources to work where the data said they would be most effective.

Adaptive

The final element of Decision Management Systems is that they are adaptive. Decision Management Systems help organizations test new approaches and learn about them. As organizations become more agile and more sophisticated in their use of analytics, Decision Management systems can also help them manage tradeoffs between their objectives.

Finding New Approaches

KPN is one of Europe's leading telecommunications and ICT services companies. In its home market in the Netherlands, KPN offers fixed-line and mobile telephony, Internet, and television services to consumers, as well as end-to-end telecommunications and ICT services to business customers. The company also operates several highly successful mobile brands in Germany and Belgium, and its subsidiary Getronics provides ICT services to companies within the Benelux region and across the globe. In total, KPN has more than 40 million customers and 33,000 employees, and reported revenues of € 13.5 billion in 2009.

KPN uses analytics to segment customers into groups based on their corporate profile, the products they have purchased, their usage of fixed-line, mobile, and broadband services, their retention rate, and numerous other criteria. Embedded in a marketing Decision Management System, this analytic approach helps KPN target its direct marketing campaigns more effectively, improving customer response by 400 to 1,000 percent.

The system also lets the company see how well new approaches might work. When qualitative research suggested that its best customers wanted to be contacted more often than the three times in the six month period limit KPN had set, the system allowed it to see that making one additional marketing interaction every six months to the right group could increase KPN's revenue from certain groups of customers by 50 to 70%.

The qualitative research suggested the possibility of improved results and the system allowed KPN to see what the impact of different approaches would be. It helped KPN find the right way to use this extra interaction with its best customers.

Testing and Learning

One of the most important ways in which a Decision Management System can be adaptive is in its support of a test-and-learn approach. Decision Management Systems often allow multiple approaches to decision-making to be defined. These approaches are tested against each other in the only laboratory that works when you are trying to see how consumers will react—the real world.

Equifax is a global leader in information solutions, managing and delivering one of the world's largest sources of consumer and commercial data. In addition to providing data to power the Decision Management Systems of others, Equifax's InterConnect® platform is a specialized Decision Management System for credit risk decisioning that is licensed to financial services and other companies to help them manage credit accounts more profitably. One of the most powerful elements of this platform is how it supports a test-and learn-approach.

Within InterConnect for Account Management, a bank or credit union can define multiple credit policies. These policies define what credit limit might be approved for an account, when a credit line increase might be appropriate, or what kind of credit product should be offered. The financial institution sets up a default approach and identifies the others for testing. What-if analysis tools compare the approaches and estimate the likely difference between them based on past results.

Just because what-if analysis identifies an approach as superior, however, does not mean it will actually work better when it is tried on real customers. As many companies have found out to their cost, consumers are not entirely predictable. Instead of relying on offline analysis,

InterConnect allows institutions to test new approaches in the real world. As consumers apply for credit from the financial institution, most are processed using the default approach, while some are processed using one of the test approaches. The system carefully tracks which approach was used for which consumer. As time passes, the institution gathers information about which approach works best—which results in the lowest rate of default, highest rate of usage, and greatest customer satisfaction, for instance.

Once the results are in for the test groups, the institution can run reports and do analysis to see how the overall results would look if the different approaches were applied to everyone. From this the institution learns which approach it should use in the future. The agility of the Decision Management System means it is easy to change the default approach to the one with the best results, and easy as well to create new approaches to see how they could be even better. A never-ending cycle of continuous improvement can begin.

Managing Trade-offs

Adaptive Decision Management Systems can help organizations find new approaches and conduct experiments to test and learn what works or will work best. As decisions become more complex, as there are more objectives to be considered, and more data about what might work, it becomes essential that they also manage complex tradeoffs.

One company uses Decision Management Systems to help airlines manage their operations and provides other services for travel companies. Airline planning and operations decisions are driven by the desire to minimize operating cost while simultaneously maximizing operating profit. Airlines have access to limited resources (aircraft, crew, airport systems) so effective planning is essential for profitability and survival.

For instance, daily airline schedules are rarely flown as planned due to weather, air traffic control, labor unrest, mechanical problems, and security procedures. Disruptions can have a significant impact on operations due to the complex interactions between aircraft, flight crews, and passengers. When schedules are disrupted, there is often no "good" answer, only complex tradeoffs to make. Decision Management Systems help airlines better manage off-schedule operations and disruptions while providing them with the ability to re-accommodate passengers and thus improve the overall passenger travel experience.

Schedules are not the only place where airlines must manage complex tradeoffs. With customers increasingly price-driven and booking closer to departure, airline travel has become a more dynamic market place. This conflicts with traditional revenue management systems, which assume more stable patterns of customer purchasing behavior. This company also delivers Decision Management Systems to help manage the revenue management tradeoffs in this new environment. These systems determine the set of revenue management controls that will maximize revenue given the current competitive situation and airline data. Strategic objectives can be expressed in terms of business rules and fed into the Decision Management System to determine feasible revenue management actions given all the various tradeoffs.

This more complex revenue management environment extends to travel agencies. Faced with declining commissions and increasing competition, agencies must strike and manage incentive deals that pay override commissions or guarantee fare discounts. Another Decision Management System evaluates pending supplier deals and constructs the best possible supplier deal portfolio from them. This allows agencies to manage and drive demand to maximize revenue. The same system also provides appropriate sales targets given the current set of supplier deals. This system allows agencies to negotiate better supplier deals and reduces deal conflicts while providing the right sales targets.

Continuously Improving Decision-Making by Adapting and Learning

Decision Management Systems are much more adaptive than traditional systems. This makes for systems that learn and improve over time. KPN used it to find new approaches and to see how effective it could be. Equifax used it to test multiple approaches and see what worked best. The complex tradeoffs of the airline and travel industry can only be resolved by such adaptive systems.

2

Your Business Is Your Systems

Many organizations regard information systems as a necessary evil. Information about customers must be managed, orders must be stored so they can be retrieved and tracked, and so on. They have a perception of themselves and a go-to-market strategy that does not reflect their information systems. They may have a poor CRM system, but they pride themselves on delivering excellent customer service. Their claims processing system may be antiquated and out of date, but their claims adjusters are excellent. Every application may have to be reviewed manually, but they take a great deal of care in how they train case workers to make sure that the eligibility of each application is assessed accurately.

This approach is increasingly impractical. Organizations of any size increasingly are their information systems—the behavior of their systems determines the behavior of the organization as a whole. The way their website behaves directly influences their prospective customers. The way their call center systems behave directly influences their ability to serve their customers. The way their marketing system behaves constrains their ability to segment and target their customers.

Decision Management Systems are a new class of system. Offering dramatic improvements in performance, Decision Management Systems are agile, analytic, and adaptive. Decision Management Systems are easier, cheaper, and quicker to change in the face of changing needs. Decision Management Systems put the data you have to work, making decisions based on the analysis of data as well as judgment and policy. Decision Management Systems adapt to constantly changing circumstances, continually trying new approaches to see what will work best as situations change. These systems represent a significant departure from previous generations of information systems.

However, the premise of this book is not just that Decision Management Systems are a new class of system. Decision Management Systems do not just change the way you think about systems, nor do they simply change the quality of your information systems portfolio. Decision Management Systems fundamentally change your organization. Using Decision Management Systems changes organizations, altering long-held assumptions about the way organizations must work and exploring new frontiers for efficiency and effectiveness.

Adding a new class of system and changing the way you think about the systems you build has a profound effect on your business because your systems are your business. Changing expectations of consumers and companies, ever increasing demands for scale and changes in the nature of organizations mean that the way your systems operate determines how your organization operates. The way your systems interact with people determines how your organization interacts with customers, suppliers, and partners.

Changing Expectations

One of the biggest changes facing organizations is the change in consumer expectations. Consumers have become accustomed to real-time responses from the online retailers they do business with. They are increasingly aware of their ability to do business globally with whomever they wish. They can do more for themselves using increasingly sophisticated self-service applications and devices. Whether acting as customers, or as suppliers or partners, consumers have new expectations that are driving organizations to rethink their systems.

Real-Time Responsiveness

It was not very long ago that the process to get personal unsecured credit was a long one. Consumers would have to fill out paper forms, submit them to a bank, and then wait days or possibly weeks to hear whether their application had been accepted. Consumer expectations were that complex decisions such as this one took a while, and this was reflected in their interactions with companies. If it took a while to order something that was out of stock or if a question required a few days waiting, then it just did. All this has changed as we enter the era of real-time, instant gratification.

Leading direct-to-consumer businesses now deliver real-time, immediate responses to consumer requests. Consumers can get instant credit in a retail store, using the new credit card to buy what is already in their basket. Online they can fill in a web form and be approved for auto insurance or have a medical claim paid directly into their bank account. Call center representatives reconfigure customer mobile devices and change service plans while they are on the phone. When they make an online payment it is processed immediately, and they have instant access to the service they have purchased. Even when they must wait for physical goods to be shipped, they get real-time notifications of the package's journey and continual updates on its status. 24/7, real-time responsiveness has become a mainstream expectation.

Whether organizations like it or not, this is the world in which they must now operate. When an insurance company gets a claim, the applicant is increasingly going to expect a real-time response. When a company wants to know whether a particular order can be shipped today, it expects its supplier to know. Companies expect this response no matter what time zone they are in and no matter what time it is for the organization they are talking to.

This move to real-time responsiveness creates a challenge for many organizations. Most organizations still have people involved in many of their processes. These people are not involved in the process to handle exceptions or to provide excellent customer service to good customers. These people are involved in the process because the process itself and the systems that support it *require* people to make the process execute correctly, to ensure that the customers get what they want.

A process that relies on people as part of its everyday operation, however, cannot complete in real-time. People just don't respond that quickly. People are more flexible and more understanding, but they simply take longer to do things, especially to do things manually. Only systems can respond in real time, so in a real-time world what matters is the behavior of systems. If the organization's systems don't allow for this kind of real-time responsiveness, then the organization will not be able to meet these expectations. If an organization's systems do not deliver appropriate, effective, real-time responses, then the organization cannot do so.

Global Customers Expect Global Service

It is a cliché that we live in a "flat" world. Many organizations are doing business all over the world. Suppliers, customers, partners, and staff could be anywhere. These global organizations look for suppliers and partners that can deliver consistent products and services world-wide. They want to know that their staff will be treated consistently in different locations and that they can move their business to a new location without having to re-think everything.

As organizations develop truly global supply chains and serve customers around the world, expectations of consistent service have only grown. If consumers can get a product delivered to their home in London, they will expect to be able to have it delivered to them in New York when they are staying with friends there. A company with stores all over the world will only value a supplier's promise of overnight restocking for a product if that offer is true for all those stores.

Delivering global or even widespread consistency puts real strain on traditional systems. Local exceptions, regulations, and norms must be accounted for while still delivering global consistency. Customers may be talking to a call center representative in one country to place an order in a second country for delivery to a third country. It is impractical for the users of the system to keep track of the rules and regulations that apply; the system must do it for them. Only an organization that can embed the management of this complexity into its information systems is going to be able to offer the consistent, global customer service increasingly expected by these customers.

Self-Service

Physical self-service transformed retailers in the 20th century. The principle that shoppers could and should select their own cuts of meat, their own vegetables, and more, completely overturned traditional models of retail operation. In the 21st century, self-service information systems are expanding this throughout every aspect of business. Consumers expect to be able to manage their accounts, track their spending, or determine the status of something they care about without having to wait on hold for an operator or talk to someone in a branch or retail outlet. Consumers want to be able to change their cell phone plan, increase their credit line, renew their web account, and manage their online identity. They deal with online retailers and other organizations that allow them to maintain their preferences, their credit cards, delivery addresses and much more for easy use. Any change they want to make to this information they can make for themselves. These consumers don't contact the call center to ask for help and they don't visit retail locations—they expect to be able to do everything for themselves online.

As soon as customers adopt this self-service mentality, they become focused not on what your organization wants to allow but on what your systems *actually* allow. Self-service increasingly means interacting directly with an organization's systems or with a user interface layered on top of those systems. What customers can do for themselves is limited to what the systems allow.

Airline check-in kiosks and automated teller machines provide an ever-increasing array of services. Company websites have grown from providers of information to hubs of electronic service. These self-service venues rely completely on underlying information systems. If the information system does not allow or cannot support something, then there is no self-service option. Inadequate systems cannot be compensated for with staff, as there is no staff present. Organizations that need to deliver effective self-service must do so by building information systems that do so.

The 24/7 World

Finally there is the reality of the always-on environment of the 21st century. The Internet, smart phones, widespread WiFi, and other technologies ensure that consumers and companies are always "on"—always able to want something, ask for something, or need something. Providing staff at the other end of a phone 24/7 is expensive, and providing them locally is unrealistic for most organizations. To support customers and operate the business 24/7, an organization needs to rely on its information systems. Systems must support the staff, and more importantly, interact directly with customers, suppliers, partners, and even physical devices and equipment. Systems must ensure the organization can respond, and respond appropriately, all the time.

Changing Scale

Changing expectations, a desire for real-time responsiveness, global service, and more self-service options would be enough to drive many organizations to focus on their information systems. The changing scale of business operations only exacerbates this situation. With the explosion of data generated by the use of the Web and new social media channels, organizations must deal with more electronic information than ever. Continuing pressure from worldwide competition to be more efficient—and increasing transaction volumes—has changed the scale at which organizations operate.

Big Data

Information systems store information about almost every transaction. Websites generate digital "exhaust" about visitors, logging every page displayed or ad clicked on. Social media sites, reviews, and discussions create an unstructured history of conversations about products, companies, people, and happenings. There has been an explosion of audio, image, and video data as digital cameras and equipment replace analog versions. The era of "Big Data" has begun.

In theory, all this information is useful to organizations. It can help determine what consumers think of a company's products. It can show how citizens are responding to new laws or what they think of a government department. Changing environmental conditions or clusters of crime can be spotted. The potential value of this data is great, but so is the scale of the problem. The volume of data has become so large that only information systems can handle it. Not only must information systems be used to store and manage this information, they also must be used to analyze and act on it. Its scale simply exceeds the ability of people to cope.

Efficiency

Organizations of all sizes are under constant pressure to become more efficient. More must be done with less, and each increase in business or operations must be supported by a smaller increase in costs. Because people are a key element of most organization's costs, an increase in efficiency means having the same number of people do more work. For the last few decades this has meant, in part, using information systems to allow people to handle more work. Interactive Voice Response systems were designed to allow the same number of call center representatives to handle more calls. Sales force automation tools let the same number of sales people handle more prospects and customers.

This pressure is not going away, and organizations must continue to find ways to use information systems to improve efficiency. Boosting customer self-service and enabling more services to be offered 24/7 without increasing staffing are critical. So are systems that allow the first point of contact with the customer to be the only one necessary, eliminating the need for referrals to supervisors. Systems that free up expensive experts to focus on higher value tasks, not day-to-day minutiae, also improve efficiency. The kinds of systems that have got us to our current level will not be able to offer continued increases in efficiency indefinitely. To drive efficiency up still further, organizations will need to adopt systems that require fundamentally fewer human interactions to process transactions.

Transaction Volumes

As organizations grow, they must handle more transactions, more products, more customers, and more employees. Where 100 customers may be known personally, 100,000 customers cannot be. While 100 orders can be tracked and kept on schedule with paper and pen, 100,000 cannot be. As transaction volumes grow, everything about the transaction must be managed by information systems. A steady increase in transaction volumes and increasing scale on the part of organizations as they merge and grow has long been one of the drivers of information systems. In the past, this has too often meant systems that could handle the volume but only with a matching loss in precision. The system might handle 100,000 customers, but it treats them all the same and customer intimacy is lost. 100,000 orders can be managed and shipped, but commitments to specific customers or local discounts cannot be accommodated.

For most organizations, transaction volumes are continuing to rise. What is changing is that customers, and even organizations, are no longer willing to give up customer intimacy or localization. High volumes must be matched to high precision with a new generation of information systems.

Changing Interactions

Changing expectations and ever-increasing scale make it difficult for organizations to meet the demands of their customers, partners, suppliers, and employees. The changing way in which people interact with organizations has, if anything, even more of an impact. As consumers become mobile and social, their interactions with organizations change. The Web has driven a massive expansion in options for consumers so they interact with more companies while interacting less with each. As organizations change their structure, becoming ever more distributed and specialized, this too creates a need for new interactions. These changes drive a need for a new type of information system.

Mobile Interactions

There has been an explosion of mobile devices. Consumers clearly want to use their mobile devices to do everything from interacting with friends to shopping, listening to music, and finding places to eat. This rapid movement of consumers from PC-based Internet access to always-on, mobile applications that take advantage of pervasive Internet connections is changing the nature of consumers' interactions with organizations.

For one thing, the nature of a mobile interaction lends itself to an interaction with an information system much more than to an interaction with a person. Mobile interactions could come from anywhere at any time. As such, responding to a mobile interaction must be automated by an information system.

Mobile devices also have a different form factor, with smaller screens and typically without a keyboard. Gestures and abbreviations that can be entered quickly, intelligent defaults, and automatic behavior that learns from the user are critical to a powerful mobile experience. The information systems that respond to mobile devices must be able to do more and act more intelligently than systems that must only support users at home on their personal computers.

Social Interactions

The growth in social channels and platforms means that organizations are interacting with consumers in new and ever-changing ways. Consumers are reviewing and discussing brands and products much more interactively. Connections between consumers let them share experiences, coupons, and information. For organizations, these channels represent a rich new set of data and can even reveal how fraudsters collaborate.

For now, these social channels are being handled manually by most organizations. They are hiring staff to monitor social networks and respond to consumers. They are putting this new data on screens for people to analyze. The question is, what happens as the scale of these interactions increases? If the explosion in social media does not stop, organizations will soon be dealing with vast amounts of data and huge numbers of interactions about their products and services. As with every new environment, efficiency demands will make it impractical to simply handle this explosion with more staff. New systems will be required that can support these new kinds of interactions.

Distributed Interactions

The Web has led to an explosion of shopping options for consumers. Where they might have always bought a particular product from one store, now they might order it from whichever store has the best deal today. They still have some loyalty to specific retailers and prefer them over others if the prices are more or less the same. What is different is that far more of them price-check first, comparing their preferred retailer to others before placing their order. The ease with which consumers can do this kind of price comparison creates at least two challenges for retailers.

When price comparison is easy and widespread, it is common for companies to "race to the bottom" and try and compete only by being the cheapest. Although this works for some companies, many will find it impossible to win this race. They need to deliver something more, some advantage for customers to shop with them. These customers interact only over the Web and increasingly use third-party aggregators and search engines. It is no longer enough to just train your staff to provide better service or rewards for loyal customers. Now you must ensure that your systems, even your published APIs, can do so.

As customers spread their business around more widely, it also becomes more difficult to build a complete picture of what they buy. Loyal customers create a history with a company that can be used to categorize them and to offer rewards and discounts. The totality of their orders is available for analysis. When these orders are spread out, the analysis becomes more complex and more sophisticated analytics are required. Companies need to be able to predict what else a customer is buying so they can fill in the gaps and build a complete picture of the customer. They must use more sources of data and use them in a more sophisticated way.

Changing Organizations

Consumer interactions with organizations are changing due to the technology they are using. The ways in which an organization interacts with consumers are also changing because organizations are. Outsourcing, global supply chains, and the end of the vertically-integrated organization have created an era of distributed business webs. Consumers interact with these new organizational structures in fundamentally different ways.

Consider a consumer electronics company. It designs and brands its products, but it outsources manufacturing to a network of other companies. It does not sell directly to consumers but sells through a set of retailers. The warranty it offers to consumers is constrained by the warranties these various manufacturers offer each other on the components they develop.

When consumers who bought the product through one of those retailers have a problem that might be under warranty, they call for support. They don't speak to the manufacturer or the retailer; instead they talk to the warranty management company that works for the manufacturer. This company sends a repair person out to look at the problem.

The person who comes to the consumer's home does not work for the manufacturer who designed the product, or the manufacturers who built it, or the retailer who sold it, or even the warranty management company—he is likely to be an independent local repair agent. When this person looks at the problem, he must make a determination whether the repair is under warranty. The manufacturer would like him to consider not only the warranty but also the value of the customer. If the repair is out of warranty but the consumer has bought many products from the same brand, perhaps an exception should be made. Without information systems that link this web of companies together and empower the repair person to act appropriately, the consumer interaction will not be optimal.

3

Decision Management Systems Transform Organizations

Decision Management Systems are a new breed of information systems. Agile, analytic, and adaptive, they are distinctly different from the systems that run most organizations today. The impact of changing expectations, changing scale, and changing interactions means that organizations increasingly are their systems—the behavior of their systems determines the behavior of the organization. Organizations that are developing Decision Management Systems are being transformed by these systems.

This transformation comes in many forms. Some organizations find Decision Management Systems let them truly create a market of one, while others are transformed because Decision Management Systems let them be "always on" or break the staffing ratios that have held them captive for years. Others are transformed by crushing fraud, maximizing the value of their physical assets, or maximizing their revenue. Some are transformed by the power of Decision Management Systems to make smart people smarter.

A Market of One

"The customer is king"—the marketing rallying call of the early 1980s—was a fallacy. It was enterprise-centric in a world driven by accounting and the number of products or services being sold. It was a world where product quality, manufacturing efficiency, and lean operations represented significant barriers to entry, and where the voice of the customer was confined to the call center or trapped in the electronic cages of Interactive Voice Response systems.

The advent of the social media revolution has given worldwide consumers a megaphone, with extraordinary immediacy and a remarkably loud voice. At the same time, analytics has started to be widely understood thanks to commercial bestsellers promoting the power of predictive analytics. Decision Management Systems powered by analytics make it possible to fulfill the marketing dream of mass customization and customer centricity—the "market of one." As illustrated in Figure 3-1, pulling together operational excellence and product leadership, Decision Management Systems can deliver the customer intimacy the senior executive is seeking.

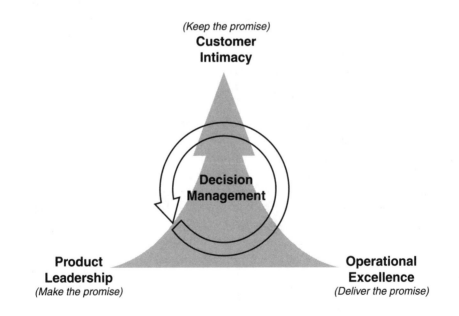

Figure 3-1 Decision Management Systems at the heart of customer intimacy.

In a massively interconnected world, CEOs are prioritizing customer intimacy as never before. Globalization and a dramatic increase in the availability of information have exponentially expanded customers' options. CEOs know that ongoing engagement and co-creation with customers produce differentiation. They consider the information explosion immensely valuable in developing deep customer insights. In a recent study (IBM Corporation, 2010) CEOs said that they will focus on customers as the number one priority to succeed in the new economic environment. More successful companies are especially determined to put their customers' needs front and center: 95% of CEOs at these companies said that "getting connected" with customers is their top priority. They are convinced that they must stay connected (or re-connect) with their customers and keep on learning how to strengthen those bonds.

The Paralysis of Choice

In the late 1950s Gaston Bachelard said, "the multiplicity of choices lead to alienation." Bombarded with an increasing number of choices, users find themselves paralyzed when it comes time to make a choice. Is this choice the best one? What am I giving up by choosing this one instead of that one? Have I visited enough sites to get enough information? A vicious cycle has become common. Consumers like a new product and admire its new features. Competitors respond with more variations and product options across the board. Consumers become paralyzed by this choice and seek a new product to cut through the confusion. Companies respond to this with yet more products and features and so on. This explosion of choice ends up working against everyone. For instance, Fidelity Investments has found the more funds its 401k products offer, the less consumer participation it gets. Each 10 additional funds results in a 2% decrease in participation.

If excessive choice paralyzes, then offering more options to customers cannot deliver a market of one. Customer intimacy means offering effective and appropriate defaults so that consumers do not have to make choices. Instead they can rely on getting defaults that are appropriate for them and profitable for the company. These defaults must be based on a one-to-one relationship centered on trust and a high degree of personalization. By flipping analysis around and looking at the buyer's interest, the right defaults can be determined.

The Experience of One

Go to any Starbucks and you will hear customers ask for coffee just the way they want it—"a venti, no-fat, sugar-free, extra hot cinnamon-peppermint (two pumps), light blend dolce latte, no whip—but please leave room for cream." More than 90,000 combinations are available so that each customer can get their perfect drink. Drinks made just for them, right here, on the spot, at their command. In reality, Starbucks is not really selling coffee but an experience. You need a healthy dose of customer intimacy to sell a coffee at premium prices, and this is what Starbucks delivers.

The online business model too is evolving toward personalization. Engines like the iTunes Genius or Netflix recommendations put personalization at the heart of cross-selling and customer acquisition. Using vast amounts of interaction data from many other consumers—the wisdom of crowds—these engines find complex and unique similarities to drive recommendations unique to the consumer. While everyone has their horror story about these engines—just because you like *The Shining* does not mean you will like every horror film ever made—these engines are improving steadily and already outperform people's choices on some measures. For instance, Netflix watchers overall are much more likely to enjoy a movie that was recommended to them than one they picked without a recommendation. Personalization is here to stay.

Beyond retail, pharmaceutical companies have already started to address the personalization of medications; in 2003, Allen Roses, then senior VP of genetics at GlaxoSmithKline made headlines when he said that the vast majority of drugs (more than 90%) only work in 30 or 50% of patients, as diseases progress along physiological pathways that vary from person to person. The way a single drug dosage affect patients, from different ages, backgrounds, lifestyles, and unique genetic predispositions is bound to have a wide variety of potency, thus introducing at best an unfortunate lack of efficacy if not radically negative side effects. Given the rise of healthcare costs, personalization of drug treatments is clearly upon us.

Decision Management Systems

Effective personalization requires the anticipation of a customer need. It is often the result of an ongoing "conversation" between that customer and an organization. It uses the combination of many data points gathered across time and a variety of channels and sources. Instrumentation and mobility are creating opportunities for more accurate targeting. Only a system, a Decision Management System, can deliver context-aware decisions for the right person, at the right place and at the right moment.

As the beauty care retailer and Carrefour found, Decision Management Systems make a market of one practical. These Decision Management Systems are delivering targeted, personalized offers and recommendations at the point of interaction with the consumer.

Always On

Global companies and globalized consumers want service providers they can access from anywhere, anytime. They expect to be able to buy their favorite products when they need them and have them shipped promptly wherever they want. They don't expect to wait in line at government agencies or in branches, and they expect to use their mobile phone to do something, not to stay on hold while they wait to talk to someone who can do it for them. They expect to file claims online, apply for credit from their smart phone, and get coherent responses even from the most complex of supply chains or service networks. They expect organizations of all sorts to be "always on."

Most governments have made big investments in "e-government" initiatives. Making forms available as PDFs, putting information on web pages, making information available to citizens for download, and much more has opened up government like never before. But government agencies around the world are using Decision Management Systems to go further.

These government agencies are using Decision Management Systems to ensure that citizens can get the help and responses they need from their government anytime and anywhere. Decision Management Systems ensure that applications for benefits can be made or changed online 24/7 and be immediately validated and approved without compromising the accuracy or completeness of eligibility checks. Permits and licenses can be applied for with instant feedback about inspections or additional information that will be required and even automated scheduling. Fees and taxes can be accurately determined, paid and validated whenever a citizen or a business is ready to do so, not when the government office is next open. E-government on steroids—active e-government where the government's systems act as always-open offices.

Banks have been 24/7 for a while, with ATMs leading the way and the rapid provision of online banking. Over time, Decision Management Systems have let these become more powerful environments. Moving from allowing simple cash withdrawals and balance printing, ATMs have become increasingly full service thanks to the automation of critical risk decisions. This same automation allows banks to offer in-store credit approval so consumers can get credit cards and loans instantly. Decision Management Systems that detect fraud allow smart phone apps that scan and deposit checks and much more.

As consumers move to mobile banking in ever-increasing numbers and social media becomes increasingly important, Decision Management Systems allow more of what consumers need their bank to allow or approve to happen when the consumer wants.

Traditional property and casualty insurers have been paper-based. Forms are used to apply for insurance, and other forms to make claims. All of these forms are mailed back and forth between insurers, agents, and consumers. Electronic versions of these forms reduced mailing costs and streamlined processes but did not fundamentally change the dynamic. With Decision Management Systems, insurers are also moving to an always-on mindset.

When underwriting decisions can be handled by a system much of the time, the online application for insurance becomes practical. Now consumers don't have to wait to see an agent or talk to an underwriter. Their application can be processed automatically as soon as they make it, and they can keep track of its status as it works through the system (assuming it does not get immediately approved or rejected). Claims too can be automated, allowing consumers to file claims from a website or their smart phone and get immediate responses—even immediate deposits to their bank account for the amount of the claim. This is more than just capturing the right data and passing it around electronically—this requires Decision Management Systems to check for fraud, manage risk, and apply regulations and policies. Only then can an insurance company be always on.

Consider the case of the largest property and casualty insurer in the Nordic region. It prides itself on a strong focus on customer satisfaction. In particular, it aims to deliver customer satisfaction in the difficult situations for which people buy insurance—when consumers need to make a claim. Its perspective is that better claims handling is key to customer satisfaction. It has taken this from a concept to systems implementation and ultimately to a key feature of its advertising campaigns.

Customers want to get their money quickly when they make a claim. The company wants to reduce the amount of money it spends processing and paying claims while increasing customer satisfaction. It allows customers to submit claims online and aims for those customers to have no further actions to take once they have submitted the claim. It developed a Decision Management System for claims decisions and embedded it in a standard end-to-end process for claims processing. A common process-oriented architecture and a focus on using business rules and predictive analytics to automate the critical decision was applied first in Finland and then expanded into other countries and types of claims. The new approach empowers underwriters and actuaries to create and update the business rules and means that they can run tests and do impact analysis across the whole portfolio. The Decision Management System is more thorough than the old approach; it's faster, the results are better, and the business people are happier with the increase of control they now have.

This approach means that no paper flows into the company related to claims. Thanks to a Decision Management System, the company can determine what percentage of these claims it wants to handle automatically. Today it chooses to process 60% of claims straight through with money flowing out to customers in just 3 seconds. The remaining 40% of claims are inspected and processed within 24 hours. The system means that the claims staff handles more claims more quickly and can focus where it needs to. It saves money in claims processing and pays out less in claims because the process is consistent and error-free. Customer satisfaction is up, and it's open and available 24/7.

This kind of always-on mindset also supports the distributed business webs that are becoming common as specialty companies take over part of the supply or distribution chain of a company. In the example of warranty claims discussed earlier, the use of Decision Management Systems would resolve critical issues. A Decision Management System could answer the critical question—should this repair be considered a warranty repair or not? Provided by the brand owner, the Decision Management System could handle the complexities of the various sub-warranties offered by suppliers as well as the brand loyalty and net promoter score of the consumer (based on all their registered products and even social media analytics). The warranty repair person would not need to see this information; he could simply say, "this is the repair needed" and the company, whose brand and customer relationship is at risk, could decide to make a warranty repair even though the product is a few days out of warranty, based on a more holistic decision. With an always-on Decision Management System, it would not matter how many layers of service providers were involved—they would all act the way the brand owner wanted them to.

Breaking the Ratios

Many industries have staffing ratios that are considered fixed, or at least very hard to change. In insurance, the number of underwriters drives the number of policy applications that can be priced and processed, while the number of claims agents is driven by the amount of business written—more policies will ultimately result in more claims. In banking, similar assumptions are made about loan officers—more loan applications, more loan officers. In government agencies, assumptions are made about the number of auditors—more auditors means more fraud detected. With Decision Management Systems, these ratios can be overturned and businesses changed in fundamental ways.

One insurance company once said to me, "I can't remember the last time we hired an underwriter." The company's business had been growing, and several underwriters had either retired or moved on to other jobs within the organization. How then had it avoided hiring new underwriters? This company had been an early adopter of Decision Management Systems. In particular, it had built a home and auto underwriting system. This system handled 80% or more of its underwriting decisions. As a result, the underwriters don't spend their time making decisions about each policy application. Instead their time is spent on analysis and business development. They analyze the world of business, seeing which agents are selling which products in which locales, and visiting agents to help explain products or discuss strategy. The need to hire new underwriters to handle new business has been fundamentally changed.

Claims is another example. Infinity Insurance, discussed earlier, got some great results from using a Decision Management System. The company also changed the relationship between claims and claims adjusters. While Infinity was building its claims Decision Management System, the industry entered a deep recession. Without the analytically-enhanced decision-making it was adopting, this would have had far more effect on its business than it did. Infinity had to lay off 25% (some 300 staff) and trim expenses. With 12,000-13,000 new claims a month, it had to get cases out to field staff quicker, improve customer service, and reduce people all at once. The automated identification of fast-track claims helped it decouple the number of adjusters from the amount of business being written.

To achieve this, Infinity started "right tracking" claims—assigning claims to fast-track adjusters. This was a new approach, created to take advantage of the new Decision Management System. These fast-track adjusters were people in the business units whose role changed from simply reporting losses to actually processing some claims. Infinity created a group who could process the claims "once and done" with no hand-off to field adjusters. This allows it to open, appraise, and pay some claims within 10 days. The analytically-enhanced decision increased the old fast-track rate of 2% to 22% in just a year of operation. The 100 fast-track adjusters now handle more than 2,500 claims a month without referral to a field adjuster. This represents a huge cost saving for the field, helps decouple business growth from the number of field adjusters, and has reduced its loss adjustment expenses from 14% to around 11%.

Banking, like insurance, is full of decisions that have historically been made by trained experts. Every loan being checked by a loan officer is the most significant in retail banking, acting as it does to cap the amount of credit that can be issued. Whether in personal loans, mortgages, commercial lending or credit cards, the use of a manual approval decision ties the amount of business to the number of trained staff. The ever-increasing use of Decision Management Systems in banking has changed this ratio.

One of the leading banks in the Baltic region offers a full range of financial services for private individuals, corporations, and other organizations. Using a Decision Management System for loan decisions changed its business in dramatic ways. It excluded human error and waiting time in issuing credit contracts and decreased the headcount involved in the credit issuing process by nearly 90%, improved employee productivity 833%, and reduced the cost per credit contract issued from 240€ to 32€.

It's not just for-profit organizations that find themselves able to reinvent core staffing ratios using Decision Management Systems. Government agencies also can do the same. Of course for most government agencies, the problem is a fixed number of staff—driven by some federal, state, or local budget process—and an expanding or unbounded amount of work. Traditionally this has reached some point of equilibrium—the inefficiencies of the process have been worked out and the available staff gets as much done as they can. The rest goes undone or is deferred.

With Decision Management Systems this can all change. Take the New York Department of Taxation and Finance, for instance. This state department processes 24 million business and personal tax returns and collects more than $90 billion in state and local tax payments every year. A finite pool of auditors is available to audit and investigate tax returns. To maximize the amount of tax revenue collected for the state and to ensure fairness, the department needs to apply these auditors effectively. The vast majority of taxpayers are entitled both to the refunds they request and a prompt response from the state. Some are not, and tax evasion techniques get more sophisticated every year.

Using a Decision Management System, the department has transformed its approach from "pay and chase" to "next best case." Instead of paying all the refunds and then chasing after the ones the auditors find to be invalid—an often futile chase as the criminal is long gone—the system proactively identifies returns that are outliers and focuses constrained audit resources on those returns that seem most unusual.

Like many of the most sophisticated Decision Management Systems, this grew out a long-term project to use information to transform the department's operations. Evolving from simple decision-making to ever more sophisticated and analytic decisions, the system now automatically rejects those refund requests that are clearly ineligible. This prevents these cases from even entering the audit process. It then uses predictive models and business rules to make a decision as to the priority of each remaining case. As case officers complete a case, the system presents the next best case—the pending case with the highest value that is most likely to be questionable. This ensures that the department's resources are always focused where they will make the most difference. With limited resources and a finite time in which to make a decision—refunds cannot be held up indefinitely—the system maximizes the effectiveness of audit officers.

The system is effective, increasing the percentage of audits that found questionable refunds. It is also efficient, with automated rejections and other efficiencies allowing fewer staff to process more cases—from 56,000 in 2003 to more than 200,000 today without increasing staffing.

Crushing Fraud

Fraud is a problem in a wide variety of industries and areas. Government must deal with benefits fraud as well as tax evasion. Banks and other credit issuers must deal with credit card fraud while insurers tackle false and overstated claims. Identity fraud is a problem for many industries, and healthcare systems spend billions of dollars on false claims for services never performed.

In every case, the traditional approach of paying and then chasing down fraudsters is largely a failure—so-called "pay and chase" approaches often recover only a few percentage points of the money lots. Manual checks and audits may work well against petty fraud, but most fraud is now the result of organized crime syndicates. These syndicates constantly change their approach, probing for weaknesses and responding to new checks with more sophisticated attacks. Crushing fraud means building systems—Decision Management Systems—that can rapidly and accurately determine that a transaction is fraudulent and prevent it ever penetrating the organization.

One such example is the New York State Department of Taxation and Finance discussed previously. Its Decision Management Systems focuses auditors more effectively but also proactively identifies those returns that are distant outliers or match known patterns of fraud and automatically rejects them. Like all systems targeting fraud, it continuously evolves to detect and prevent new patterns of fraud. The department has steadily increased the amount of data involved in the decision-making process. The data now includes a taxpayer's past interactions with the tax department—allowing a history of honest interactions to drive future decisions—as well as data on businesses and employees and data from other internal silos. In the five years the system has been operating, it has saved the state of New York more than $600 million—$600 million of taxes that would have been lost to the state and would have had to be made up with more taxes on honest taxpayers or cuts in state services. The system's support for multiple approaches also allows the department to evaluate the effectiveness of different audit programs, setting the stage for ongoing improvement and for tackling evolving fraud threats.

In insurance, the fraud comes from invalid claims. Rings of criminals stage fake accidents and file inflated claims for damages and for fake injuries (supported by the testimony of participating doctors).

Legitimate policy holders overstate damages and under-report other insurance coverage that might be expected to pay some of the cost. Insurance companies have to tell which claims are valid and should be paid and which should not, while still providing good customer service and meeting state and federal guidelines for time to pay.

As discussed earlier, Infinity Insurance's use of a Decision Management System to flag claims as potentially fraudulent was very powerful. It doubled the accuracy of fraud identification, contributing to a return on investment of more than 400%. It also reduced the referral time to send those claims to Infinity's Special Investigative Unit from 45–60 days to 1–3 days while improving customer service through fast payment of legitimate claims.

Even when insurance companies develop sophisticated predictive analytic models to detect fraud, the absence of a Decision Management System makes it hard to apply these models to claim as they are processed. One large North American insurance company was struggling with a legacy claims processing system that hard-coded the rules for approving claims. The analytics team had found patterns of claims fraud—specifically provider fraud. Provider fraud is where organizations filing claims for patients are claiming for services not provided, or at least not provided as extensively as is being claimed. This fraud is complex to find, as each claim may look perfectly valid and it is only by looking at the patterns of claims made by a provider that the fraud can be detected. Integrating these models with the claims approval rules in a Decision Management System allows these models to be applied earlier in the claims lifecycle, preventing seemingly valid claims from providers who are committing fraud from getting into the payment queue.

Banking and financial services are also plagued with fraud problems. Identity fraud, where fake applications are made for credit, loans, or mortgages, is widespread. Credit card fraud, where card details are stolen and then used to make purchases, is also common. Some of the earliest Decision Management Systems were created to tackle this kind of credit card fraud. Using data pooled from multiple issuers, companies have developed systems that detect fraudulent behavior patterns and allow card issuers to identify and stop fraudulent transactions. If you have ever had your credit card company call you about a transaction, it was because one of these systems flagged it as potentially fraudulent.

Credit card fraud is not the only kind of fraud for banks and financial services. As we saw with Bancolombia earlier, detecting and preventing money laundering and similar criminal fraud is also an important issue.

As in many fraud scenarios, one of the most important aspects of a Decision Management system in preventing fraud is its agility. Fraudsters and criminals are often very sophisticated, constantly changing and adapting their techniques to penetrate the systems put in place to stop them. No matter how good an initial implementation might be, it will not last long unless it can be changed quickly.

One example of the power of this kind of flexibility is a top ten investment and brokerage. This company used a Decision Management System to enforce "know your customer" and anti-money laundering policies across multiple systems. This centralized approach meant it could demonstrate compliance with regulations and improve its transparency. But the real value in preventing money laundering came from a more than 50% improvement in time to market with new rules. This ability to respond quickly to new advice from law enforcement and new internal policies meant that the systems could be adapted to meet new threats and counter new schemes on the part of criminal organizations. Keeping up with the crooks was essential to keeping this kind of fraud out of the systems and the fact that the organization could implement rule changes in real time or just days rather than the months a traditional approach would have taken was critical to its success.

Maximizing Assets

It can sometimes seem that the most powerful examples of Decision Management Systems all come from information-centric industries. Banking, insurance, and even government examples related to making decisions about information products rather than about physical assets. In fact, Decision Management Systems can be effective tools in maximizing the value of physical assets also. In telecommunications, where expensive and extensive networks are essential to providing high quality services, and in energy and utilities, where smart grid approaches are taking off, the management of the network is critical. In manufacturing and travel, the optimal use of physical assets from machine tools to silicon chip fabrication equipment to airport gates drives profitable operations. Decision Management systems maximize the value of these assets and drive success.

In telecommunications, especially mobile telecommunications, the effective development and management of a network underpins everything else. Bharti Airtel is India's largest integrated telecommunications company, offering communication and entertainment services to more than 100 million mobile, landline, and TV customers. With three billion calls a day, scale is a critical issue for Bharti Airtel. Bharti's customers range from large enterprises to small businesses and urban consumers, along with a rapidly growing number of rural consumers whose mobile phone might be the only communications technology they own. To support this extremely distributed growth, and differentiate itself from its competitors, Bharti focuses on information.

Bharti Airtel uses Decision Management Systems to effectively target its marketing to this diverse customer base, driving a 1:1 program called My Airtel My Offer. Besides these customer-facing systems, Bharti Airtel uses analytic Decision Management Systems in its core network planning and optimization, IT infrastructure management, partner management, and financial systems. With its heavily instrumented infrastructure, analytics are increasingly used to merge the customer-facing and back-office worlds, with marketing campaign analytics considering the impact on network operations and optimization, for example.

Bharti's meteoric and continuing growth, as well as its expansion into broadband, IP-TV and more, relies on its backbone of analytic Decision Management Systems. Analytics play a central role in network planning and in rolling out targeted content services, as well as in the development of the right IT infrastructure. Financial analysis, revenue assurance, supply chain optimization, and even human resources have all been transformed.

Energy networks are changing as old style grids are being transformed into "smart grids." One of the most straightforward ways to do this is to invest in what is known as smart metering. Smart meters measure power use like traditional meters but track exactly when the power was used. This allows power suppliers to introduce variable pricing—charging more for power when demand is high and less when demand is low. Not only does this allow consumers to manage their power costs more effectively, it has been estimated that it would mean we could avoid building any new power generation capacity for a significant period and could retire some of our worst polluting generating capacity.

Smart meters aren't that complicated, but they change the kinds of systems utilities need. Instead of billing being a fairly mindless calculation, now the rules for billing need to be applied. Given how people and businesses behave, these rules will change constantly—utility companies will tweak the rules to manage their workload and maximize their profit; cities and states will require specific rates for certain people at certain times, or will require that certain times should always get the best prices; large electricity buyers will negotiate their own contracts. Unless there is a system that can make a smart decision on the back end, this constantly evolving set of rules will cause problems. Utilities need Decision Management Systems to handle this billing if they are to take advantage of smart meters and maximize the value to their networks.

The longer-term consequences are just as interesting. Suddenly there is all this data about who uses what power when. Using predictive analytics to find trends, segments with specific behaviors, and to predict how people might react to specific price changes will become the norm. Integrating the results of this analysis back into the pricing models and the pricing decisions will start the process of moving towards optimal pricing, balancing the needs and behaviors of consumers with the intent of regulators and the profit of utilities.

Networks are not the only kinds of assets that can be maximized using Decision Management Systems. In manufacturing, lines and machine tools must be scheduled efficiently to maximize output and minimize downtime. It is one thing to do this overnight to set up the next day's schedule. But the production objectives of a manufacturing facility, quality issues, offline machines, and much more must be taken into account to truly maximize the value of the facility. As the situation evolves during the day, so too must the way in which the assets are being utilized.

IBM Microelectronics develops, manufactures and markets semiconductors and application-specific integrated circuits, or ASICs. One of its key product sites is a 300mm semiconductor manufacturing facility in upstate New York that produces chips using photolithography. This kind of manufacturing uses multiple intricate production processes and a great deal of capital-intensive equipment. Managing all the various steps to ensure optimal usage of raw materials and scheduling of time-sensitive procedures was a challenge.

The site integrated a Decision Management System into its manufacturing execution system. Data from the facility is continually fed into the system for analysis. Every few minutes the system assesses the state of the manufacturing processes and establishes what materials are available, what other constraints exist, and what the facility is scheduled to produce. Based on this, it creates an optimal schedule for the systems and assets in the facility—everything from furnaces and lithography tools to chemical baths. Best practices developed by expert engineers are applied and the resulting schedule is automatically fed back into the execution systems.

Because the system continually monitors and reschedules every few minutes, the system ensures the facility runs with maximum effectiveness and efficiency even as the situation changes or problems are encountered. The system increased production throughput and reduces cycle time while using less raw material.

In fact, any kind of asset can be maximized using Decision Management Systems. Telecommunication networks, energy grids, factories and fabs— even airport gates, a finite resource that determines how many planes can land or take off on time. With a Decision Management System, some airports are dynamically allocating gates and ground crew to speed the arrival and unloading of planes. Replacing a pre-defined schedule with one that balances bringing planes in near their scheduled gate with staff schedules, identifying planes that have been delayed and are still occupying gates, confirming which flights are expected on the ground soon, and much more.

Maximizing Revenue

Decision Management Systems can also help maximize revenue. Dynamic pricing based on demand and load is common, for example, in telecommunications and travel. Determining the best price, one that will maximize revenue given current and predicted loads as well as current capacity, is complex. Many policies and best practices must be applied, and these change regularly. Tradeoffs between different possibilities must be assessed and managed to see which will generate the most revenue. Predictions about long- and short-term changes in demand must be accounted for. Only a Decision Management System can deliver this kind of dynamic revenue maximization.

For instance, some characteristics of today's travel distribution environment conflict with the workings of traditional revenue management systems. Customers are increasingly price-driven and book closer to departure—resulting in a more dynamic market place. A Decision Management System uses shopping data to overcome the shortages of traditional revenue management systems. It determines a set of revenue management controls that maximizes revenue given current competitive situation and carrier data. The user expresses strategic objectives in terms of business rules, and the system determines the feasible set of revenue management actions.

Travel agencies are faced with declining commissions and increasing competition. Striking and managing incentive deals that pay override commissions or guarantee fare discounts has become crucial to large agencies' success. A Decision Management System evaluates pending supplier deals and constructs the best possible supplier deal portfolio; determines optimal sales targets given the set of deals to manage/drive demand and maximize per booking revenue; and allows an agency to negotiate better supplier deals, reduce deal conflicts, and provide sales targets for merchandising tools.

Making Smart People Smarter

There is one last critical area in which Decision Management Systems can transform organizations. So far, all the examples have focused on automation, where the ability of Decision Management Systems to make unattended decisions is critical to their value. Many Decision Management Systems actually complement the decisions of people. These Decision Management Systems analyze data and apply best practices to make recommendations to the professionals working in organizations. One of the best examples is in healthcare, where clinical decision support systems are increasingly sophisticated.

First-generation systems in healthcare, as in many other expert-oriented industries, focused on delivering information. Electronic medical records and other related systems store and present all the available information to a doctor or nurse. Although this can be useful, these systems are too passive to truly transform healthcare. What is needed are clinical Decision Management Systems that can make intelligent healthcare decisions as data changes and that can make specific recommendations to medical professionals based on the content of these electronic medical records.

One healthcare provider, for instance, used a Decision Management System to provide alerts to nurses and doctors for potentially harmful combination of drugs and changes in patient's conditions based on critical lab results. As new lab results were added to the electronic medical record, the system automatically applied medical best practices and analysis to see whether anything should be done. This automated alerting decreased the amount of time it takes for nurses and doctors to react to potentially life-threatening conditions. It also improved the detection of critical patient conditions, such as sepsis. The system reduced the need for more expensive procedures and reduced the time patients spent in the hospital—lower costs but better care.

Sequoia Hospital, located midway between San Francisco and Silicon Valley, also uses Decision Management Systems. With 140 beds, Sequoia Hospital provides healthcare support for residents of Redwood City and its surrounding communities. Each year, clinicians at its celebrated Heart and Vascular Institute perform procedures ranging from stents and catheterizations to valve replacements, angioplasties, and coronary bypass surgeries. Sequoia Hospital wanted to gather patient-specific intelligence on the effectiveness of its cardiovascular treatments and protocols but was hampered by tools that couldn't adequately manage the quantity and complexity of the data. New automated statistical and analysis tools now make it possible to manage and analyze surgical and treatment data on 14 years of data on 10,000 cardiac patients for better patient outcomes.

Sequoia used a Decision Management System to refine crucial pre- and postoperative procedures, reducing complications, and extending the length and quality of patients' lives. The hospital can generate fast, accurate reports on expected outcomes for any given patient and thus personalize the treatment that patient gets. The hospital reshaped its treatment protocols and cut its overall mortality rate from 2.9 to 1.3%. In 2010, the hospital received the highest ranking in the nation for aortic valve replacement survival rates; in 2009 it received a Blue Distinction Center for Cardiac Care designation from Blue Cross and Blue Shield of California. It also replaced anecdotal information on its successes with verifiable data, boosting referrals and marketing opportunities.

Conclusion

Decision Management Systems are more agile, more analytic, and more adaptive that traditional information systems. As the role of information systems changes in organizations and as the market perceptions of organizations increasingly reflect the behavior of their systems, Decision Management Systems can transform organizations. Delivering on the promise of a market of one, breaking long-held staffing ratios and maximizing the value of assets drive impressive transformations. Helping support the always-on, self-service environment demanded by modern consumers while reducing fraud and maximizing revenue, Decision Management Systems should be a critical element in an organization's information systems portfolio.

4

Principles of Decision
Management Systems

*Organizations that have adopted Decision Management Systems have gained
tremendous results from doing so. The use of business rules in Decision
Management Systems has given organizations the agility to respond rapidly to
competitive and market changes, to avoid business risks, and to take advantage
of narrow windows of opportunity. The use of analytics to predict risk, fraud,
and opportunity in these Decision Management Systems has kept companies profitable despite the risks they face and has allowed them to maximize the value of
their customer relationships through a laser focus on opportunity. The ability of
Decision Management systems to adapt to change and to be part of a learning
environment has allowed organizations to experiment with new approaches, learn
from their successes and failures, and continuously improve their business. Any
organization would want the benefits of these kinds of systems.*

*However, it is not immediately clear how to build Decision Management
Systems. Although there are specific technologies involved, the use of these technologies is not sufficient to ensure that Decision Management Systems are the
outcome of using them. Decision Management Systems appear to deal with different issues, and have different characteristics, across different industries and
business functions. It can be hard to see what an underwriting system in use by*

the agents of a property and casualty insurer has in common with a real-time offer management system supporting a website. Yet when the basic principles of Decision Management Systems are understood, they can be correctly identified and delivered with maximum return on investment.

Four specific principles are at the heart of identifying and building Decision Management Systems. If a system exists, it can be assessed against these four principles and can be said to be a Decision Management System if these principles guide its design and implementation. If an information systems project is being considered, then the integration of these principles into the project will ensure that what is delivered is a Decision Management System.

The four principles address the characteristic capabilities of a Decision Management System:

1. *Begin with the decision in mind.*

   Decision Management Systems are built around a central and ongoing focus on automating decisions, particularly operational and "micro" decisions.

2. *Be transparent and agile.*

   The way Decision Management Systems make each decision is both explicable to non-technical professionals and easy to change.

3. *Be predictive, not reactive.*

   Decision Management Systems use the data an organization has collected or can access to improve the way decisions are being made by predicting the likely outcome of a decision and of doing nothing.

4. *Test, learn, and continually improve.*

   The decision-making in Decision Management Systems is dynamic and change is to be expected. The way a decision is made must be continually challenged and re-assessed so that it can learn what works and adapt to work better.

Principle #1: Begin with the Decision in Mind

Most information systems have been developed, and are continuing to be developed, around business functions, business data, or business processes. Functional systems support a set of related business functions such as accounting or human resources. Data-centric systems focus on particular kinds of data, such as customer information. Business processes such as order-to-cash have been layered on top of both kinds of systems, and newer systems are developed to deliver additional specific business processes. Each of these approaches has pros and cons, but they all share a common challenge—they assume either that *people* will make all the decisions involved in the functions and business processes being automated or that how these decisions are made can be fixed. As a result, none of them are Decision Management Systems.

To develop Decision Management Systems, we must take a different approach—not one based on functions, data, or processes. To develop Decision Management Systems we must begin with the decision in mind. Decision Management Systems are built to automate and improve specific business decisions. As a decision involves making a selection from a range of alternatives, these systems make that selection—they choose the action or actions that can or should be made given the data available and the context of the decision. Decision Management Systems do not assume that every decision must always be taken by a human. Decision Management Systems make these decisions using the same business logic humans would apply without human intervention.

Clearly, however, we are neither willing nor able to build information systems to make every decision on our behalf. Only certain decisions can and should be addressed by Decision Management Systems.

What Kinds of Decisions Are We Talking About?

Information systems are good at handling repetitive tasks. They excel at doing the same thing over and over without variation and without making mistakes from one transaction to the next. Something that cannot be defined in a repeatable way is not a good target for any kind of information system; thus, only those decisions that are repeatable are good candidates for being automated and managed using a Decision Management System.

Repeatable Decisions

A repeatable decision is one that is made more than once by an organization following a well-defined, or at least definable, decision-making approach. Business decisions can be categorized in various ways; one effective way to look at decisions is to categorize them as strategic, tactical, or operational (Taylor & Raden, 2007). This divides decisions into three categories based on the value of each decision made—the difference between a good and a bad decision—and the number of times such a decision is made by an organization:

- **Strategic decisions** are those high-value, low-volume decisions that guide the overall direction of the company. These ad-hoc, typically one-off decisions are made by senior management or the executive team of an organization. Lots of information is assembled and analyzed while many options are considered. Once the decision is made, it is never made again in the same context—even if it is revisited later, this is really a different decision as circumstances are different. Organizations may know that a strategic decision is going to be needed well in advance, but often these decisions arise from unexpected opportunities or challenges. Strategic decisions are not candidates for Decision Management Systems as they lack the key element of repeatability.

- **Tactical decisions** are those focused on management and control. These medium-value decisions still have significant business impact. They too involve data and analysis, typically by humans in management or knowledge worker positions. However, these decisions do repeat—the same kind of decision is made repeatedly during normal business operations. Decisions about the discounting approach being used or the staffing levels of a call center might be examples, and these decisions must be made every month or every week. The same or very similar analysis is performed each time, and company policies may play a significant role in how the decision is made. More repeatable and consistent tactical decisions are certainly targets for Decision Management Systems.

- **Operational decisions** are those of lower individual value and typically relate to a single customer or a single transaction. They are critical to the effective operation of an organization, especially an organization of any size. Because of the number of times they must be made, consistency and repeatability are critical. Policies and well-defined decision making criteria are typically developed to ensure this consistency. Despite their low individual value, they are extremely valuable in aggregate. A decision made thousands or millions or even billions of times a year has a total value that often exceeds even the most important strategic decision. Furthermore, strategic and tactical decisions (for example, to focus on customer retention or discount more aggressively) will only have an impact if a whole series of operational decisions (how to retain this customer or what discount to offer this distributor) are made in accordance with the higher-level decision. For these reasons, operational decisions are the most common subject of Decision Management Systems.

To begin with the decision in mind, we must understand what operational or tactical decision is to be the focus of our Decision Management System.

BUSINESS STRATEGY AND STRATEGIC DECISIONS

This focus on repeatable operational and tactical decisions can and should be combined with a focus on business strategy. A business strategy must be supported by many operational and tactical decisions if it is to be put into practice. For instance, if a focus on growing per-customer revenue is central to your business strategy, then there may be strategic decisions that must be made to support this strategy. There will definitely be many operational and tactical decisions that will be influenced by and contribute to this strategy. For example, unless operational decisions about customer retention and cross-sell offers are made effectively, you cannot deliver on this customer-centric strategy. As discussed in Chapter 5, "Discover and Model Decisions," the right operational decisions to focus on are those that support the objectives and key metrics of the organization.

Operational Decisions

Operational decisions are by far the most common kind of repeatable decision. Every order placed, every customer interaction, every claim, or credit card transaction involves operational decisions. Operational decisions are the day-to-day, run-the-business decisions that are taken in large numbers by every organization.

Operational decisions are highly repeatable—in fact, being consistent by following a set of guidelines or applying the relevant policies and regulations is a defining characteristic of an operational decision. Operational decisions can also involve an assessment of risk, as many forms of risk (loan default or credit risk, for instance) are acquired one transaction at a time. Operational decisions often must be made in real time or near real time, while customers are waiting for the decision to be made.

Although many operational decisions are made about customers, they can also be made about shipments, suppliers, or staff. As more physical devices are connected to the Internet with sensors or RFID chips, operational decisions are often made about "things"—about vehicles, packages, railcars, or network components.

Micro Decisions

Micro decisions are a particular kind of operational decision (Taylor & Raden, 2007) where the desire to personalize an interaction with a customer requires a focus on making a decision for that customer and that customer only. Often an operational decision is repeated for all customers, with the decision being based only on the data available for the particular interaction or transaction concerned. A micro decision, in contrast, uses everything known or predictable about a customer to make a unique decision just for them. Two customers making the same request or involved in identical transactions would get two different outcomes.

This focus on the information about the customer is what makes micro decisions a distinct form of operational decision. Everything known about the customer must be synthesized into actionable insight about the customer and fed into the operational decision alongside the information about the transaction. For example, when an order is placed, two operational decisions might be made—what shipping options to offer on the order and what discount to offer. The first of these might be managed as a standard operational decision with information about the order such as delivery address, weight, and value used to determine which of the various shipping options would be allowed. The second could be managed similarly but could also be handled as a micro decision. The customer's history with the company could be used to compute their likely future profitability and the risk that they might consider a competitor. This information, as well as information about the specific order, would then feed a micro decision to calculate a discount specific to *this* customer placing *this* order at *this* moment.

Tactical Decisions

Although most repeatable decisions are operational or micro decisions, some are more tactical in nature. These repeatable tactical decisions often relate to management control of operations, such as assessing the staffing level required by a call center for the coming shift. They may also include knowledge worker decisions, such as those in clinical situations where a doctor is advised as to the likely interactions of a set of medications she has just prescribed to a patient. Although these tactical decisions are not as high-volume as operational or micro decisions, they are often of slightly greater value and so still offer an opportunity for Decision Management Systems.

CHANGING DECISION CRITERIA

Another set of tactical decisions under managerial control are those for revising the decision criteria used in operational decisions. The world is dynamic, so the decision criteria for operational decisions need to change regularly. For example, customer preferences and fraud patterns change over time, as do the criteria for deciding what offers are to be made. Some tactical decisions are about setting the right decision criteria to be applied in an operational decision.

Because these systems are more complex and less repeatable, however, it is likely that the system will not completely automate the decision. Instead it will guide and support the decision maker by restricting the available options or by focusing them on a specific set of information, which will be useful to making the final determination.

Different Types of Decisions Interact

Operational decisions are made every time a business process or transaction executes, and tactical decisions are made periodically to change operational decision criteria or to attend to exceptional business situations and take corrective actions. Over a longer horizon, this is not sufficient to improve business outcomes. Business strategy guides tactical and operational decisions and may need to change to respond to the dynamic marketplace and the external world. For example, competitors may introduce new products and services, influencing customer choice and putting competitive pressure on revenue and profitability. This may mean changing business strategy around providing targeted discounts and customizing products. This in turn creates change in processes and associated operational decisions. These strategic, tactical, and operational decisions must be aligned.

One way to understand the relationship between operational, tactical, and strategic decision-making is shown in Figure 4-1. This Observe-Orient-Decide-Act (OODA) model was originally introduced by military strategist and USAF Colonel John Boyd. Business outcomes are "observed" to detect changing situations that may lead to new tactical decisions, represented by "decide" or strategy "reorientation" with changes in business processes and additional decisions. "Act" represents operational decisions following the decision criteria set by the "decide" stage. There's more on the OODA Loop in Chapter 10, "Technology Enablers."

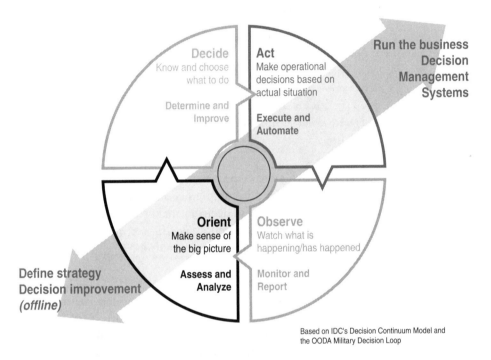

Based on IDC's Decision Continuum Model and
the OODA Military Decision Loop

Figure 4-1   The Decision Lifecycle From strategy definition to decision automation.

If We Are Talking About Decisions, Aren't We Just Talking About Decision Support Systems?

The line between Decision Management Systems and Decision Support Systems (or Executive Information Systems) can be blurry. This is especially true when considering the kind of Decision Management System that handles tactical decisions, or where an operational decision is not completely automated—where the user is presented with multiple valid options, such as possible offers to make.

Decision Management Systems are distinct, however, and they differ from traditional Decision Support Systems in five ways:

1. Decision Support Systems provide information that describes the situation and perhaps historical trends so that humans can decide what to do and which actions to take. Decision Management Systems automate or recommend the *actions* that should be taken based on the information that is available at the time the decision is being made.

2. The policies, regulations, and best practices that determine the best action are embedded, at least in part, in a Decision Management System where a Decision Support System requires the user to remember them or look them up separately.

3. The information and insight presented in a Decision Support System is typically backward looking, and Decision Support Systems are generally reactive—helping human decision-makers react to a new or changed situation by presenting information that might help them make a decision. In contrast, Decision Management Systems use information to make predictions and aim to be proactive.

4. Learning is something that happens outside a Decision Support System and inside a Decision Management System. Users of Decision Support Systems are expected to learn what works and what does not work and to apply what they learn to future decisions. Decision Management Systems have experimentation or test-and-learn infrastructure built in so that the system itself learns what works and what does not.

5. Decision Management Systems are integrated into an organization's runtime environment. They make decisions for applications and services in the organization's enterprise application architecture. In contrast, Decision Support Systems are often desktop or interactive applications that execute outside the core application portfolio.

Why Don't the Other Approaches Work?

Before considering the remaining principles, it is worth considering why it is essential to begin with the decision in mind. What is it about a focus on functions, on process, or on data that prevents the effective development of Decision Management Systems?

Objective

A Functional Focus Is Not Enough

One traditional approach to building systems is to focus on a cluster of related functions—those to do with human resources or those to do with managing a factory, for instance. Such systems contain stacks of capability focused in one functional area and owned by a single functional department. This approach could result in the development of Decision Management Systems if the decisions involved were wholly contained within a single business function. However, while some decisions are concentrated in this way, many cut across functions. A discount calculation decision, for instance, might involve inputs from supply chain functions, from finance, and from customer management. As such a focus on functions will rarely identify and encompass decisions in a way that lends itself to the construction of Decision Management Systems.

A Process Focus Is Not Enough

Functional applications have gradually fallen from favor as organizations have moved to focus on end-to-end business processes. Business processes such as "order to cash" or "issue policy" often cut across several functional areas, linking elements of one function together with elements of another to create a useful business outcome. Although this cross-functional approach can help with the identification of decisions, a pure process focus tends to entwine decisions with the process itself. If no real distinction is drawn between decisions and the processes that need those decisions, it is hard to create true Decision Management Systems. A strong separation of concerns, keeping business processes and decisions linked but separate, is required if enough of a focus on decisions is to be maintained.

Some processes keep decisions separate and manage them separately by assigning these decisions to people in manual process tasks. A focus on human decision-making, even in high-volume operational processes, also does not result in the construction of Decision Management Systems.

/ Analytic

A Data Focus Is Not Enough

Particularly when constructing their own custom systems, organizations often focus on the data that must be managed. These systems become focused almost entirely on the management of the data elements or entities concerned. Providing what is known as CRUD functionality

(Create, Read, Update, and Delete) for the core objects becomes their rationale. The data contained is managed only so that it can be edited and displayed while analysis is limited to reporting. Such systems often provide data for decision support systems but they, like process- and function-centric systems, defer decision making to actors outside the system.

Principle #2: Be Transparent and Agile

Most information systems in use today are opaque and hard to change. The use of programming languages—code—to specify their behavior makes them opaque to any but the most technically adept. This opacity, and the difficulties of confirming that changes made to the code do what they are expected to do, make for long change cycles and a lack of responsiveness. The combination means that extensive information technology projects must be planned, budgeted, and executed to make changes to the behavior of a system.

These characteristics are unacceptable in a Decision Management System. Opacity is unacceptable because many decisions must demonstrate that they are compliant with policies or regulations. If the code is opaque, then it will not be possible to see how decisions have been made and it will not be possible to verify that these decisions were compliant. Decision Management Systems also make decisions that are based on detailed business know-how and experience. If the code is so opaque that it cannot be understood by those who have this know-how or experience, then it is unlikely to be correct.

Organizational decision-making changes constantly, so agility is also essential. As regulations change, the behavior of any Decision Management System that implements that regulation must also change. Organizations also want Decision Management Systems to make good decisions—effective ones. Effective decisions based on the expectations of customers must be competitive, yet the behavior of competitors and customer expectations change constantly. And moreover, customers and competitors are not obliged to tell organizations when their expectations or plans change. An ability to rapidly change Decision Management Systems to respond is essential.

Decision Management Systems must therefore be both transparent and agile:

- The design must be transparent so that it is clear that the system is executing the behavior expected of it.

- The execution must be transparent so that it is clear how each decision was made.

- They must be agile so that their behavior can be changed when necessary without delay and without unnecessary expense.

Design Transparency and Why It Matters

A Decision Management System must exhibit design transparency. It must be possible for non-technical experts—those who understand the regulations or policies involved or who have the necessary know-how and experience—to determine whether the system is going to behave as required. Those without IT expertise must be able to manage the way in which decisions are made so that it is clear to all participants involved. The drivers or source of this behavior must be identifiable so that those reviewing the behavior of the system can clearly assess its effectiveness in meeting objectives.

Tracking the source of decision-making behavior also means that changes in those sources can be quickly mapped to the changes required in the system. Design transparency means it is possible to determine the way in which a proposed change will ripple through the Decision Management System. One regulatory change might affect many decisions, for example, and decisions may be dependent on the same data elements because they have information needs in common.

Organizations must be sure that their Decision Management Systems will make decisions accurately and effectively after a change is made. This requires that the ripples and impacts of any change can be determined before it is made. Design transparency is essential to being able to trace these impacts.

Execution Transparency and Why It Matters

When a decision is made by a person, that person can be asked to explain the decision. If a person rejects an application for a loan, for instance, he can be asked to appear in court, to write a letter explaining, or simply to answer the customer's questions. This is not possible when a system makes a decision. A Decision Management System must therefore provide an explanation of a decision that will satisfy customers or suppliers who are materially affected by it. When a decision is regulated, such as when deciding which consumers may have access to credit, a Decision Management System must provide an exact description of how each decision was made so that it can be reviewed for compliance. Decision Management Systems must deliver real execution transparency in these cases.

Not all decisions require execution transparency. When marketing or promotional decisions are being made, it may not be necessary to understand exactly why a particular offer was made to a particular site visitor. When a Decision Management System is being used to decide when to bring a human into the loop, for fraud investigation for instance, it may also not be necessary to understand why as the human acts as a second "pair of eyes."

Even when a Decision Management System does not require execution transparency, an understanding of how each decision was made can help improve the decision-making of the system. Building in execution transparency is therefore generally a good idea, whether it is required or not. Any approach to developing Decision Management Systems must support execution transparency as well as design transparency.

Business Agility and Why It Matters

An increase in transparency is likely to result in an increase in business agility—if it is easier to see how something works, it will be easier to change how it works when this is needed. A faster response to a needed change improves overall business agility. Transparency is necessary for agility but not sufficient. Once a change is identified and its design impact assessed, it must be possible to make the change quickly and reliably. Decision Management Systems can require real-time changes to their behavior in extreme cases. Daily or weekly changes are very common. When sudden market changes occur, such as major bankruptcies or an outbreak of hostilities, the resulting need for changes to Decision Management Systems can be extreme. Money—and perhaps lives—will be lost every minute until the change is made.

Decision Management Systems must change constantly to reflect new regulations, new policies, and new conditions. This rate of change must be both possible and cost-effective. For most businesses and other organizations, it will not be acceptable if the needed agility in Decision Management Systems comes at too high a price. For a Decision Management System, change must be easy, it must be reliable, it must be fast, and it must be cost-effective.

AGILE DECISION-MAKING FOR TRULY AGILE PROCESSES

Many organizations invest a great deal in developing agile business processes. Decision Management Systems further increase this agility as business changes often involve updates to business decisions. These decisions are often the most dynamic part of a process, the part that changes most often.

For instance, a company's pricing rules are likely to change far more often than its order-to-cash process. If only the business process can be changed quickly, then the company will not be able to respond to the far more numerous pricing changes without changing its process, an unnecessary step. Developing Decision Management Systems allows an organization to control business processes and the critical decisions within them. This increases the agility built into a process and allows for a stable process even when decision-making is constantly changing and evolving.

Explicitly identifying decisions and describing the logic behind them allows this logic to be managed and updated separately from the process itself, dramatically increasing the agility of an organization.

Principle #3: Be Predictive, Not Reactive

In recent years, organizations have spent heavily on technology for managing and using data. Beginning with Database Management Systems and moving through Information Management, Data Quality and Data Integration to Reporting, and Dashboards, these investments are now mostly classified as Business Intelligence and Performance Management. These investments have taken data that was once hidden in transactional systems and made it accessible and usable by people making decisions in the organization.

These investments have been focused on analyzing the past and presenting this analysis to human users. They have relied, reasonably enough, on their human users to make extrapolations about the future. Users of these systems are making decisions based on this data, using what has happened in the past to guide how they will act in the future. Many of these systems can also bring users' attention to changes in data quickly to prompt decision-making. The value of this investment in terms of improved human decision-making is clear.

These approaches will not work for Decision Management Systems. When a decision is being automated in a Decision Management System, there is no human to do the extrapolation. Passing only historical data into a Decision Management System would be like driving with only the rear view mirror—every decision being made would be based on out-of-date and backward-looking data. It fact it would be worse, as a human driver can make guesses as to what's in front of her based on what she sees in a rear view mirror. She will be reasonably accurate too, unless the road is changing direction quickly. Systems are not that smart—without people to make extrapolations from data, Decision Management Systems need to be given those extrapolations explicitly. Without some view of the future and the likely impacts of different decision alternatives, a Decision Management System will fail to spot opportunities or threats in time to do anything about them.

Predicting likely future behavior is at the core of using predictions in Decision Management Systems. You need to predict individual customer behavior such as how likely they are to default on a loan or respond to a particular offer. You need to predict if their behavior will be negative or positive in response to each possible action you could take, predicting how much additional revenue a customer might generate for each possible action. You want to know how likely it is that a transaction represents risky or fraudulent behavior. Ultimately you want to be able to predict the best possible action to take based on everything you know by considering the likely future behavior of a whole group of customers.

Decision Management Systems require predictions. They must be given predictions in the context of which they can act instead of simply reacting to the data available at the time a decision is made. They need access to predictions that turn the inherent uncertainty about the future into a usable probability. They cannot be told, for instance, which claims are definitely fraudulent—this is uncertain. They can be given a model that predicts how likely it is that a specific claim is fraudulent.

There are three specific ways in which Decision Management Systems can be given predictions. They can be given models that predict risk or fraud, that predict opportunity, and that predict the impact of decisions. They can use these predictions to direct, guide, or push decision-making in the right direction.

Predict Risk or Fraud

Most repeatable decisions do not have a huge economic impact individually. Despite their limited scope, many do have a significant gap between good and bad decisions. The value of the decision varies significantly with how well they are made. This gap arises when there is a risk of a real loss if a decision is made poorly. For instance, a well-judged loan offer to someone who will pay it back as agreed might net a bank a few tens of dollars in profit. A poorly judged offer will result in the loss of the loan principal—perhaps thousands of dollars. This mismatch between upside and downside is characteristic of risk-based decisions. Similarly, a poorly made decision in detecting fraud can result in large sums being transferred to an imposter or large purchases being made using stolen credit cards.

When Decision Management Systems are being used to manage these decisions, it is essential that the decision-making be informed by an accurate assessment of the risks of the particular transaction or customer concerned. Such models might be focused on fraud, using analysis of patterns revealed in past fraudulent transactions to predict how likely it is that this transaction is also fraudulent. They might be focused on the likelihood of default, using a customer's past payment history and the history of other customers like him to predict how likely it is that he will fail to make payments in a timely fashion.

Many techniques can be used to build such models from historical data, but all of them require knowledge of which historical transactions were "bad"—fraudulent or in default. These known cases are used to train a model to predict how similar a new transaction is to these "bads." Once such a prediction exists, a Decision Management System can use it, treating those transactions or customers with particularly high, or particularly low, risk differently.

Predict Opportunity

Many decisions do not involve an assessment of downside risk, but they still have some variability. Not driven entirely by compliance with regulations or policies, these decisions require an assessment of opportunity before an appropriate choice can be made. There is typically no absolute downside if a poor decision is made, simply a missed opportunity. When Decision Management Systems are being used to manage these opportunity-centric decisions, they will need to have some way to manage these tradeoffs.

These decisions are largely, though not exclusively, about how to treat customers. Deciding which offer to make to a customer or which ad to display to a visitor are examples of decisions where the "best" decision is one which makes the most of the opportunity to interact with the customer or visitor. Historical data can be used to predict how appealing a particular offer or product might be to a particular person or to a specific segment of customers. The value to the company of each offer, combined with the likelihood that a particular customer will accept it, can then be used to identify the most effective offer—to make the best decision.

When many such offers are being considered, it may be complex to identify the "best" offer. It may be difficult to manage the tradeoffs between the various decisions. In these circumstances, Decision Management Systems can take advantage of optimization technology that allows the tradeoffs to be explicitly defined, and then the "optimal" or best outcome can be selected mathematically.

Predict Impact of Decisions

Sometimes the effect of an action taken by a Decision Management System cannot be precisely determined. For instance, the value of a subscription for a mobile phone will vary with the use made of the phone. When an action is available for a decision and has this kind of uncertainty about its value, a further prediction is needed.

The likely impact of each action on the profitability, risk or retention of a customer can be predicted by analyzing the behavior of other similar customers who were treated the same way—for whom the same action was taken. The prediction of the likely impact of each action can be combined with predictions of risk and opportunity to improve the quality of decision-making in Decision Management Systems.

Principle #4: Test, Learn, and Continuously Improve

Most information systems have a single approach to handling any decisions that have been embedded in them. Every transaction is treated the same way, with possible alternative approaches largely eliminated during design to find the "best" approach. Once this singular approach has been implemented, information systems continue to work the way they were originally designed until someone explicitly re-codes them to behave differently. The only way these systems are changed is when an external agent—a human—decides that a change is required. These systems also accumulate large amounts of data about customers, products, and other aspects of the business. This data might show that certain actions are more effective than others, but the system will continue with its programmed behavior regardless—every customer is treated like the first.

This approach is not an effective way to develop Decision Management Systems. When we make decisions about our own lives or interactions, we often assess a large amount of data, either explicitly or implicitly. We learn from this data what is likely to work or not work—the data accumulated provides clues to how an effective decision can be made. A Decision Management System cannot afford to ignore the accumulated historical data.

Decisions involve making a selection from a range of alternative actions and then taking the selected action. It is often not immediately obvious if the decision was made effectively. Some decisions have a significant time to outcome, and no assessment of the effectiveness of the decision will be possible until that time has passed. For instance, an early intervention designed to ensure a customer renews her annual contract cannot be assessed until the customer reaches the renewal point, perhaps many months later. If the action taken turns out to be ineffective, then a different approach will need to be considered. A Decision Management System cannot afford to "single thread" this analysis by only testing one decision making approach at a time.

Whether a decision is a good one or a bad one is a moving target. A decision may be made to discount a particular order for a customer that may be competitive today but much less so tomorrow because a competitor has changed their pricing. As markets, competitors, and consumer behavior shift, they affect the effectiveness of a decision. This constant change in the definition of an effective decision means that Decision Management Systems must optimize their behavior over time, continuously refining and improving how they act.

Decision Management Systems must therefore test, learn, and continuously improve. The analysis and changes may be done by human observers of the Decision Management System or by the system itself in a more automated fashion. Decision Management Systems must collect data about the effectiveness of decision making. They must use this data, and other data collected by traditional information systems, to refine and improve their decision-making approach. Decision Management

Systems must allow multiple potential decision-making approaches to be tried simultaneously. These are continually compared to see which ones work and which ones do not. Successful ones persist and evolve, unsuccessful ones are jettisoned. Finally, Decision Management Systems must be built on the basis that their behavior will change and improve over time. Decision Management Systems will not be perfect when implemented but will optimize themselves as time passes.

Collect and Use Information to Improve

The first way Decision Management Systems must learn is through collecting and then using information about the decisions they make. When a Decision Management System makes a decision, it should record what decision it made, as well as how and why it made the decision it did. This decision performance information will allow the long-term effectiveness of a decision to be assessed as it can be integrated with the organization's performance metrics to see which decisions result in which positive, or negative, performance outcomes. This information allows good decisions to be differentiated from bad ones, better ones from worse ones. It is often said that if you wish to improve something, you must first measure it. Decisions are not an exception to this rule.

Information about the decisions made can and should be combined with the information used to make the decision. This information might be about a customer, a product, a claim, or other transaction. This is the information that is passed to the Decision Management System so that it can make a decision. Combining this information with the decision performance information will identify differences in performance that are caused by differences in the information used to drive the decision. For instance, a decision-making approach may work well for customers with income below a certain level and poorly for those above it. Storing, integrating, analyzing, and using this data to improve decision-making is the first building block in building Decision Management Systems that continuously improve.

Support Experimentation (Test and Learn)

When a Decision Management System is being defined, it may not be clear what approach will result in the best outcomes for the organization. Several alternative approaches might all be valid candidates for "best approach." Simulation and modeling of these approaches, and testing them against historical data, might show which approach is most likely to be superior. Even if the historical data points to a clear winner, the approach is going to be used against new data and may not perform as well in these circumstances.

A Decision Management System, therefore, needs to be able to run experiments, choosing between multiple defined approaches for real transactions. The approach used for each transaction can be recorded, and this information will allow the approaches to be compared to see which is superior. This comparison may not be definitive, and one approach may be better for some segments of a customer base, while a second works better for other segments. Results from these experiments can then be used to update the Decision Management System with the most successful approach or combination of approaches. Because Decision Management Systems handle repeatable decisions, there will always be more decisions to be made that will be able to take advantage of this improved approach.

Optimize Over Time

In a static world, one round of experimentation might be enough to find the best approach. A set of experiments could be conducted and the most effective approach selected. As long as nothing changes, this approach will continue to be most effective. However, the effectiveness of a decision-making approach can vary over time for many reasons, and you have little or no control over this. The old "best" approach may degrade suddenly or gradually, and when it does, you will need to have alternatives. Even when experimentation finds a clear winner, a Decision Management System needs to keep experimenting to see whether any of the alternative approaches have begun to outperform the previous winner. Alternatives approaches could be those rejected as inferior initially or new ones developed specifically to see whether a new approach would be superior in the changing circumstances. The effect of this continuous and never-ending experimentation is to optimize results over time by continually refining and improving decision-making approaches.

Summary

Decision Management Systems are different from traditional information systems.

- Traditional information systems have a process, data, or functional focus. Decision Management Systems are decision-centric, built with a repeatable decision in mind.

- Traditional information systems are opaque and hard to change. Decision Management Systems improve collaboration and compliance by being transparent and agile.

- Traditional information systems present historical data as analyses to people. Decision Management Systems embed analytics that predict risk, opportunity, and impact deep into the system itself.

- Traditional information systems are static and don't use the data they store to improve their results. Decision Management Systems test new approaches, learn what works, and continuously improve.

Developing Decision Management Systems requires a new approach; this is the subject of Part II, "Building Decision Management Systems."

II

Building Decision Management Systems

Decision Management Systems radically alter the way an organization's systems support and enable its operations. Decision Management Systems are agile, so they can be easily changed as needs change; analytic, in that they use the data an organization has to be more effective; and adaptive because they learn what works and what does not over time. Such systems demonstrate the four principles of Decision Management Systems:

- First and foremost, they are built with the decision in mind—they are decision-centric systems that automate and improve specific decisions.
- Secondly, they are transparent, exposing their logic so that business and IT teams can collaborate effectively, and agile, so they can be changed easily.
- Thirdly, they are predictive, turning historical data into usable future probabilities.
- Finally, they test and learn, track results, and experiment to make sure they stay effective as time passes.

Building Decision Management System requires a new approach. Although most of the techniques and disciplines of software development remain relevant, a new set of techniques must be applied and a new framework adopted. This framework has three elements—decision discovery, decision service construction and decision analysis. When applied, this framework delivers agile, analytic, and adaptive systems that demonstrate the four principles of Decision Management Systems.

> This part of the book contains descriptions of deliverables and work products, techniques, and tasks. It is not, however, a complete methodology for developing Decision Management Systems. It focuses on core techniques and on the most important things to remember. Aimed as it is at business leaders and those at the intersection of business and technology rather than at developers, it is not a substitute for an effective development methodology.

5

Discover and Model Decisions

The most fundamental of the four principles of Decision Management Systems is the first—begin with the decision in mind. Decision Management Systems are focused on automating and improving specific decisions. Decision Management Systems do not execute complete business processes; they provide decision-making to allow other processes to execute more effectively or to run straight through without manual intervention. Decision Management Systems do not replace complete legacy systems; they replace hard to change decision-making components of legacy systems with more manageable, more agile components.

To build Decision Management Systems, we must know what decisions are being managed. We must identify appropriate decisions, then document, design, and understand them. Existing software approaches do not focus on decisions at this level of detail. A new phase or discipline is required—Decision Discovery.

Decision Discovery involves identifying, describing, and modeling decisions that will repay an investment in developing a Decision Management System.

Characteristics of Suitable Decisions

Organizations make many decisions of many different types. Not all these decisions are suitable for automating in Decision Management Systems. Before committing to building a Decision Management System for a specific decision, it is important to be sure it has suitable characteristics. In particular decisions need to be repeatable, nontrivial, and measurable to be good candidates. The organization must also be able to accept automation for the decision. If the organization fundamentally believes a decision should be made by a person, you can end up with a Decision Management System that no one uses.

Repeatable

By far the most important criterion for a suitable decision is repeatability. If a decision is not repeatable, there is no value in developing a Decision Management System to automate it. To be considered repeatable, a decision must pass four tests:

1. It is possible to say when the decision will need to be made.
2. Each time the decision is made, the same information is available, considered, and analyzed.
3. The set of possible actions remains consistent between decisions.
4. The way in which the success of these actions is measured in terms of business outcomes remains consistent.

For example, the decision about which cross-sell offer to make to a customer at checkout passes all four tests:

1. The decision is made every time a customer checks out with a new order.
2. The customer profile, his past orders, and his current order are analyzed to determine the most appropriate cross-sell.
3. The cross-sell is always a product selected from the current catalog.
4. Success is defined as an increase in the value of a customer order after the cross-sell offer is made relative to the value of that order before the cross-sell offer was made.

Note that the content of the information in steps 2 and 3 change from decision to decision, but the structure or scope of the information does not.

The Decision Is Made at Defined Times

An organization knows when a repeatable decision must be made. Such a decision might be made for all transactions of a certain type. A decision might be required for a process to complete or move to the next step, allowing an organization to define it in terms of a process context. For instance, decisions about claim validity are made for every submitted claim. In more event-centric environments, a decision might be required when a specific event is received or event pattern is identified. For instance, a pattern of sensor events might identify a particular piece of hardware as being close to failure, and a decision must then be made regarding which engineer to dispatch to look at it. Finally, a decision may be made on a regular schedule such as hourly, daily, or weekly. For instance, a bank may check to see whether it has wealth management recommendations for its best customers every week. The need to make these decisions is knowable in advance.

It is also possible to know that a decision must be made many times in the course of a year without knowing exactly when such a decision will need to be made. These decisions may be made in response to some external driver over which the organization has no control, such as competitive changes or the weather. Decisions may also be proactive, driven by considerations of individuals not knowable to the organization's systems. These decisions may still be repeatable if the organization can define the circumstances in which a decision will be made. For example, an outbound marketing campaign may launch based on a wide range of factors, but if the organization knows it will decide to launch an outbound campaign multiple times each month and can articulate the circumstances in which it will do so (a competitor launches a new product or changes pricing, a news item is relevant to a product, and so on), then this decision can pass the test for being made at defined times as the organization knows what the conditions are that will trigger the need for a decision.

The Same Information Is Used Each Time

The second test for repeatability is information. For a decision to be repeatable in the context of Decision Management Systems, it must use a consistent set of information. This will allow the implementation of an interface to pull this information into the Decision Management System when the decision is automated. The corollary of this is that a consistent set of information must be available each time the decision is made.

This does not mean that every time the decision is made, an identical set of information is presented to it. It does mean, however, that a set of information can be defined that is a superset of the information that will be presented each time.

For example, a decision about a customer retention offer will use the customer's profile and the products she has purchased as part of its decision-making. This is consistent from decision to decision, although the completeness of a customer profile and the number of products owned by a customer will vary from customer to customer. The specific information about a customer and her products will differ each time, but the basic structure of the information will remain consistent. This decision about a customer retention offer could only be made when this information was available.

AVOID INFORMATION SUPERSETS

The intent of this test is not to define a massive superset of information to link disparate decisions into a set. If it is not possible to define a fairly coherent set of information that is used repeatedly, the decision will not pass this test.

Defined Set of Actions

A decision always selects from a set of possible actions. These might be a list of customer treatments, loan terms, offers, or products. They might also be a range of values, such as a price or discount level. The act of making a decision selects one or more of these possible actions. Repeatable decisions have the same set of actions each time. Different actions will be selected each time the decision is made, but the set of actions remains consistent between decisions. For instance, each loan originated will make different selections of the appropriate terms and prices based on the specifics of the loan application. Nevertheless, the set of possible terms and prices is the same for each decision.

DECISIONS CHANGE OVER TIME

This test for repeatability does not mean that the allowed actions for a decision do not vary over time. Decision-making is dynamic and new possible actions may be defined and existing ones "retired" as the decision-making approach is refined. This kind of evolution does not mean that a decision is not repeatable. A repeatable decision is one in which the same actions are available each time a decision is made between such changes in the decision-making approach.

Consistent Measurement of Success

The final test for repeatability is that good and bad decisions can be consistently identified. Nothing can be improved if it cannot be measured, and decision-making is no exception. It is essential to understand how to measure the success of each decision in terms of outcomes that make sense for the business. This is true of all decisions, even one-off ad-hoc decisions. For repeatable decisions, the measurement of success is consistent over time. For example, a decision about which supplier to use for a particular part is measured by assessing on-time delivery and by counting any quality problems with the supply. This assessment is consistent for every supplier selection decision.

Nontrivial

The second test for a suitable decision is that it is nontrivial. Decision Management Systems represent an investment of time and money. Organizations will only a see a return on this investment if the decision being automated is one that has a degree of complexity. Typically, the drivers of this complexity are policies and regulations, the need for domain knowledge, the need to analyze large amounts of complex data, the need to select from very large numbers of possible outcomes, and the need to trade-off competing objectives. Even if none of these drive complexity in the decision, the decision-making approach may need to be updated so often that it should be considered nontrivial on that basis.

Nontrivial decisions do not need to pass all of these tests. Very complex regulations or very difficult trade-offs might be enough to classify a decision as nontrivial regardless of other factors. Similarly, no one test need be very severe if a decision has elements of several. A decision based on a few policies, some straightforward analysis, and a simple trade-off may be nontrivial thanks to the combination of factors.

Policies and Regulations

Perhaps the most common drivers of complexity in repeatable decisions are the existence of policies and regulations that must be followed when making a decision. Organizations often have policies that constrain decision-making as a way to ensure consistency and to avoid known problems or pitfalls. For instance, organizations may have policies that define the minimum size of companies who can act as suppliers of critical parts, or that insist on specific terms being included in loans above a certain size. Ensuring that decisions made are always compliant with these policies can be complex.

Many decisions an organization makes are also constrained by regulations, particularly when those decisions relate to individual consumers or to interactions with government agencies. For instance, the ways in which companies decide who gets credit is heavily regulated to prevent bias, while other regulations control exactly what kinds of medical services the government will pay for. Organizations want to be sure they follow these regulations when making decisions as the consequences of not doing so can include fines, rejected payment requests, and even legal action. Increasingly, governments are insisting that organizations not only comply with these regulations but *demonstrate* that they are complying with these regulations. This need for execution transparency can make even fairly straightforward regulations a driver for Decision Management Systems.

Domain Knowledge and Expertise

Some decisions are hard to make the first time you try. More experience making the decision often makes it easier to make a decision quickly and increases the chances that you will make a good decision. For instance, making a decision as to the cause of a problem in a piece of machinery is hard when you are unfamiliar with the machinery and with how to debug it. As you gain experience, the decision becomes easier, and you are more likely to correctly identify the root cause of a problem. Decisions like these require domain knowledge and expertise. Some require relatively little domain knowledge, the kind that can be acquired in a few days by watching an experienced operator. Others seem to require years of experience or extensive mentoring to build a suitable level of expertise. These kinds of decisions are nontrivial, as making a good one requires deep understanding of a particular domain.

Analysis Is Required

Although some decisions can be made solely by following the policies or regulations defined for the decision, many require some analysis. If a decision involves making the "best" or "most appropriate" selection, then some judgment or analysis is going to be needed. The decision can be made only after the information available is considered and analyzed. This need for analysis does not mean the decision is not repeatable, or automatable, just that it is a somewhat more complex decision. Repeatable and well-defined analysis can be part of a decision without requiring manual decision-making, as the analysis can be defined in advance.

Several kinds of analysis are possible. The analysis might be to categorize someone or something so that a decision can be made based on that categorization. For instance, someone's driving history might be analyzed to see which risk segment they should be put into when underwriting an auto policy for them. Analysis might result in an assessment of risk, fraud, or opportunity. For instance, a business might be analyzed to see how likely it is to pay back a commercial loan. Analysis might also assess a propensity or likelihood. For instance, the propensity of a particular customer to buy a particular product might be needed before deciding which product to offer.

The analysis can be of the current information (such as all the data in an application or an order) or of historical information (such as all the prior transactions of a customer). A requirement for either kind of analysis will tend to make a decision nontrivial.

Large Amounts of Data

Some decisions involve the consideration of large amounts of data. When the values for large numbers of data elements must be considered to make a decision, it is likely to be nontrivial. For instance, a decision to approve an application may be nontrivial simply because the application contains hundreds of data elements that must be validated and cross-checked.

Large Numbers of Actions

A decision that requires selection from a small number of possible actions is generally simpler than one requiring selection from a large number of possible actions. As the number of possible outcomes rises, so does the likelihood that a decision is going to be nontrivial. It is often said that people have a hard time with lists containing more than seven or so items. Any decision that involves selecting from more options than this is likely to be complex enough to be a good candidate for a Decision Management System.

Of course, a decision can be extremely complex and still only have a couple of possible actions. The underwriting of a complex commercial development project may only have two actions—yes or no—and yet remain an extremely difficult decision to make. The point is more that the mere fact of large numbers of possible actions will make a decision more complex.

Trade-offs Must Be Made

Many decisions involve trade-offs. These decisions are selecting from possible outcomes, none of which are "perfect." Either each outcome has potential downsides that must be balanced against potential upsides, or each outcome has downstream consequences that must be balanced against their value. For instance, a sourcing decision may have to consider both the price a new supplier is offering and the impact the order would have on cumulative discounts from existing suppliers. Some trade-offs are extremely straightforward and easy to make, and others are much more complex. Sometimes there is an optimal or best trade-off, but often there is only a need for a reasonable one. The need to make a trade-off almost always means that a decision is a nontrivial one.

Continued Updates

Even if a decision appears trivial using all the previous criteria, the need for continued updates to the decision-making approach may be enough to make the decision suitable. Some decisions have a stable decision-making approach that does not change very much over time. New regulations or policies may be issued once a year, for instance. Sometimes the decision-making approach must change much more often. Regularly scheduled monthly, weekly, or daily changes are not uncommon in decision-making. For instance, pricing guidelines for heavily traded products might change every day, while new fraud detection approaches could be released every week. Such regular updates can easily justify considering a decision nontrivial.

In addition to regularly scheduled changes, some decisions have a need for continued updating in a less predictable way. For instance, some fraud rules are not released on a regular schedule but must be updated rapidly once announced. Decisions that have a need for immediate updates, even if those updates are fairly rare, are generally nontrivial.

Measurable Business Impact

Because building and evolving Decision Management Systems involves investments, it must be possible to show a return on this investment. Repeatable decisions are more likely to show this return, as there are decisions to make in the future that Decision Management Systems can be designed to make. Similarly, nontrivial decisions are more likely to show a return, as their complexity means that relying on less well-defined decision-making approaches is likely to result in poorer-quality decisions. Although being repeatable and nontrivial are necessary for a decision to be suitable, they are not sufficient.

A suitable decision needs to have a definable and measureable business impact. It must be possible to see the cost of bad decisions and the value of good ones. For a suitable decision, the organization can see the impact of a decision in terms that relate to the measurement framework the organization already has. If an organization values customer loyalty, then the business impact of a customer retention decision could be measured in terms of an increase in customer loyalty. If an organization focuses on being a low-cost provider, then decisions could be measured in terms of their ability to reduce costs. A suitable decision has a defined and measurable impact on the organization.

The business impact of a decision may not be immediately apparent. It can take months or even years to see the total impact of improving how a decision is made. Improving the initial product configuration decision for a subscription product may improve long-term customer retention, for example, but this won't be apparent until the customers affected by the improved decision reach their annual renewal point.

It may also be difficult to measure the impact of a single decision. It is not reasonable, for instance, to consider the improvement in portfolio risk caused by a single loan origination decision. An improvement in the quality of loan origination decisions will, however, show a cumulative improvement in portfolio risk over time.

BEGIN WITH MEASUREMENT INFRASTRUCTURE

It is sometimes possible to see that a decision is important to the business, and perhaps to understand what impact it has, without being able to measure that impact. Experience suggests that it is best to begin by creating an infrastructure that allows the measurement of the impact first before building a Decision Management System to automate and improve the decision.

This measurement infrastructure should capture and report on the right data to assess decision effectiveness. This includes being able to track what actions were taken as a result of a decision and being able to link future outcomes back to these actions.

Candidates for Automation

There is one final test for suitable decisions. If a decision is repeatable, nontrivial, and has a measurable business impact, it will not be suitable unless the organization accepts it as a candidate for automation. There is no value to creating a Decision Management System that is not used. If the decision is one that the organization fundamentally believes requires human judgment, it is not a suitable decision for building Decision Management Systems.

SUITABILITY CHANGES OVER TIME

This is not as simple a test as it appears. The way organizations think about decisions and decision-making evolves. The expectations of younger workers who grew up with computers are different from those who began work with manual processes. Industry norms change over time as proof points from early adopters become widely known. Corporate cultures can hold automation back but can be changed or overridden with enough of a crisis. Observing how a decision is made manually can show that an automated decision would be better and build enthusiasm for it. Just because a decision is not a good candidate today does not mean that it will not become one in the future.

Decisions can often be decomposed into a set of simpler decisions on which the main decision is dependent. The top-level decision may not be a candidate for Decision Management Systems because the organization is unwilling to have a machine make that decision. Lower-level decisions, however, may be suitable simply because the more limited scope of those decisions makes an organization more comfortable with having a computerized approach. For instance, a large commercial underwriting decision may be one that an insurer does not consider a candidate for automation. In this case, an underwriter is going to be charged with making the decision. The organization might be comfortable using a Decision Management System for some elements of this decision, such as selecting the right terms for the kind of project or identifying the amount of reinsurance required.

A Decision Taxonomy

Many decisions made by an organization are suitable for automation in a Decision Management System. Decisions that have suitable characteristics fall into several distinct categories. Decisions in each of these categories have a distinct style or profile. Understanding these profiles can help in identifying and describing decisions. The most common categories are eligibility, validation, and calculation decisions. Risk, fraud, and opportunity decisions are less common but still a part of most organizations' decision inventory.

Eligibility

Many decisions are about determining eligibility. Products and services cannot always be sold to every customer. Government benefits are not payable to all citizens. Not every organization can bid on certain kinds of contract. Determining whether a particular person or organization is eligible is a decision.

Eligibility decisions are often good candidates for Decision Management Systems. They are highly repeatable, as every person or organization that applies should be assessed the same way. Outcomes are well defined—typically only "yes" and "no with reasons"—and the information available to make the decision is both consistent and well defined. Eligibility decisions typically have a very fixed approach with little room for judgment as they are heavily regulated or constrained by policy.

An example would be a decision regarding banking products that might be offered to a customer. Offering a product as a cross-sell that the customer is not eligible for will result in poor customer service, so a decision about the products a particular customer is eligible for is required. Based on information known about a customer, regulations that prohibit certain products in certain states, minimum age requirements, and the bank's policies for each product, it is possible to determine which products should be considered for cross-selling.

ELIGIBILITY AND RISK DECISIONS OVERLAP

There is an overlap between eligibility decisions and risk decisions (described in the following sections). For instance, there may be a minimum or maximum level of risk that can be tolerated for a product. In these circumstances, a customer may be ineligible for a product because a risk assessment made is outside the permitted range. It is generally more useful to consider these to be risk decisions, as the critical issues are those to do with the risk assessment and its integration into decision-making.

Validation

Very similar to eligibility decisions, validations are well-defined and highly repeatable decisions. These decisions are typically used as gates controlling sequence or process. Until or unless the transaction or customer can be validated, the process cannot continue. Validation decisions are mostly driven by policies, although these policies can come from outside the organization, such as an industry standards body.

For example, a claim may be validated before processing. This ensures that the claim contains a complete set of information and that basic checks such as a valid address have been performed before more time-consuming and complex tasks are scheduled.

Calculation

Calculation decisions are often missed in the identification of decisions for Decision Management Systems. It is easy to think of calculations as completely fixed and therefore trivial in the context of Decision

Management Systems. However, some calculations are based on policies that change regularly, and some are more specific to a customer than might at first appear to be the case. Rather than asking, "what is the price for this product?" and regarding this as a trivial look-up in a database, it can be more informative to ask, "what is the correct price for this product for this person at this time?" Such a calculation is clearly a non-trivial decision with opportunities to personalize the pricing or have it reflect rapidly changing demand or competitive environments.

Risk Decisions

Although calculation, eligibility, and validation decisions are driven by policies and regulations, risk decisions are driven by the need to assess how risky a particular customer or transaction is. The potential for a significant loss drives the need for risk assessment, and these decisions have a large gap between the value of a good decision and the value of a bad one. For instance, when a loan is offered to someone, there is a risk that he will not repay the loan. If the loan is not repaid, the lender suffers a significant financial loss. If the loan is repaid, the lender gains financially from the interest paid. The upside potential of such a decision is typically significantly less than the downside risk. A good loan might result in tens or hundreds of dollars in fees, while a bad one might result in a multi-thousand dollar write-off. This difference between the upside and the downside of a risk decision is its defining characteristic.

There are often policies and regulations that must be applied in a risk decision. These might constrain the decision or define how the risk assessment itself can be made. Risks can be assessed judgmentally, using experts as a source. Predictive analytics are widely used to assess risk, and such a data-driven approach is generally to be preferred whenever possible. The use of predictive analytic models to predict how risky a particular transaction or customer is likely to be is at the heart of risk decisions. Most organizations need to be able to explain risk decisions after the fact. As a result, only explicable predictive analytic models that clearly show what is driving the prediction will be acceptable. In addition, organizations will want to be able to show causation in these models—that the drivers of these models have some clear link to the riskiness of behavior.

MANAGING PORTFOLIO RISK IS NOT ENOUGH

When many organizations think about risk decisions, they often focus on portfolio-level risk decisions; for instance, deciding on a sub-prime lending strategy to manage their exposure to high risk but profitable loans. Although these are important risk decisions, the kind of repeatable decision we are discussing is more important in many ways. Organizations do not generally acquire risk in large lumps but one transaction, one loan, one customer at a time. Deciding on the terms for a specific sub-prime loan is the decision that must be made correctly if the portfolio is not to become unbalanced. The portfolio decision constrains this repeatable decision, but it is the repeatable decision that prevents bad loans from entering the portfolio in the first place.

Fraud Decisions

Fraud and abuse decisions are those where the action to be taken is dependent on whether the transaction or customer is considered to be other than they seem. Examples include a decision whether customers are who they say they are, or whether this claim is for a medical procedure that has genuinely been carried out. Although fraud is deliberate, many situations where the system is being abused or where there is a failure to follow best practices look similar to fraudulent transactions because they fall outside the norms. Considering fraud and abuse a single category can therefore be helpful as the approaches are often similar.

Fraud decisions are very similar to risk decisions in that there is a large downside if a decision is made poorly and it is the risk of fraud that is being assessed with an analytic model. These decisions are a different category for two reasons:

- First, when detecting fraud and abuse, there is generally no need to be able to explain the predictive models involved. As long as they work well—they predict a lot of "bad" transactions accurately while mislabeling only a small number of "good" ones—they are acceptable, and there is little or no interest in establishing causality.

- Second, there is a difference in volatility. Risk decisions involve regulations (especially where the decision is about consumers) and long-term risk-management policies that do not change all that often. Fraud decisions involve policies that are based on the changing behavior of fraudsters, tips from law enforcement, and other highly volatile sources. For these reasons, it is worth considering fraud and abuse decisions as being distinct from risk decisions.

Opportunity Decisions

Some decisions are only lightly constrained by policies and regulations. If there is no assessment of risk required—if the decision has little or no possible downside—then the key driver for the decision will be an assessment of opportunity. The potential value of each possible outcome, each action that could be taken, will be used to select between them. Opportunity decisions often ask, "how profitable might this customer be if we take one of the possible actions?"

Opportunity decisions are generally those that are customer-centric such as cross-sell and up-sell decisions. Opportunity decisions also use expert judgment, and increasingly, analytics to predict the likely response of a customer and the potential size of the opportunity. It is also common for opportunity decisions to have to change rapidly to take advantage of competitive and market circumstances. Some opportunity decisions do not relate to customers; for example, it is possible to assess the opportunity for future discounts from a supplier as part of selecting a supplier.

OPPORTUNITY DECISIONS ARE DIFFERENT

There is often little difference between good and bad opportunity decisions. For this reason, it is helpful to think of these as separate from risk decisions and fraud decisions. You could "reverse" how you look at an opportunity to make money and consider it a risk that you will not make any money. It is not helpful to do this, however, as the kind of analysis you do when trying to avoid a loss is and should be different from the kind you do when you are examining two alternatives to see which will benefit you the most.

Repeatable Management Decisions

Calculations; eligibility and validation decisions; risk, fraud, and opportunity decisions are all operational decisions. Operational decisions make up the majority of suitable decisions for Decision Management Systems, but not all. Some suitable repeatable decisions are tactical decisions. A planning decision that is made every day or a decision about budgeting for customer retention might be examples of tactical decisions that are repeatable.

These decisions are not going to be as repeatable as operational decisions and are likely to involve more degrees of freedom for the decision-maker. They are likely to be made by a knowledge worker or manager with the skills and know-how to use business intelligence tools and spreadsheets. The role of any Decision Management System built to handle these decisions is likely to be one of supporting a decision maker rather than one of trying to completely automate the decision. For instance, a Decision Management System might constrain the available outcomes so that the decision maker can focus on only those that are valid, given company policy and risk models. Alternatively, the Decision Management System might assemble the right subset of the available information and present it to the decision maker so that they focus on the highest risk elements of the decision. It can be helpful to think of the resulting system as a blend of traditional decision support systems with Decision Management Systems.

Micro Decisions

When searching for repeatable operational decisions, it is important to consider how fine-grained a decision you are really making. Often what appears to be a single decision is actually many "micro decisions" (Taylor & Raden, 2007). A micro decision is a decision from a customer's perspective. For instance, when consumers receive a piece of direct mail, they respond as though that piece of mail was sent just to them. If it is not relevant, they class it as "junk" and downgrade their opinion of the company that sent it (especially if they are already customers of that company). The contents of this letter are the result of a micro decision.

This perspective of the customer is typically not shared by the company. The marketing department of this company probably thinks it made a single decision to send a particular offer to everyone in a particular segment—10,000 or 100,000 pieces of mail from a single decision.

When evaluating this marketing decision to see whether it is a suitable decision for a Decision Management System, it is much more informative to consider the micro decision perspective. After all, there is no particular reason why the company could not, in fact, make each micro decision differently. It could generate a letter for James, a letter for Erick, a letter for Jean—one letter per micro decision. A Decision Management System could handle this decision and generate a targeted, intensely personalized letter for each of the 10,000 or 100,000 customers. As long as the marketing decision is thought of as a single decision for all the letters, this kind of 1:1 marketing will not be possible.

Most micro decisions are about customers, although there are often analogous decisions for suppliers or partners. Micro decisions can be risk or opportunity decisions, although most missed micro decisions are opportunity decisions.

Finding Decisions

Organizations of even quite modest size make many decisions that are suitable for automation using Decision Management Systems. Repeatable, nontrivial, and measurable decisions of many different types are widespread. However, most organizations have never attempted to inventory these decisions. As a result, it is hard to build Decision Management Systems without first engaging in an exercise to find an appropriate set of decisions.

There are several ways to find suitable decisions, including a top-down approach, process-centric or event-centric analysis, analyzing legacy systems, or using an organization's metrics and key performance indicators (KPIs) to find decisions. All these approaches have value, and most decision inventories are built using multiple approaches. Using several approaches cross-checks and validates the decisions found and engages different people in the discussion, reducing the likelihood that a decision will be missed.

Although the objective of applying these various approaches is to develop a complete decision inventory, it is definitely not a good idea to try and develop an organization-wide decision inventory as a single exercise. Like most such horizontal efforts, you are likely to become bogged down and spend far too long without showing a return on the time invested. Instead, focus on a specific area of the business or a small, tightly coupled set of business processes. Focus on the decisions within this area that make a difference to a goal or objective that you can meas-ure. After you have a first version of a decision inventory for this area of the business, continue on to develop some high-ROI Decision Management Systems to prove the approach. Iteration and incremental development of a decision inventory over time are critical to success with Decision Management Systems.

Top-down

Perhaps the most obvious, although not necessarily the easiest, way to find decisions is simply to brainstorm them. Working with a group of executives and decision-makers, start making lists of decisions made. Most of these decisions will not be suitable for Decision Management Systems as they will not be sufficiently constrained or repeatable. Focus on the day-to-day decisions that implement the executive decisions identified as well as drawing out the hidden micro decisions behind these decisions; this will start to draw out more and better candidates.

With an executive audience, it is also helpful to ask them what deci-sions their staff makes and to ask them about the exceptions they have to handle. Anything referred up the management chain is likely to be an example of a decision that is mostly made at a lower level in the organi-zation. For instance, a risk officer who talks about handling approvals for really complex commercial loans is telling you that all commercial loans must be approved and that this happens somewhere further down the organization.

You can also ask executives about customer complaints. What deci-sion or set of decisions provoked the customer's unhappiness? How about service outages or major company crises? Often these were trig-gered by a series of bad decisions, and executives are happy to tell you what decisions were involved.

A top-down approach is often very informative but almost never suffi-cient. Only in the most decision-centric industries (consumer credit cards or property and casualty insurance, perhaps) will facilitated ses-sions and interviews of executives get you a reasonably complete deci-sion inventory. A focus on the business processes in the area you have selected is likely to be essential.

THE TOP-DOWN APPROACH AND EXECUTIVE GOALS

One of the key issues in any project is getting funding. A top-down approach has the advantage that it clearly begins with the things that matter to executives, with their goals and objectives. Any decisions identified will therefore be linked to and clearly supportive of these goals. This strong connection between the decisions found and the organization's strategic goals will help make the case for funding and help deliver strong executive sponsorship.

Process-centric

One of the best ways to find suitable decisions is by analyzing existing process designs. By and large, processes are only designed and automated if they are themselves repeatable. These processes are about the day-to-day operations of the organization, and as such, almost any decision that is relevant to these decisions will also be a suitable, repeatable decision.

Most processes have been designed without an explicit focus on decisions, however, so the decisions will be hidden in the process design to a greater or lesser extent. Four approaches can be used separately or in combination to find the decisions in a process—looking for explicit decision points, evaluating similar processes, looking at local exceptions and examining every escalation or referral step.

Explicit Decision Points

Some processes have explicit decision points embedded in them. Decision points have two characteristics. First, there is a task in the process that is immediately followed by a branch or gateway that uses the result of that task to send the process down one of several paths. Second, this task typically uses a "decisioning" word in its name. For instance:

- **Determine** whether someone is eligible for a benefit
- **Validate** the completeness of an invoice
- **Calculate** the discount for an order

- **Assess** the risk of a transaction
- **Select** the terms for a deal
- **Choose** which claims to fast track

Determine, validate, calculate, assess, select, and *choose* are all decisioning words. Any such decision point should be immediately identified and added to the decision inventory.

Multiple Similar Processes

After the explicit decision points have been documented, it is worth looking at the process inventory to see whether there are groups or clusters of similar processes. Often these similar processes have a decision that is different, while everything else in the process is the same. Because the decision-making has been embedded in the process design, however, the processes all look different. For instance, a government agency might have multiple permit-issuing processes. These processes are different because the eligibility criteria for each permit are different. If checking these criteria is handled with process steps, the processes will look quite different.

If multiple similar processes are found, look for a decision that is being made as part of the process. It is likely to be made slightly differently in each case, but often can be reduced to a single decision—such as "is a company eligible for this permit?"—that is common across all the processes. Visual inspection of the processes can be used to confirm how similar the processes would be if the decision were to be externalized from the process.

Local Exceptions

Another common consequence of not identifying and managing decisions is a process with large numbers of local exceptions. These have often made what at first seemed to be a straightforward process look very complex. Each country, division, or product group might have defined its own exceptions to the global standard process that everyone is using. For example, a standard supplier onboarding process might be overloaded with hundreds of local exceptions to handle country-by-country requirements for supplier information.

It is often possible to define a decision that applies these local exceptions and thus allow everyone to use the standard process. For instance, the decision "do we have enough information about this supplier?" could be defined, and as long as that decision included country-specific guidance, everyone could use it. With access to such a decision, it may well be that every group is happy to use the standard process, as all the exceptions to the process were really a way to capture how this decision should be made in each case. Once again, identifying and externalizing the decision will simplify the process.

Escalation and Referral

The final sources of decisions in a process are manual escalations and referral tasks. When a process must sometimes stop while an issue with a transaction or question about a customer is escalated, a decision is clearly involved. Generally the person executing the process (such as a call center representative) is not considered sufficiently senior or well trained to make the decision, so it must be escalated. These decisions are almost always good candidates for Decision Management Systems.

Similarly, any time a process is paused while work is put on a worklist so that a human can be brought into the process, a decision is implied. Sometimes a human is brought in to apply her judgment or to interact with the real world in some way. A mortgage process might assign someone to go and inspect a property to decide what condition it is in. These decisions are unlikely to be suitable for Decision Management Systems. Most often, however, little or no judgment is required, and there is little freedom of action for the person assigned. She is instead expected to apply policies and regulations, or guidelines from a cheat sheet to make the decision and push the transaction back into the process. These decisions are almost always a good candidate for Decision Management Systems.

Externalizing these decisions will not generally make a process simpler, as the escalation or referral will still be required for some decisions—those the Decision Management System cannot make. A Decision Management System will generally make more transactions run straight through without such an escalation or referral, however, improving throughput and increasing efficiency.

Event-centric

For organizations that are adopting event-centric design and building event-processing systems, analyzing existing event-based systems can also result in the identification of additional decisions. Event-based systems are generally high-performance, low-latency systems, so any decision they require is going to be an excellent candidate for Decision Management Systems.

Event-based systems involve many decisions about the events and how to handle them. These are largely internal to the systems themselves. Because of the need for high—often extreme—performance, event-based systems often include business decision-making along with event correlation decisions. Three approaches can be used separately or in combination to find the decisions in event-based systems—looking for places where event and non-event data are presented together, event streams that are coming under increasingly precise scrutiny, and examining a finite state analysis of the entire system.

Event and Non-event Data in Combination

Event-based systems have data flowing into them that they interpret by monitoring changing states—this data is said to be "stateful." Often some of the data required to determine a specific action is not contained within an event-based system. A good indication that a decision is embedded in an event-processing system is that it must look up this kind of stateless data externally. If the decision is not extracted, the event systems will embed the decision-making logic within their event processing logic and execute it after the data has been retrieved.

For example, an event-based system is ideally suited to monitor a package delivery system. In this way, various undesirable states can be detected and acted on in the shortest time possible. Specific data on each package in transit is continually available as a data feed. As the data passes through the event-processing system, the system builds up a memory of what occurs—both for the individual package itself and systemically for the entire system. The event-based system can correlate data across every package, and it can determine that the time difference between packages arriving and leaving a particular hub is increasing exponentially. This could be caused by snowstorms that have closed the airport, with a few trucks being used to route the packages out to another hub. The system now needs to prioritize which packages will be moved first on to trucks so they can proceed without any further delay.

The information needed to prioritize packages does not exist within the event-based system. For instance, the company may choose to prioritize by customer membership levels, to ensure that its best customers are given top service. Thus, a gold-level member's package would be retrieved from a stranded airplane and loaded on a truck ahead of a package heading to a customer with basic-level membership. Information on customer membership levels is typically held in a separate customer database. The event-based package monitoring systems now calls out to this database using the customer information on each stranded package. The ones returned as gold-level customers have their packages rerouted first.

In fact, there is a separate decision here—a decision to determine which customers should be prioritized. This should not be embedded in the event-processing system. Instead, the decision should be externalized. The clue to the decision was the external look-up for additional stateless data.

Event Streams Under Increasing Scrutiny

Businesses have various data sets that are produced during operations that reflect the changing nature of their business. Identifying these data sets and their data ranges, and building data dictionaries, is a common first step to bring visibility to key information assets. Consider, for example, a manufacturing facility that monitors the fatigue, heat, and stresses of the machinery in an assembly line. Data coming in from each sensor have some maximum and minimum tolerance levels. Knowledge of these constantly changing data sets and their tolerable ranges is the first level of data awareness.

Many companies begin by monitoring sensors and real-time changes are graphed by operators. Operators may observe certain key data interaction patterns. For instance, the heat in an axle rises with a corresponding increase in its acoustic activity under load. Watching both graphs increase, the operator realizes that the structural health of the axle is deteriorating and the axle is about to break. This is a key event that plant maintenance can act on to ensure safe operation.

After this pattern is identified, it is inefficient to watch for these data interactions graphically. Instead, operators can build a scorecard that tracks the increase of the both heat and acoustic sensors above certain levels. Instead of watching two graphs, the operator gets a warning light in the scorecard dashboard when the specific condition occurs. Other combinations of sensors lead to other lights in the scorecard turning on. Ultimately, many of these state changes are combined together to generate manufacturing KPIs such as availability and mean time between failures.

These KPIs become the metrics by which a business is operated. Typically, businesses monitor KPIs and then take action as KPIs change. Any time a business progresses through these increasing levels of scrutiny—from processing specific raw data to managing KPIs—a decision is in the offing, and it can be identified and isolated.

Finite State Analysis

Finite state diagrams provide insight into event-driven systems and show the possible situations that can arise. Modeling an event-driven system in this way allows you to identify decisions that must be taken to keep the system functioning as intended. First, the key states that are important to track must be determined. The system is simplified to this set of key states, and then the transitions that move the system from one of these states to another are established.

This finite state model can be exposed to everyday expected stimuli using a simulation. If simulation runs cause undesirable results, some changes would need to be made to the system to ensure that the sequence of events that caused a problem was being dealt with in a different way. This gives clues to changes in the decision-making in the system and the decision logic can then be isolated.

A simple example is the intersection of a traffic light with the pedestrian crossing. Modeling the state diagram for the system shows that it is an event-driven system, where the lights must change between a known set of states. Immediately it is evident that some states are undesirable—a pedestrian "walk" light with a "green" traffic light should never occur to prevent pedestrians from being run over, for example. The decision-making in the system must ensure that the system can never be in this state.

The finite state machine can also show how to refine the decision-making to meet changing conditions. To extend the traffic light example, the duration of each state change in the traffic light system could vary depending on the traffic patterns during the day. Introducing this variable into the traffic modeling helps make adaptable decisions on how long a light should stay green given the traffic volumes. Main artery roads could have longer green lights during peak traffic times and revert back to a more equitable distribution at other times.

Analyzing Legacy Systems

It is always possible that some suitable decisions are already automated in legacy systems. Generally, legacy systems do not handle decisions well. Legacy systems are neither agile nor transparent. They were rarely designed with an explicit focus on decision-making. Particularly in very high throughput scenarios, however, some decisions may have been embedded in legacy code. When building a decision inventory, it may be useful to identify those parts of a legacy system that automate decisions. The two best signs of this are large numbers of change requests and table-driven code.

High-Change Components

Decisions are high-change elements of the business. Anytime there is a legacy module that is the subject of constant change requests, especially when these change requests come at regular intervals, there is a strong likelihood that the module is implementing a decision or decisions. For instance, if a regulated decision is implemented in code, then each time new regulations are issued, a large number of change requests will likely be generated. IT will gradually work through these but will often get behind.

To find these decisions, use an application portfolio analysis tool if you have one, or review the change request and project logs to see where the efforts are focused. Examine these modules to see what they do and why they are being changed. If policy or regulatory change is the main driver, or if a business unit just needs the changes made to stay competitive, you will likely be able to describe a decision that is implemented by the module.

Table-driven Code

Because code is hard to change and because decisions are high-change components, IT departments will sometimes attempt to define all the expected variations for the decision-making logic and then build table-driven code. Any time a module has been built with table-driven approaches, it is worth evaluating it to see whether it is automating a decision.

Although table-driven code is used to make code easier to change—something that it is important for automated decisions—it does not improve transparency very much. Often table-driven code is even harder to read, as code must be cross-referenced with data tables before it can be understood. In addition, it is often impossible to define all the possible variations so that they can be built into the tables; this means that code changes will still be required, even if many changes can be made simply by updating tables. If the table-driven code implements a decision, add it to your inventory.

Using Metrics and Performance Management Systems

Key business decisions and the effectiveness with which these decisions are made have a direct impact on the business outcomes that can be measured using KPIs and associated metrics. For example, an inability to identify likely fraud in the context of claims processing results in the payment of fraudulent claims that are hard to recover subsequently. Such a failure will be reflected in the various KPIs that monitor claims effectiveness, such as the number of "likely frauds" measured through post-analysis, loss ratio measured in near real-time and the number of adjudicated claims. In contrast, an ineffective decision that identifies too many false positives results in unnecessary delay in the claims process, incurring too much overhead and poor customer satisfaction—all reflected in other KPIs and metrics.

Understanding the key decisions that are responsible for the business outcomes being monitored with KPIs and other metrics helps differentiate good decisions from bad ones, and shows which decisions to focus on when metrics or KPIs are out of acceptable bounds. Where an existing performance management environment exists, it can be used to identify decisions. Simple mapping of decisions and KPIs, analysis of past data, and root cause analysis can be used to find decisions.

Mapping Decisions and KPIs

One of the simplest ways to find decisions using KPIs and metrics in a performance management system is simply to map them to the decisions found to date. If the top-level decisions identified are listed on the vertical axis of a table and the KPIs and metrics for the business are listed on the horizontal axis, an empty table is created. Each decision can be examined to see whether it affects each KPI or metric. A decision affects a metric if a change in the quality of decision-making would move the metric. These relationships can be direct (where every change in decision-making shows up clearly in the metric) or indirect. In addition, they can be correlated (where improvement in the decision improves the metric) or inversely correlated (where improvement in the decision makes the metric worse). For instance, improving a customer retention decision might improve the retention metric, while damaging the retention budget metric.

After the existing decisions have been analyzed, it is interesting to examine the gaps. Metrics and KPIs that have no decisions should be examined and discussed to see whether there are decisions that have not yet been identified. It is possible for something to be monitored even though no decisions are made that affect it, but it is unlikely. Similarly, decisions that do not affect a metric may need to be examined in more detail. It may simply be that a metric is missing, but it may also be that the decision is poorly understood or affects metrics and KPIs in other business units.

Analysis of Past Data

KPIs, whether mapped to decisions or not, can be analyzed over time for additional insight. The historical values of KPIs can reveal periods when the values were particularly good or particularly poor. Analysis of these values can also show inflexion points where something changed and significantly altered the trajectory of the KPI. Finally, if a structured approach to KPIs has been taken, then variation of KPIs between regions, teams, shifts, or organizations may be identified.

Any or all of these variations in KPIs might be indicative of a decision that should be added to the inventory. When a period shows particularly good or bad results, it may well be that some decision was being made differently during this period. Discussing the period with those involved might reveal some initiative or change that is thought to be responsible. If the current decision inventory does not contain any decisions that would have been affected by this initiative, then there may well be another decision or set of decisions that can be identified—those that were affected by the initiative.

When there is a variation between organizations, the likelihood is that these organizations make some decision or decisions differently. Analysis of the decisions already identified might make it clear where this variation exists. If none of the decisions identified so far vary between the organizations, an additional decision can be identified. Any additional decisions identified in this way should be associated with the relevant KPIs.

Root Cause Analysis

Some changes in the external environment cannot be addressed simply by improving or optimizing operational decisions. Sometimes a larger set of changes to business operations may be necessary to support a realigned business strategy as your organization responds to the changed business environment. For instance, you may have to restructure claims processing to introduce early fraud detection to counteract a rise in certain types of fraudulent claims. A new operational decision—"likely fraud"—has to be performed for each claim transaction. One of the most effective ways to discover the need for this kind of change is to perform root cause analysis on KPIs.

Analysis of KPI data over time combined with drill-down analysis of associated data can provide insight into the underlying root causes. Detailed analysis of a "time to process" KPI might show that while the average is satisfactory, there is a growing problem with occasional long delays for some loan applications. The delays might be observed as outliers in an aggregate completion time report, for instance. Further analysis can drill down to see what is causing these delays. The delay may come when all the necessary documentation is not collected before routing the application to a loan approver. The solution may be a change in the process to generate a checklist and ensuring all documents are collected before the loan approver gets involved. Implementing this involves a change to the process but also identifies a new decision—what is the correct checklist for this application?

WHAT-IF ANALYSIS OF ALTERNATIVES

With this kind of analysis, you can often come up with many alternative proposals to address a specific root cause. Not all changes will be equally effective, and business modeling and simulation through "what-if" analysis is essential to select a feasible and optimal approach. Considering the decisions that each approach would require and the degree to which those decisions might be automatable will help ensure the best choice.

Documenting Decisions

Before deciding which decisions should be the basis for Decision Management Systems, it is important to understand those decisions. Like any other requirement or specification, decisions can be described in a number of ways to help clarify how they can be automated. Decisions can also be decomposed so that the way in which a decision is made can be seen more clearly. Understanding the dependencies of a decision on other decisions and on sources of information and know-how helps ensure that the Decision Management System will work correctly. This decomposition of a decision into smaller, more focused decisions can also help balance human and automated decision-making. Decisions are also a part of a broader business design, and the linkages between decisions and business processes, events, and more help establish its context.

Decision Basics: Question and Answer

As with most requirements, decisions can be given a name and described. Identifying the "Approve Claim" decision and describing the basic decision-making approach for approving a claim is a good place to start with documenting this decision. Because decisions select from known and defined alternatives, the most powerful information to add to this is a question and a set of possible answers. Extending our example, you could add, "Should we approve this claim for payment at this time?" as a question and identify "yes" and "no" as possible answers.

The question that goes with a decision needs to be as precise as possible. It is helpful to be specific about the subject of the question—the claim in our example—and about the question itself. Identifying a singular subject is also important. If we are approving a specific claim rather than deciding whether a group of claims is approved, we should be clear in the question. Time periods and the possibility of reassessment can also be included in the question. In our example question, we make it clear that claims approval can be decided at multiple times. Questions, like names and descriptions, can also evolve as our understanding improves and clarity is important enough that changes should be allowed.

The set of answers should be complete. The example is a simple one—only yes and no are allowed. In most questions, the answers are more complex and more varied. The list of allowed answers can be defined explicitly with every possible answer listed, or it can be defined implic-itly by reference to some set. A list of allowed answers, for instance, might be "a valid product in the product catalog." When implicit de-finitions are used, they too should be precise—not "a product," but "a valid product in the product catalog."

Various forms of answers are possible:

1. A number from within a range of numbers
   For instance, the discount rate to be offered to a customer or the price for a product configuration
2. A single answer value from a set
   For instance, yes, or a product from the product catalog
3. A combination consisting of multiple answer values and numbers (the set is considered a single answer)
   For instance, a product from the product catalog and a specific price for that product
4. Multiple candidate answers from a set
   For instance, the most suitable three products from the catalog with a price for each. Each answer is of the first three kinds of answer—a number, an answer value, or a combination of numbers and values

SPEND TIME GETTING THE ANSWERS RIGHT

It is worth spending a fair amount of time getting the answers right for a decision, as a clear understanding of the available answers will make it much easier to define and manage the decision going forward. The answers show how broad and how complex the decision will need to be. The answers are also how one decision supports another, and so a clear understanding of the answers will allow the dependencies between deci-sions to be evaluated.

Many decisions involve not only coming up with answers but sup-porting those answers with explanations or, perhaps, supporting facts. A decision to grant credit, for instance, may result in a number for the amount of credit granted along with five explanatory statements that explain why the amount was neither higher nor lower. Although this information is not part of the answer, it should also be documented as part of the decision.

Linking to the Business

Decisions are independent objects that will repay an investment in being managed independently of other requirements, business processes, events, and systems. They are also essential to these other requirements and it is vital that it is understood how decisions support other elements of the business. The initial discovery of decisions will provide some links to the business. Decisions found in the context of a process are clearly linked to that process, while decisions found in legacy systems analysis are linked to the system in which they were found. Decisions are often reused, so additional links between processes, systems, events, and decisions should be expected and documented when found.

Establishing a number of other links will make it easier to manage the decisions and easier to determine how best to measure them and improve them over time. Decisions can be linked to the organizational units—departments, people, teams—that are responsible for them. This responsibility might be one of ownership—being responsible for the definition of exactly how the decision should be made—or one of execution—making the individual decision. These are often not the same for repeatable decisions. For instance, a marketing team might own the definition of a cross-sell offer decision, while the call center team owns the execution of that decision.

Measurement of decisions is critical. All decisions have an impact on the metrics and measures that judge success or failure in an organization. If an organization has any control over a metric or an objective, then it must be making decisions that influence that metric. Understanding which decisions affect which metrics, as well as how and why, is an essential ingredient in measuring decisions. More importantly, the linkage of decisions to metrics and key performance indicators underpins continuous improvement. Changes to decision-making or experiments in decision-making approaches need to be assessed to see which ones should be kept and which rejected. Without a link to the organization's metrics, such assessment will remain technical in nature, where it should be business-focused.

Modeling Dependencies

The day-to-day operations of any organization rely on a portfolio of repeatable decisions. These decisions have a measurable impact on the organization and clearly support its business processes and events. However, the repeatable decisions that support a business are not generally independent of each other. A decision is dependent on another decision if it cannot be made without knowing the outcome of the other decision. Decisions are also dependent on information if they cannot be made without that information and similarly, on know-how. Understanding these dependencies links the otherwise isolated decisions discovered into a true portfolio and identifies sub-decisions to give structure to the internal workings of decisions.

The process for finding decision dependencies involves five steps:

1. Determine dependencies
2. Find decision dependencies
3. Find information sources
4. Find know-how
5. Iterate

The end result of this analysis is a decision dependency diagram, such as that shown in Figure 5-1. In this example, decisions are shown as rectangles, with information sources as ovals and know-how as hexagons. The shapes are not standardized but should be different to allow rapid identification.

Determine Dependencies

The most effective way to determine the dependencies of a decision is to work with a group of people who understand how that decision is made today or should be made going forward. Such a group can be asked to list everything needed to make that decision. Each element required for the decision can be listed out. The list will contain elements that are the outcomes of other decisions, elements that are information about the transaction or customer-sconcerned, and elements that are knowledge-related. Each element can be classified and then expanded on depending on its classification.

In the absence of a suitable group of experts, it may be possible to determine the dependencies from existing processes and system implementations.

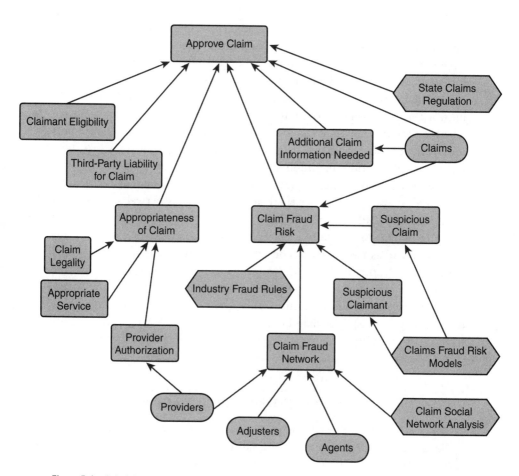

Figure 5-1 A decision dependency diagram

Find Decision Dependencies

The most common kind of dependency is a dependency on another decision. Most decisions have dependencies on other precursor decisions or on more granular "sub-decisions." For example, the decision to validate a claim can be decomposed into a decision to confirm the claimant, another to establish completeness of data, and a third to validate that individual data elements such as address are valid. It is entirely possible that these decisions have already been identified as part of our decision inventory—the confirm claimant decision might have been separately identified as part of defining how a request for service is handled, for instance. When a decision exists already, the dependency can simply be documented between them. More common is that these other decisions have not yet been identified. In this case, the basic question and answers for each new decision identified need to be documented.

Decision dependency networks can get quite complex. As the dependency network grows, evaluate the outcomes of all dependent decisions to see whether they are enough to support the parent decision. As your understanding of each decision improves, it may become increasingly obvious that there is missing information that implies another dependent decision.

The decisions on which a particular decision is dependent can also be evaluated as a set. Sometimes there are dependencies between those decisions that should be modeled. In our validate claim example, for instance, we might initially identify confirm the claimant and check for identity fraud as two decisions on which the "validate claim" decision is dependent. On further analysis, we might decide it makes more sense for the confirm claimant decision to be dependent on the check for identity fraud decision. In these circumstances, we would remove the direct dependency between validate claim and check for identity fraud, as we have an implied dependency through the confirm claimant decision.

DON'T CREATE DEPENDENCY LOOPS

One challenge with dependency networks, especially deep ones, is that loops can be created, where decision A depends on decision B, which depends on decision C, which in turn depends on decision A. Such loops cannot be valid, and decision dependency networks should be checked regularly to ensure such loops are not being created.

Find Information Sources

Decisions are often dependent on other decisions. In addition, they are often dependent on information sources. Business decisions cannot be made without some information being presented for consideration. This data might be of various types and can be internal or external to an organization. Information might be about customers, transactions, or the organization itself. All such information sources should be identified and linked to make it clear which information sources are essential for which decisions.

AVOID DETAILED DATA DESIGN

It is not useful to try and drive a detailed data design at this stage, so business-level information sources such as "customer data" or "claims data" are entirely appropriate. If an information source must be heavily analyzed before it can be used, this is a sign that know-how (see below) is required—that the decision is actually dependent on the insight derived, not the source information. For instance, a credit decision is dependent on the likelihood of default, which is derived through the analysis of past payment history.

Information sources come in a variety of categories and can be described in terms of the kind of data involved (structured data, structured content, and unstructured content) as well as ownership (internal, external, and pooled).

Structured data is stored in a database, typically a relational one, and the structure of the data—its attributes and allowed values—is known or at least knowable. Every record or instance matches the defined structure, and the data can be manipulated record by record, attribute by attribute, typically very efficiently and rapidly.

Structured content is document- or file-based and typically stored in a content management system. This content also has a repeatable structure that is defined—a contract, for example, has a repeatable structure with parties, clauses, and sub-clauses, and so on. XML documents or documents with standard contents can be considered structured content.

Unstructured content has no pre-defined structure, such as call notes or the body of an email. Analysis of this information and its use in Decision Management Systems is more complex than the use of structured data and content, but it is increasingly common. Analysis includes entity extraction, text analysis, sentiment analysis, and assessing how likely it is that the text is discussing a particular topic.

Internal sources are those owned by an organization. It can change the layout and the values of the data and has access through a range of interfaces. Many systems often share a single source, and costs are typically not entirely dependent on the volume of data involved—there are significant fixed costs. External sources, in contrast, are owned by someone else, and access is tightly defined and restricted to a limited and defined set of interfaces. The data provider manages change to its structure, and records are added and removed without the organization's participation. There are fees associated with the data that are almost always record or data volume-based. In addition, access to external data is likely to be less timely than internal data with performance implications for Decision Management Systems that use it.

POOLED DATA SOURCES

Pooled sources are an interesting subtype of external sources. Data from multiple sources is sometimes pooled for analysis as pooling data supports additional insights. For instance, credit card transactions are pooled to fight fraud so that patterns can be seen across credit card issuers. Pooled data has privacy and access issues and generally does not support access to specific transactions or consumers. Pooled data is used exclusively to derive analytic insight and, as such, will not appear as a dependency for a decision—instead the know-how derived from the data will do so.

MANAGING EXTERNAL DATA COSTS WITH DECISION MANAGEMENT SYSTEMS

There is a whole class of Decision Management Systems focused on decisions about external data. Some external data sources can improve a decision but cost a significant amount per transaction. It can be very valuable to determine whether the external data will actually make any difference before paying for it. Many Decision Management Systems are built to make this determination. For instance, in auto insurance, it costs a significant amount to request a motor vehicle report on a driver to confirm their driving record. A Decision Management System may be built to determine whether the information in such a report will make any difference to the underwriting process, or even if it will make a difference larger than the cost of the report. This will eliminate unnecessary costs.

Find Know-how

Decisions depend also on know-how and expertise. As you decompose decisions, identify the sources of know-how on which those decisions are dependent. Know-how falls into four broad categories—policies, regulations, analytic insight, and expertise. For instance, a decision on the eligibility of a person to claim a government benefit is dependent on the regulations that define the criteria for that eligibility.

Policies and regulations are available in documents and publications. Regulations might be produced by local, state, or national governments. Policies may be internal to the organization, passed on to it by a parent or related organization, or be published by an industry group. These documents may define limitations on how specific decisions can be made and provide guidance on how to make a good decision. The documents are unlikely to only contain decision-related material. More typically, policies and regulations contain requirements for processes as well as more general guidance for organizations. Policy and regulation know-how should be defined at a level that makes sense. For instance, an organization might differentiate between the regulations from the federal government and those from state governments, while not listing every individual state regulation as a separate source.

Analytic insight is know-how derived from data analysis. It could be developed using business intelligence, data mining, predictive analytics, text analytics, or some combination of approaches. When it is the *insight* gained from information that a decision is dependent on rather than the *information* itself, it should be modeled as know-how. For instance, a cross-sell decision might be dependent on customer segmentation derived from customer behavior data, or on models that predict the risk of default for this customer for various financial products. These would be modeled as analytic insight know-how.

CAPTURING THE DATA NEEDS FOR ANALYTIC INSIGHT

When you identify analytic insight as being necessary for making a decision it is important to think through the data that this analytic insight will require. This information may be modeled as an information source already, but it may not be. For instance, a decision on customer retention may require analytic insight about the risk of a customer canceling his service. This insight may require analysis of his social network—his friends and family members—to see whether anyone in the network has left recently. This information is not an information source used directly by any of the decisions being modeled. Document this kind of information as part of the analytic insight as you refine your understanding of how you will derive the insight you need.

The final category is that of expertise. Many decisions are dependent on the accumulated experience and wisdom of those who have been making the decision for a while. This might be called collective wisdom or tribal knowledge. Decisions are typically dependent on this kind of know-how because it helps make good decisions. Often the best way, at least while data is being gathered and analyzed, to tell how to make a good decision is to use the experience and judgment of those who have been making effective decisions. For example, the best practices of the procurement department might be the best source of know-how for selecting suppliers, and decisions in this area would then be dependent on this know-how.

Iterate

As the decision dependency network is developed, it will be necessary to repeat this decomposition at each new level. When a decision is decomposed to show which decisions it is dependent on, it is likely that new decisions will be created. These decisions must not only be described, they must also be decomposed in turn. Eventually a set of "atomic" decisions—that cannot be usefully broken down any further—will be identified, or all the dependent decisions will exist, or some combination of the two. At that point, the decision inventory for the area of the business being analyzed can be considered stable. It is likely to change in the future, but decision discovery can move on to understanding and documenting the critical attributes of the decisions that have been identified.

Decision Characteristics

Besides the basic information of the decision, it is worth spending time understanding some of the characteristics of each decision. Important characteristics include things like volume, timeliness, consistency, time to value, value range, and degrees of freedom.

Volume

Although all the decisions being considered for Decision Management Systems are repeatable, there is a significant difference between a decision to assign a particular team to a call center shift for the week and a decision to alert a network operator that a piece of equipment is at risk of failing. The shift assignment decision may be made every week or 52 times a year, but the alert/don't alert decision could be made every second for thousands of pieces of equipment—tens of billions of decisions each year. The volume of a decision constrains how a Decision Management System that automates that decision must behave, as well as playing a key role in determining whether any human can be involved at all.

Timeliness

The volume of a decision is paired with its timeliness. Generally, the more often a decision is made, the less time can be spent making the decision. It is worth noting the timeliness requirement of a decision separately, however, as some low-volume decisions can have short time windows in which they can be made. Responding to an emergency signal might not be a decision that happens very often (most years it may not happen at all), but when it does, the decision as to which equipment to shut down must be made nearly instantly. Timeliness will act as a major constraint on the behavior of a Decision Management System.

Consistency over Time

Some decisions remain remarkably consistent over time with only slow incremental change in the decision-making approach being required. Others are in a constant state of flux with new regulations, policies, or analysis being incorporated all the time. Even within apparently very similar decisions, there can be significant variation. Pricing decisions, for instance, range from product pricing guidelines that are updated once a year to pricing in dynamic markets where prices are updated every day based on competitive situations or deals with suppliers. You may be wrong about how consistent a decision is going to be in the future, but an initial assessment of the extent to which the decision-making approach will remain consistent over time will help you design an appropriate Decision Management System.

Value Range

The difference between the value of a good decision—of the best decision possible—and a bad one varies tremendously. Some decisions offer only small opportunities for improvement. A bad up-sell decision is of zero value, while a good one increases the profit on a transaction by a small amount. A bad choice in subject lines means an email won't be opened, a good one means it will. For these decisions, the value range is small. Other decisions have a much larger value range. The difference in value between a good loan origination decision that might be worth a few tens of dollars in fees and interest over and above the intra-bank lending rate, and a bad decision where the whole loan has to be written off, is thousands of dollars. Multiply that by thousands or tens of thousands of loan origination decisions, and the total value runs into millions. The value range for a decision makes a big difference to the kind of Decision Management System you end up building, in particular to the degree to which predictive analytics can and should be part of the system.

Time to Value

The impact, the value, of some decisions is felt immediately. The decision of which ad to display to a website visitor either works (he clicks on it) or fails at once. In contrast, a loan origination decision won't show a positive or negative outcome for some time—not until you see whether the borrower will make payments reliably. When the time to value of a decision is short, you get immediate feedback on how well you are making the decision. This allows for rapid experimentation and highly adaptive Decision Management Systems. In contrast, a decision with a long time to value must be monitored for an extended period, and any experiments are going to have to run for a while to gather the data you need to evaluate them. How quickly your decisions will have an impact on your business is worth knowing for all the decisions in your inventory.

Degrees of Freedom

Some decisions are highly constrained by the policies and regulations that must be followed. After all the rules for eligibility for a benefit are followed, there may be no choice remaining—either the person applying is eligible or she is not. For such a decision there will be little or no analysis and no reason to experiment. Other decisions have a large amount of freedom. There may also be uncertainty in judging the success or failure of a decision. Judgment, analysis, and experimentation all play a role in determining how these decisions should be made now and in the future. Understanding the amount of freedom and the nature of that freedom is helpful when designing Decision Management Systems that automate the decision.

Prioritizing Decisions

Most business areas will contain more decisions that can be addressed in a single Decision Management System project, or even a set of such projects. This means that the decisions identified will need to be prioritized so that incremental progress can be made. In general, decisions can be ranked in various ways for prioritization and a "hotspot" analysis can be conducted.

BEGIN WITH THE PROJECT'S GOALS

Before beginning the prioritization process, revisit the project's success criteria and goals. Make sure you understand what the project's primary objective is and that you are clear what will make the team and others regard the project as a success. Understanding the most important criterion or project goal will help drive effective prioritization.

The enterprise-level purpose of the project—whether it is to increase customer retention, increase profit per customer, reduce cost per unit, or some other target—is a critical driver for prioritization. Use this to identify the measures and KPIs that most closely align to the project's overall purpose.

By analyzing the decisions that support these measures and KPIs, you identify the decisions that relate most closely to the project purpose and to set aside, at least temporarily, decisions that relate to this goal only loosely. Part of the association between a decision and a measure or KPI is an assessment of how direct the association is and of the contribution the decision makes. Those that make a larger and more direct contribution to the critical measures should be put in a preliminary list of prioritized decisions.

To further rank the decisions from highest to lowest priority, you can consider a number of factors:

- How measurable is the decision's impact on the measures it affects?

  In general, it is helpful to target decisions that are going to be easy to measure, as it will be easy to show that the project made a difference.

- How big is the difference between good and bad results in terms of revenue, risk, or loyalty?

  The bigger the gap, the larger the potential payoff for improving the quality of decisions.

- How often do you make the decision?

  More decisions act as a multiplier, and this means more impact from a Decision Management System.

- How much spending is committed as a result of the decision?

  Decisions that commit the organization to large amounts of spending, such as expensive investigations or purchases, can be worthwhile even if the improvement is quite modest.

- How much does it cost to make a decision?

  If a decision currently costs a great deal in terms of staff or expert time, then a Decision Management System may offer a high payoff.

- How hard will it be to develop a Decision Management System for the decision?

  A quick and dirty assessment of the technology and process change required to implement a Decision Management System can help prioritize those decisions that will be easier to implement.

In addition, the candidate decisions can be plotted to try and show the "hotspots." This is an analysis showing which decisions should be the focus of immediate projects, given organizational and technical realities. For instance, the value of each decision could be ranked into high, medium, and low. The difficulty of implementation and time to market could be similarly assessed. Each decision can then be plotted on a bubble chart, such as the one shown in Figure 5-2.

In this example, the technical difficulty is on the horizontal axis from most difficult to least difficult, the time to market is on the horizontal axis from slowest to fastest, and the bubble represents the value of the decision, with larger bubbles for higher value. With this approach, the larger bubbles that are closer to the top-right are those most suitable to prioritize.

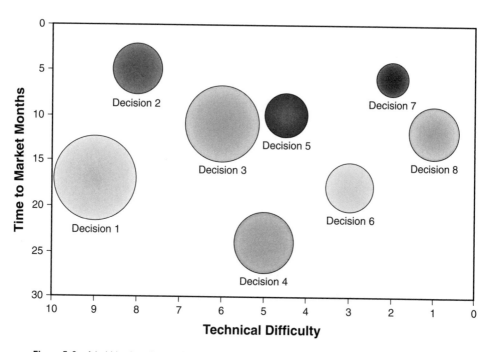

Figure 5-2 A bubble chart for a collection of decisions to show the hotspot of high-priority decisions

The exact prioritization approach taken should be varied based on a number of factors:

- Organizations developing their first Decision Management System should prioritize based on which decisions seem most readily implemented and least controversial. Early success is important, and this should drive the prioritization.

- Organizations with extensive portfolios of Decision Management Systems should include the ability to reuse and exploit existing development assets and infrastructure.

- Organizations that struggle with organizational change should prioritize those decisions that are already implemented, if done poorly, as there will be less organizational disruption involved in replacing one automated decision with another.

6

Design and Implement Decision Services

An organization with a decision inventory for a line of business or a related set of business processes is ready to create Decision Management Systems. Those decisions that have been prioritized for implementation represent the requirements for one or more Decision Management Systems. The characteristics and decomposition of those decisions provides a detailed specification of the decision, how it is made, its actions, and more.

At the core of these systems are Decision Services—service-oriented components that make decisions. The main step in implementing a Decision Management System is to define and build a Decision Service that delivers the selected decision as an IT component. This Decision Service will also need to be integrated with the rest of the IT environment, and there are some well-established best practices that should be followed.

Decision Services require decision scaffolding to handle the flow of the decision as well as the business rules, predictive analytic models, and optimization models that determine how the decision should be made. For many decisions, a test-and-learn infrastructure will also be required.

Build Decision Services

At the core of a Decision Management System is a Decision Service. This service-oriented component implements one or more of the decisions identified in the decision inventory. A Decision Service answers a set of questions for other systems, processes, or services—the questions defined for the decisions it implements.

Decision Services are not implemented for every decision identified in the decision inventory. In general, the highest-level decisions possible should be turned into Decision Services—those decisions that are required by a process or an event, or that replace a module in a legacy application. These high-level decisions—the ones found early in the decision discovery process—are those that offer the most value when built as Decision Services. Lower-level decisions are useful for designing these Decision Services but may not be worth deploying as a Decision Service in their own right. A Decision Service should only be built if there are processes, events, or systems that need access to these sub-decisions other than in the context of the top-level decisions. Often a single Decision Service can have multiple entry points to allow access also to these lower-level decisions. The ability to reuse business rules, analytic models, and optimization components means that there is no need to incur the overhead of a Decision Service to access these sub-decisions.

Building a Decision Service involves laying out the decision itself, building the scaffolding for the decision-making components, and then developing the business rules, predictive analytic models, and optimization models necessary to make the decision. By far the best way to develop Decision Services is iteratively, gradually improving the quality of decisions or the percentage of decisions handled over time.

Build Decision Scaffolding

The core elements of the Decision Service are implemented as business rules, predictive analytic models, and optimization models. To ensure these elements are used together in an appropriate way, a Decision Service requires some scaffolding. This scaffolding brings the right decision-making components together in the right order to produce the intended result.

The definition of the decision contains much useful information that can be used to derive the necessary decision scaffolding. It contains a definition of the allowed actions and a model of the various sub-decisions, information, and know-how that the decision is dependent on. In addition, the context(s) in which the Decision Service is accessed are defined in terms of the business processes, events, and systems that will use the decision being implemented.

Define Service Contract and Test Cases

The first step is to define a service contract for the Decision Service. Such a contract states that given a certain set of information, the Decision Service will answer a particular question and commit to returning one of the allowed answers along with any supporting information. It defines the outputs produced and inputs required by the Decision Service.

- **Outputs:**   An examination of the question and allowed answers defines part of the service contract. The allowed answers show what can be returned by the Decision Service in business terms. These are used to derive a more formal definition of the output from the Decision Service. For instance, a claims processing decision might have allowed answers of "Fast Track," "Refer," and "Investigate." As part of defining the service contract, we might decide to return a string containing one of these three allowed values or a number with each value representing a particular answer.

  Many decisions return supporting information in addition to the formal answer. This supporting information should be analyzed similarly to formally define the additional information that may be returned. For instance, if the claims processing decision also involves returning some reasons for the action recommend along with association reason codes (a common set of additional information), we will define an array of reason code—reason text pairs as an additional part of the contract.

- **Inputs:**   While our model of a decision gave us a very specific set of outputs, we have only a high-level definition of the inputs required by the decision. Examining the dependency network to see all the information sources on which the decision is dependent or on which its dependent decisions are themselves dependent will give us a starting point. In addition, a review of the contexts in which the decision is required will show what information is likely to be available at that point in the process or system or when the event occurs. Based on the analysis of these inputs, a contract can also be defined for the input data.

DON'T OVER-CONSTRAIN INPUT DATA

Although it is a good idea to define a contract for the Decision Service first, the data used by a decision may evolve as the Decision Service is constructed. It may become apparent as rules are written or models integrated that additional data must be available beyond what was originally expected. Although Decision Services can reach out and gather additional data, while making a decision it is generally preferable to have the data required be passed in as part of the inputs.

To reduce the need to change the contract, it is better to specify all the input data available within reason so the contract will not need to change as new requirements are identified within the decision. For instance, if customer data is required by the decision, then include all the customer data typically available in the input data even if there is not yet a defined need for the data within the decision.

For instance, a Decision Service implementing a decision to make a cross-sell offer to a customer as he checks out would have a simple output data contract—enough information to identify the offer being suggested. Its input data would be the standard set of information about a customer, as well as the contents of the customer's current shopping basket and his order history.

After the contract is defined, it is possible to do several things. First, a stub can be developed that acts like the Decision Service. This takes the defined inputs and returns the default answer. In our example, this might be "Refer" on the grounds that the person to whom the claim is referred has the option to "Fast Track" or "Investigate" it as she sees fit. A Decision Service that returns this answer every time may not be very useful, but it can be integrated with other services and components. Once such a stub exists, other components can be built or amended to use the Decision Service.

In addition, it is possible to start defining test cases. Knowing the test cases in advance, or at least creating the core set of test cases, makes it much easier to tell when a Decision Service has reached the minimum level for deployment. This is important, as Decision Services are rarely as complete or accurate when first deployed as they will become over time. The first version deployed need not be complete or fully refined, but it must meet a basic level of completeness. Defining an initial set of test cases and a test strategy based on the decision description and the contract definition will allow the development of a "version 1" Decision Service that can safely be deployed to start adding value.

NOT ALL DECISION SERVICES CAN BE DEPLOYED INCREMENTALLY

Some Decision Services are replacing existing components. In these cases it will not be possible to deploy the Decision Service until it at least meets the level of the component it is replacing. The test cases should reflect that.

Turn Dependency Network into Flow

After the contract of the Decision Service is defined and a set of test cases established, the next step is to define the decision flow. Although some decisions contain a single step, most do not. For every Decision Service that requires only the execution of a single optimization model or a single rule set, there are many that involve multiple steps that must be executed against a common set of information to determine the right answer to the question.

A decision flow consists of a series of decision making tasks linked together with conditional branches if necessary. A decision flow can be thought of as a kind of decision process. Unlike a true business process, it should not have the ability to assign work to people nor should it include tasks that might take extended periods to execute. Instead, the decision flow should be a set of tightly linked tasks that execute rapidly based on a common set of data to return an answer such that the calling system or process can reliably wait for an answer from the Decision Service.

In the decision discovery phase, we established a dependency network for the top-level decision being implemented in the Decision Service. This dependency network can now be used to drive the initial decision flow design. Those sub-decisions on which the decision is dependent make up the tasks in the flow. These sub-decisions may simply go earlier in the flow or may be more appropriately represented by a sub-flow with additional tasks.

Decisions are often dependent on multiple precursor sub-decisions with no particular reason for one of those sub-decisions to be made before another. As the decision flow is a design element, it is now time to make choices about which should go first, second, and so on. For instance, one of the sub-decisions on which the main decision is dependent may cause transactions to be rejected. Putting such a task early in the flow would allow rapid rejection of transactions that would be rejected eventually. Tasks may also be defined to execute in parallel. In Figure 6-1, for instance, the decision being modeled had a dependency to decisions to calculate a base premium and to make a coverage adjustment. These are now represented as tasks in the flow.

As the decision flow is laid out, it will be clear that some of these tasks are going to be represented by business rules while others are going to be predictive analytic models or optimization models. The dependency on know-how of the sub-decision represented by the task will give a clear indication of this—dependency on analytic insight will mean that the task is going to be represented by a predictive analytic model, while dependency on policy or regulation will imply business rules.

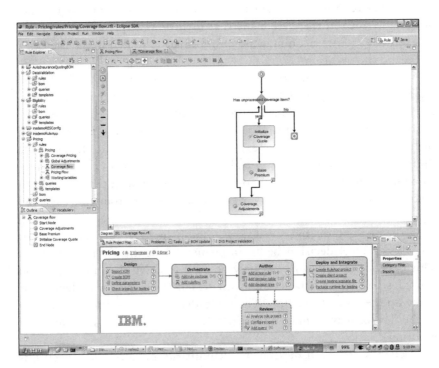

Figure 6-1 A decision flow showing several tasks within a decision

The data available throughout the decision flow should also be defined. The primary data involved in the flow is going to be based on the contract defined earlier. The input data will be available from the start of the flow, and the output data structure will need to be available so that it can be populated by the various tasks making the decision. Additional information is also produced by the tasks—this information represents the answers produced by the sub-decisions being implemented. Sometimes this data is also part of the output, but sometimes it must be added to the data flowing through the decision.

Build Test-and-Learn Infrastructure

Some decisions are completely and tightly regulated or driven by policies. These decisions will likely have a single path through the decision flow for any given set of input values, as only one approach is possible—that defined by the policies and regulations. For instance, a decision to determine whether a citizen is eligible for a particular benefit will have a single path for all citizens with the same values in the input information.

Some decisions, however, involve judgment or analytic know-how. If the know-how on which the decision is dependent includes analytic insight or human judgment—not just policy or regulation—then an ability to experiment will be necessary.

It is often not be possible to determine the right or "best" answer for a decision that involves analytics or judgment for some time. When we reach the point of being able to assess how effective our decision-making was, it will be useful if we can compare several different approaches to see which worked best. In the absence of a time machine, we cannot go back and re-test a new approach on the same customers. We must therefore experiment, treating two similar customers differently so we can see which approach will work best. When experimentation is necessary, a test-and-learn infrastructure will need to be built into the Decision Service scaffolding.

To build in test-and-learn infrastructure, examine the decision flow and identify the sections of that flow where multiple possible approaches could be considered. This might be the whole flow but might also be just part of it. In a decision there might be several sections where a single approach makes sense and several where an ability to try several approaches will be useful. For each section, the beginning and end are defined and the enclosed tasks identified. For instance, our claims decision might include some validation and eligibility tasks initially that will always be the same for all claims. After a claim is determined to be eligible, we may have some tasks to make an assessment of the likelihood of fraud. In this latter section, we might want to create an ability to try several different approaches to detecting fraud. This will allow us to compare approaches see how much fraud they catch and how many false positives they generate.

Next you must decide how many different approaches you will want to be able to run at once. You might want the ability to do A/B testing, where two equally valid approaches are run side by side to see which performs better. A/B testing is often used in marketing to compare approaches. Although A/B testing implies two approaches, some decisions conduct this kind of testing of equally valid approaches for three or more approaches—A/B/C testing, if you will.

Alternatively, you might expect to have a default or "champion" approach that most transactions will use, and then some number of alternative or "challenger" approaches. In this situation, you will want most transactions to be handled using the champion approach while only a small number of transactions flow through the challengers. This ensures you gather data about the effectiveness of alternative approaches while continuing to use the approach you think is "best" on most transactions.

In either case, you create a branch in the decision flow that will route transactions through one of the available approaches based on a random assignment. A further branch then brings all the approaches together again to continue with any additional tasks.

KEEP TRACK OF THE APPROACH USED

You will need to keep track of the decision-making approach used for each transaction. This can be recorded as part of logging the Decision Service behavior, or it can be passed out of the Decision Service as part of the data associated with the answer. If the latter, it should be part of your service contract.

At this point, you have a decision flow outlined that shows how various tasks are executed to take a set of defined input data and generate an allowed response, along with any defined supporting data. This now needs to be fleshed out with business rules, predictive analytic models, and optimization models.

Build Business Rules

After the basic scaffolding is developed for a Decision Service, the next step is to build out the individual decision tasks within the decision flow. These tasks can be the execution of a set of business rules, the execution of a predictive analytic model, or the execution of an optimization model. By far the most common is the execution of a set of business rules—a rule set.

A *rule set* is a set of rules that should be evaluated together and executed as a set. Rule sets may need to be executed before another rule set—this is what the decision dependency and decision flow define—but the rules within a rule set can and should be considered to be a single unit. Reuse of rules is at the rule set-level, and it is rule sets for which access control, security policies, and governance approaches should be defined.

Building a rule set for use in a Decision Service involves three main steps: determining the source rules, defining executable rules, and integrating the executable rules as part of the Decision Service.

THERE'S A LOT MORE TO WRITING BUSINESS RULES

It is not the intent of this book to define a complete approach for finding, documenting, or developing business rules. For instance, we will not be discussing the development of fact models (a common step in defining source rules) nor the details of appropriate rule syntax for either source or executable rules. The bibliography contains many books with good information on the details of developing business rules.

Find Source Rules

The Decision Service will need executable business rules to operate. Sometimes it makes sense to define these executable business rules directly. In general, however, it makes more sense to define source rules first and then define the executable business rules that implement these source rules. You can think of source rules as a kind of requirement artifact, one designed specifically for use when the end implementation is expected to involve executable business rules.

Source rules are natural language statements of what should be done when a specific set of conditions are true. They may be written in an "If this is true, then do that" format, or as "When this is true, do that" but they can also be expressed in terms like "Always do this" or "Never do that, except when this is true." When developing source rules, the most important thing is clarity to those who run the business. No restriction should be placed on how source rules are documented; restrictions of this type can reduce the clarity for the business people involved in the project. This does not mean that you cannot define a style for these source rules or insist on using defined terms and vocabulary. You should just ensure that these restrictions improve business clarity and are supported and understood by the non-technical business experts critical to effectively identifying your source rules.

Each knowledge source in the decision dependency network will have a set of source rules associated with it. Additional source rules might also be defined and linked to existing systems, especially when legacy systems are being re-engineered and some of the behavior of the legacy system will be replaced with a Decision Service. Source rules can, therefore, be found in legacy systems and in three types of know-how—policies and regulations, expertise, or tribal knowledge and data analysis.

In Legacy Systems

Various tools exist for extracting business rules from legacy code. These tools provide useful input to the process of defining a Decision Service, but it is generally not helpful to use the extracted rules as source or executable rules going forward. The extracted rules tend to be too technical for business users to review or edit, and too linked to the legacy implementation to make good executable rules in the new environment.

LEGACY SYSTEMS CAN PROVIDE DATA INSIGHT

Legacy systems can also provide useful information on the data that has historically been used in the decision, as well as the set of allowed actions for a decision.

Instead, the intended and observed behavior of the legacy system can be used to define the source rules implied by the legacy system. These source rules can be validated against the extracted rules. Where there are differences of behavior, not just differences in detail, this is likely to be either because the legacy system has problems (these are likely to be known) or because the legacy system contains fixes that are not known to those outside of IT. It is not uncommon, for instance, for regulations to have inconsistencies. An implementation might, therefore, have additional rules encoded to deal with these inconsistencies. Capturing these additional business rules so that the new Decision Service can handle those same inconsistencies is important.

Sometimes staff turnover or situational complexity means that the only way to see what the legacy system does is to analyze the code and extract rules. In these circumstances, begin with the extracted "technical" rules. Then manually derive source rules from them by replacing technical terms with their business equivalent and by generalizing specific processing behavior into the business behavior it represents.

LEGACY SYSTEMS ARE A POOR SOURCE OF BUSINESS RULES

In general, legacy systems are a poor choice for source rule identification and should be used only when there is no alternative. However, analyzing existing code to see what "technical" rules are implied by that code *is* an effective check on business rules developed directly from policies or regulations.

In Policies and Regulations

The most productive way to derive source rules in many circumstances is to begin with the policies or regulations that must be enforced in the decision. Regulations come from outside the organization, whereas policies come from inside. They can be treated in very similar ways when it comes to extracting source rules. Both policies and regulations contain things that must be enforced as well as suggestions or advice. Both also contain information about how to execute processes, handle data, or perform other non-decision-making tasks.

Extracting source rules from policies and regulations is mostly an exercise in identifying those statements that say how a decision should, must, or could be made from the other statements in the document. Often done as part of a broader analysis of a policy or regulation, this extraction process results in a set or perhaps several sets of statements—source rules.

Often a single set of source rules can be defined for a policy or regulation. Sometimes it makes more sense to divide the source rules into several categories or groups. For instance, a regulation about a benefit may define exclusions or eligibility criteria as well as the basis for calculation. It will be helpful to keep these two distinct kinds of source rule separate.

From Experts

As with many information systems projects, interviewing experts is almost certain to be important when seeking source rules. Typical knowledge elicitation techniques can and should be applied to help experts tell you what rules they follow. Most will be able to document a large number of rules and guidelines quickly, at least for the core or most common transaction types.

Getting the source rules for the less common or corner cases and so ensuring that all the rules have been gathered is a different issue. Most experts will never be able to define all their rules in a top-down fashion. Instead, use actual cases to help elicit the remaining rules. Apply the core source rules extracted to a corner case and show the resulting decision to the expert. If there are additional rules that are relevant to that corner case, the expert will be able to reject the proposed decision and explain why they did so. This explanation will identify the remaining rules for that case. Repeated over a number of corner cases, this will result in a more complete set of rules.

DON'T WAIT TO CAPTURE ALL THE RULES

As with all rules-based approaches, it is not necessary to capture all the source rules before beginning. One of the most important features of a Decision Service is its ability to be evolved and improved over time. As long as the Decision Service has a safe default response that it can offer when it cannot make a decision, it is easy to gradually enhance its ability to handle more cases. For instance, initial versions of a Decision Service may not handle any of the corner cases where applicants provide supporting information, referring all those applicants to a manual process. Over time the various corner cases may be investigated and additional business rules added to improve the ability of the Decision Service to handle these cases.

From Data

One of the most neglected sources of business rules is the historical data that an organization has collected about what was done in the past. This contains the results of applying the rules in place at the time, as well as representing a record that can be mined for what works and what does not.

There are a number of data mining techniques that automatically create business rules explicitly or in the form of decision trees from data. The techniques are broadly similar in terms of the output they generate—the key difference between the various methods is the way in which they create the business rules or decision trees.

DATA MINING PRODUCES EXECUTABLE BUSINESS RULES

The rules produced by data mining are typically executable business rules or at least are much closer to executable business rules than to source rules. It may be helpful to regard the output of the data mining or the model itself as the "source rule." Often the implementation of the data mining results as executable business rules involves a 1:1 mapping—the executable business rules are the same as the original model output. Sometimes there are differences, however, and keeping them separate but linked will be helpful.

Some data mining algorithms are more amenable than others in being able to be represented as business rules. Decision Tree-based algorithms, such as CART, CHAID, and C5, are also known as Rule Induction models because they generate a model suitable for representation as a set of rules. Each algorithm will use slightly different methods to build the tree (or the rules), and will have different options that affect how the tree is grown. In each case the end result is the same—a predictive analytic model that can be represented as a series of If...Then rules that select segments of cases that you wish to target or exclude.

Association rule algorithms such as Apriori and Carma are also good candidates for generating rule-based predictions. These algorithms are often used to find the items that occur together in a transactional set of data, such as items in a shopping basket. They can also be used to identify events that occur together in a particular sequence, useful for identifying patterns in time-based processes. Depending on the situation, these algorithms can help to identify the most common patterns or find the rare outliers that may indicate that something has occurred that shouldn't have. For example, the model might identify the products that most commonly get purchased together to better cross sell-related products. The algorithm usually separates the "Condition" (or Antecedents) from the "Conclusion" (or Consequence). Here is a typical representation of an Association rule:

```
Tan Beach Sandals <= Black Maxi Dress & Striped Layer T-Shirt (1450, 0.5%,
0.34)
```

Here, the Conclusion is that the purchase of the Tan Beach Sandals occurs in 34% of cases when customers have the Black Maxi Dress together with the Striped Layer T-Shirt (the Condition) in their basket. The Black Maxi Dress and Striped Layer T-Shirt are purchased together in 0.5% of all cases, 1450 individual transactions. To represent this as an executable rule, for example, to prompt those customers who haven't yet added the sandals to their basket that they might want to, it can be simply represented as:

```
If Black Maxi Dress = True AND Striped Layer T-Shirt = True
Then
Offer = Tan Beach Sandals
```

SOME PREDICTIVE ANALYTIC MODELS ARE NOT EASY TO REPRESENT AS BUSINESS RULES

There are a number of common predictive analytic models that cannot easily be represented and executed as business rules. These include Linear and Logistic Regression Models, Time Series models, and other statistical-based algorithms that must be represented as a statistical equation as well as those based on neural networks. In addition, segmentation models such as K-Means, Two Step, and Kohonen are generally not easy to represent as business rules because their execution relies on statistical equations or on neural networks. You may be able to use Decision Tree techniques to help identify the rules behind the segments that are generated but this will usually result in an unacceptable level of error being introduced.

Figures 6-2 and 6-3 show an example of a rule set that has been derived analytically to determine the profile of a person with a bad credit rating and an equivalent decision tree.

For organizations who have invested in business rules, this is often a quick start for them to benefit from the output of predictive analytics within their operational environment. Representing predictive analytic models as business rules also has a number of benefits and possible issues. Non-analysts not familiar with the data mining techniques involved or with the predictive analytic workbench being used may well find the presentation of the output as business rules less intimidating. This can increase the acceptance of a model and improve the odds that it will be used. Presenting the model in this way can also allow for partial implementation if one part is more controversial than another.

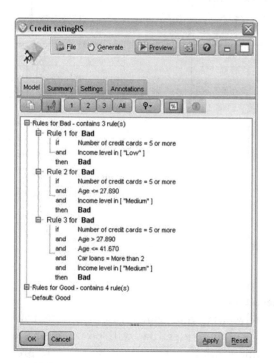

Figure 6-2 An analytically derived rule set to determine the profile of a person with a bad credit rating

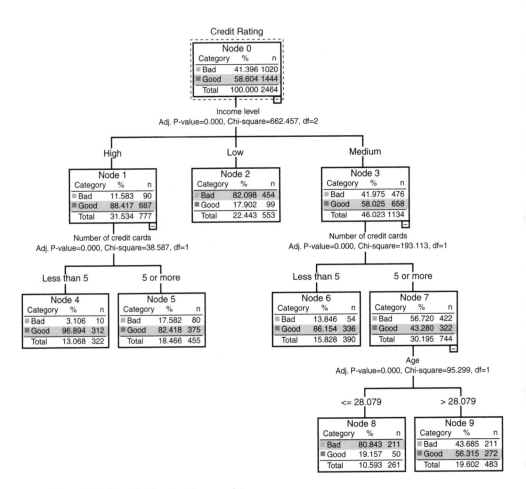

Figure 6-3 A decision tree from the same data

Define Executable Rules

After you know what your source rules are, it is time to implement them as the executable rules that will power your Decision Service. Executable business rules are supported by software products known as Business Rules Management Systems (BRMS). A BRMS stores the executable rules in a rule repository and provides tooling to allow you to author, manage, test, verify, simulate and deploy the executable business rules you develop.

An executable business rule consists of a set of conditions that check the values of attributes defined in the objects available to the Decision Service and one or more actions to take or consequences to enforce if all those conditions are true. The actions are generally defined in terms of values to be stored in specific attributes available to the Decision Service, either temporary ones of use only within the Decision Service or those defined as part of its output. Executable business rules might also have a name, a description, and other metadata such as owner or version history to assist in ongoing management.

How to effectively develop executable business rules for a real project could fill a book on its own, and if you look at the bibliography you can find several excellent references. At a high level, five steps are at the heart of developing executable rules: working with objects, selecting representations, writing the rules themselves, linking to source rules, and validating that the rules are correct.

Determine Objects

Source rules do not generally refer to the actual objects that exist in the systems with which a Decision Service will be integrated. Executable business rules, on the other hand, must execute against these objects—they must be able to manipulate the objects that exist in the rest of your information systems, the objects that are being passed around your business processes.

To make this work, you link the objects in your systems—the objects that are being passed to your Decision Service as part of its contract—to the terms and vocabulary that make sense to those who will be writing and reviewing the business rules. Each object and each attribute for each object has a technical definition that allows it to be accessed. The mapping gives each object and each attribute a description useful to someone familiar with the business but not the underlying technology. This mapped vocabulary will replace technical IT terminology with something that matches the way the business team thinks about the things being manipulated with business rules.

The process of creating predictive analytic models or using data mining techniques usually requires the creation of a number of new attributes. This might range from creating a variable such as Age by taking a customer's date of birth away from today's date, to more complex attributes such as "Number of times in the last 180 days that the customer's payment has been more than 30 days late." These new attributes will need to be added to the objects available to the Decision Service.

Select Business Rules Representation

Many BRMS offer multiple business rule representations, or ways to manage executable business rules. Some BRMS specialize in specific representations or use a single representation in all circumstances. Given your choice of BRMS, you will have to choose from one or more representation for executable business rules each time you author a rule set.

KEEP AN OPEN MIND ABOUT REPRESENTATION

In general, it is a good idea to keep an open mind about which representation will make the most sense for each rule set. Each rule set will have different volatility and update frequencies, for instance. This information is part of the analysis of decisions and will help guide the right representation choice for a rule set. Most organizations find that they need to use different representations or to use the same representation in quite different ways for different rule sets.

The major representation approaches are as follows:

- **Decision Table:**   A decision table is a look-up table where each cell represents an executable business rule. The conditions of the rule are columns or rows in the decision table and the intersection of the rows and columns shows the consequence of the rule. Decision tables are very compact ways to show a lot of rules where the number of attributes involved in conditions is modest, although the number of different values to be checked in conditions can be high. Figure 6-4, shows all the rules for pricing mechanical breakdown coverage across all vehicle values and annual mileages.

- **Rule Sheet:**   A rule sheet is often called a decision table, as it has similar characteristics. In a rule sheet, each row is a rule. Condition and action columns are defined, each containing an attribute. A rule is specified by putting values in the columns that map to the conditions of the rule and putting the consequences in the action columns to show the actions to be taken. Much more complex rules can be written simply by adding more columns. Because many rule sets have large numbers of rules with a similar structure, this can be a very effective representation for managing executable business rules. Sometimes the rows and columns are reversed, with each column representing a business rule and each row representing a condition or action.

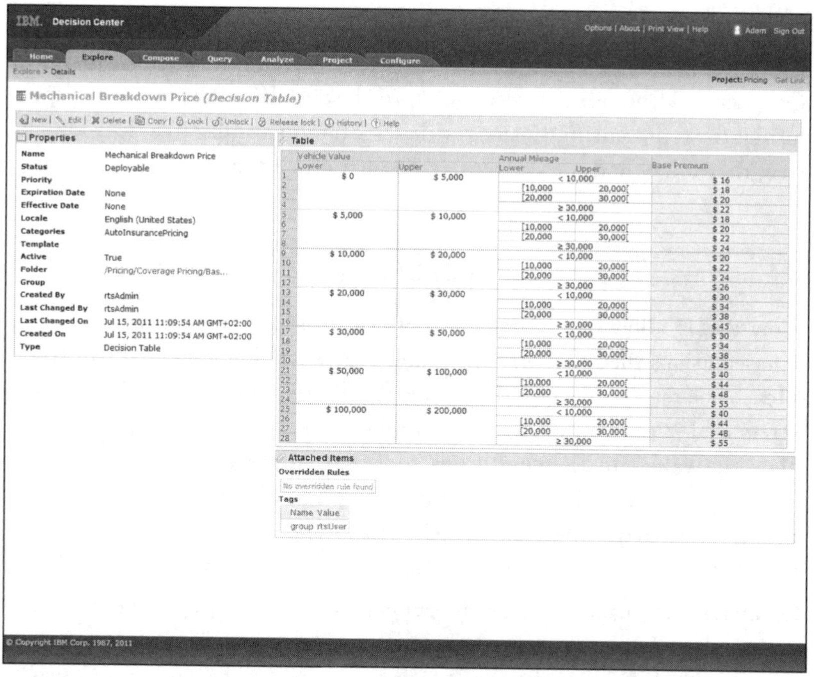

Figure 6-4 A decision table showing rules for pricing mechanical breakdown coverage

- **Decision Tree:** A decision tree represents a set of executable business rules using a branching format. A decision tree consists of a set of linked nodes, where each node is a condition and has multiple branches from it, each representing a possible outcome of the condition. The final layer of the tree is a set of action definitions. Every path from the first or root node to each end action corresponds to one rule. These rules have the same root node—they share a condition—and each group will have one or more additional layers of shared nodes. Decision trees work well when groups of rules in a rule set share some but not all conditions—they are not symmetric.

- **Freeform Rules:** The simplest representation is one that simply allows a set of business rules to be written one after another in a list. Each rule can use any available attributes in its conditions and there is no require-ment for the consequences of the various rules to be similar. Each BRMS has its own syntax for freeform rules. Many have a syntax that is "English-like," and most are extremely readable, allowing less technical users to read and write business rules without interpretation from IT staff.

- **Graphs:** Although not very widespread, some BRMS support a graph format for representing business rules. Although similar to a decision tree, they allow nodes to be reused, resulting in a more compact format.

TEMPLATES

Many BRMS allow templates to be defined for some or all of the rule set representations they support. Templates typically allow some parts of the rules in the representation to be changed and may allow rules to be added or removed in controlled ways. For instance, a freeform rule template may allow the values in the conditions for a rule to be changed while not allowing the rule to be deleted or its action to be redefined. A decision tree template may allow new branches to be added while restricting the user to the set of actions already defined.

Templates can make it easier to support less technically capable rule writers. By reducing the scope of changes and supporting the author with predefined values or selections, syntactic errors can be largely or even wholly eliminated.

Write Executable Business Rules

Although a representation has been selected for a particular rule set, an initial set of executable business rules needs to be developed. These need to implement the behavior defined in the source rules identified and support the test cases defined earlier. In addition, they must conform to the overall contract of the Decision Service. Each sub-decision implemented as a rule set must also confirm to its own set of allowable answers—it must not be possible for the executable business rules written to return an answer not included in the list of answers for the decision the rule set represents.

BUSINESS RULES FROM DATA MINING

Provided that the attributes used by the rules created using data mining techniques are available within the data model of your BRMS, re-creating the rules created by data mining within the BRMS is trivial. The business rules found through data mining are typically close to if not actually executable business rules. These business rules can be created either manually or automatically from within a data mining tool.

To create business rules manually, you follow the logic of the generated decision tree from the root of the tree to each of the leaves in turn. For example, from the tree in Figure 6-3: If the Income level is medium, and the number of credit cards is 5 or more, and the age of the applicant is less than 28 (rounded down), then there is more than 80% possibility that the person is a bad credit risk. Each such rule can be implemented.

Many predictive analytics workbenches can export the definition of a decision tree in Predictive Model Markup Language, or PMML (an XML representative of a predictive analytic model), and this can often be loaded directly into a BRMS as executable business rules.

In either case, however, a manual process has now been introduced into the deployment of the Decision Service. As the predictive analytic models change (and they will, as customer behavior changes) the rules will have to be re-created within the BRMS. A manual process can increase the time it takes to deploy updates to the Decision Service and introduces a step where human error can cause inaccuracies.

Link to Source Rules

Rule management—the ability to find and change rules as circumstances change—is typically much more important for Decision Management Systems than rule execution. It is important, obviously, that the initial version of the business rules is accurate and that it executes rapidly and effectively. Many business rules are volatile, and there is often the potential for external drivers to cause change in business rules. As a result, managing the business rules— identifying the rules that must change, finding those rules, and accurately changing them— is often more important for long-term project success. Keeping links between source rules, and thus sources, and executable business rules is essential. With these links in place, it will be easier to do impact analysis—seeing which executable rules will need to be changed based on a change to a particular policy or regulation—and it will be easier to find the executable rules that must be changed when a best practice changes.

TRACEABILITY OF BUSINESS RULES

Many BRMS allow you to extend the repository to keep track of this information, and you are strongly urged to do so. Managing all the executable business rules will help improve agility and make it easier to change without this linkage to sources. Managing the executable business rules and maintaining these links will make it much easier. Traceability from source rules to executable rules makes it easier to find, scope, and manage the changes you will need to make to your business rules.

Validate and Verify

Each rule set should be validated, verified, and tested as a unit in addition to being tested as part of the Decision Service. Many rule sets are reused, and it is a best practice to make rule sets as reusable as possible.

1. Validate that all the business rules have been written in a valid way. They should use the correct syntax, only refer to objects and attributes that exist, use valid comparators (no comparing numbers to strings, for instance), and more. This is typically either enforced by the editor in the BRMS or easy to check using an automated routine.
2. Verify the executable business rules. This involves focusing on the rule set or a group of rule sets in a decision flow and verifying that it is complete and correct by examining the structure of the rules. For instance, if a rule set is expected to set a particular attribute, and it is known that the attribute can have one of five values, the rule set can be verified by checking that each value is at least possible given the rules. Similarly, if numeric ranges are being checked, then the rules can be verified to ensure that there are no potentially confusing overlaps or gaps in the ranges tested. There are many other tests, and each BRMS implements its own.
3. Although it is possible to verify the accuracy of a rule set in structural terms, it will typically also be necessary to verify that it behaves correctly by developing and running tests. These are akin to unit test cases developed for pieces of code, and most BRMS manage and run these tests after they have been defined.

Deploy and Integrate Continuously

If you begin by defining the Decision Service contract and test cases, it should be possible to immediately integrate the "empty" Decision Service. This means that each new set of executable business rules or modifications to existing business rules can be deployed and integrated with your other systems and processes immediately. A continuous process to deploy and integrate your business rules as you develop them is highly recommended.

A continuous integration and deployment process helps ensure that each new or updated rule set works and can be used. It also supports the kind of iterative development of business rules that works best when developing Decision Management Systems. With a continuous deployment approach, each new set of rules will be available to the Decision Service quickly and will improve the running Decision Service immediately, whether it is running in production or only in a development/testing environment. Because these changes are contained within the Decision Service, they will not require re-integration, as the scaffolding will remain the same.

Build Predictive Analytic Models

Although many of the tasks in a decision flow will be represented by rule sets, some will be represented by predictive analytic models. These mathematical models take a set of information about a customer, a transaction, or some other object and use that information to calculate a score or propensity. The intent of the model is that this score is a usable probability that something is true. For instance, a predictive analytic model might use information about a claim to predict the likelihood that it is fraudulent. Such a prediction is not absolute but it clarifies our uncertainty. We know some claims are fraudulent, but we are uncertain which ones. The predictive analytic model turns this uncertainty into a usable probability—the likelihood that a particular claim is fraudulent.

Building a predictive analytic model requires access to historical data that includes information on what you are hoping to predict. For instance, if you wish to predict fraudulent claims, you will need historical data on claims that were determined to be fraudulent as well as data on claims that were valid. This historical data is used to build the model using a variety of mathematical techniques.

BUILDING PREDICTIVE ANALYTIC MODELS

It is not the intent of this section to describe the complete process for building analytic models. Existing methodologies and suitable texts that do describe the complete process are listed in the bibliography.

The core steps for building a predictive analytic model are exploring and understanding data that might be predictive, preparing this data, applying various mathematic analysis techniques, building and testing the model, and deploying it.

Explore and Understand Data

Most predictive analytic models are built from multiple data sources. After a problem has been clearly identified as one requiring a predictive analytic model, it is essential to explore existing data sources to see how those data sources might contribute to an effective predictive analytic model. In a Decision Management System, the business need is clear: some decision must be made that is dependent on some analytic insight.

Each potential data source should be examined for format, quality, and quantity, both of records and of attributes. Basic statistical analyses can be performed to see whether attributes have relationships to each other or whether there are large numbers of missing values. The normal range of continuous values in a particular attribute or the set of explicit values used should be determined.

Prepare Data

The raw data available in most data sources is not immediately consumable by the tools and techniques that develop predictive analytic models. It must be cleaned and integrated, sampled if there is a great deal of data, split into training and validation sets, and more. In addition, additional attributes are likely to be created from the data that have greater predictive power than the raw attributes contained in the original data source.

Different analysis techniques require data of different cleanliness; the first step in preparing the data is to make sure that the data is clean enough to be used. This might involve simple steps such as substituting for missing values, or more complex ones, such as estimating missing data using modeling techniques.

The data from various data sources needs to be integrated so that a combined data set can be presented to the modeling techniques that will be used to build the predictive model. Typically this involves flattening data that is hierarchical. For instance, when merging a customer data set with an accounts data set, it is likely that some customers have multiple accounts. Flattening this data set would take the important information about accounts and repeat it one, two, three, or more times so that each account would be stored in its own set of attributes. This kind of denormalization is important for most predictive analytic workbenches and techniques.

One of the most important steps in preparing data is the generation of additional attributes. Most predictive analytic models use a set of attributes, only some of which are in the original source data—the rest are calculated. These range from simple calculations such as age (using today's date and birth date, for instance) to much more complex ones such as number of times a customer has been more than 30 days late on a payment in the last 180 days. Many such attributes might be created to see whether they are potentially predictive and automation of this task is increasingly common.

Finally, it is common and generally recommended to split the data into two sets—one to train the model and one to test it. By excluding all the test data from the model training, we give ourselves a way to test with data that the modeling technique has never "seen." This prevents what is known as "overfitting," where the model is very predictive but only of the data that was used to train it—the model works for the data that built it but not for more general data sets.

Select Technique(s)

Many different predictive analytic techniques exist. Although most are not suitable for some situations and some are particularly good for a type of problem, most predictive analytic models could be developed using one of several techniques. Multiple techniques can also be assembled into what is known as an ensemble model.

Build and Test

The various techniques can now be used to build models. Often the same technique can be used to build multiple models with different assumptions or parameters. Once built, all these different models can be compared to see which seems most predictive. The key criteria are the extent to which the model will help improve the decision-making at issue. A model might be more predictive of fraud, for instance, but generate too many false positives and so be rejected in favor of a less predictive model that generates fewer false positives.

Models with good potential are validated using the test data held back from the initial modeling effort. Ensembles of multiple models can be constructed and similarly tested. The end result is a preferred or most predictive model.

Deploy

Deploying the model into production so that it can be part of the Decision Service is critical. Without this step, the model will languish on the sidelines, potentially predictive but not being used. Multiple options for deploying the model can be considered, depending on how current the model needs to be and the specifics of the decision being automated.

- Predictive analytic models can be executed natively by generating code or SQL for the model that the Decision Service can call when the result of the predictive analytic model is needed.

- Predictive analytic models can be represented as business rules or as functions within a BRMS. This can be achieved through manual or automatic import of models to create rules and rule artifacts that are executable. The increasing prevalence of PMML is making this option more practicable.

- Database scoring, perhaps the most traditional approach, involves running the predictive analytic model in a batch mode so that the resulting score is available in the database and can be passed in to the Decision Service as part of its input data. This is easy to do and widely used, but it results in scores that could be out of date when accessed in fast-moving situations.

- Separate modeling services can be deployed that are invoked by the Decision Service.

IN-DATABASE ANALYTICS

In-database analytics is a rapidly growing approach to building and deploying predictive analytic models. The approach is described in more detail in Chapter 10, "Technology Enablers." The primary use case for in-database analytics is to score data in a database with a predictive analytic model without having to remove the data from the database—the predictive analytic model is executed on the database server in either as a batch process or, increasingly, just in time when the score is required.

Build Optimization Models

There are three main use cases for optimization in Decision Management Systems:

- Optimization within a single decision

  Optimization can be used within a single decision to optimize its response on the basis of information about the single transaction for which a decision is required. In this case, an optimization model represents a task in the decision flow.

- Optimization across many decisions

  When batches of decisions are being made, optimization can be used to optimize the decisions being made by considering all the transactions as a set. This would show up as a task only in a batch decision, perhaps before a section of decision flow that repeats for each transaction in the batch.

- Optimization of future decision-making approaches

  Finally, after decisions have been made, optimization can be used to analyze historical results and optimize the way decisions should be made in the future—essentially optimizing the business rules being used to make decisions rather than the decisions themselves. This third option is discussed in Chapter 7, "Monitor and Improve Decisions," as part of monitoring and improving decisions.

OPTIMIZATION IN A SINGLE DECISION

When a decision has a single, simple action such as an offer to be made to a customer, it is likely that optimization will need to be applied to a batch of such transactions. It makes sense, for instance, to consider what offers might be made to a group of customers to optimally allocate limited high-value offers where they will have the most business impact. If a single customer is being considered each time and only a simple action being determined, it is unlikely that optimization will make sense within the Decision Service.

When the action is a complex one, however, optimization may well be very effective inside a Decision Service for a single transaction. If the desired output is "present a feasible configuration of a product for this customer, minimizing cost," the decision will involve a whole set of configuration parameters and options. Optimization may well be powerful or even necessary to generate the optimal solution in this case.

Optimization in this context refers to mathematical optimization or constraint programming. In both these approaches, an optimization model is a mathematical model that defines a problem. The model is typically defined as

1. A set of *decision variables* that represent the choices to be made
2. An objective or measure of success
3. A set of constraints defining what is allowable

Once crafted, an optimization model can be instantiated with data, and a solver is then used to find the best possible or optimal solution for the defined problem—a set of values for the decision variables that satisfies the constraints and maximizes the objective.

Optimization can help find the balance between conflicting trade-offs or the most effective way to use a set of resources. Depending on the context, the resources you optimize might be capital and risk (in financial investment), physical space (transportation, warehousing, retail space planning), machine capacity (manufacturing planning and scheduling), or labor cost (workforce scheduling). Many optimization problems will naturally consider a combination of resource constraints and objectives.

The process of building mathematical optimization models has similarities with its predictive analytics counterpart, but there are a few major differences worth highlighting to avoid confusion:

- Although predictive models are *generated* by applying an algorithm to a data set, an optimization model is *formulated* by hand to represent a business problem by defining the decision variables, the objective, and the constraints.

- Although the scope and input to a predictive model is often relatively small (such as information about a customer), the scope of an optimization model is usually a complex transaction or a set of transactions.

- Predictive analytic models generally require access to large amounts of historical data that can be used to train the model. Optimization models can be run against historical data but do not require it.

- Although *invoking* a predictive model in a Decision Service is relatively fast and simple—it simply involves evaluating a formula or interpreting a decision tree—*solving* an optimization model can consume significant time and memory, depending on the complexity of the model and size of the data. The optimization model must search a large set of possible actions to determine the one that best fits the constraints and goals.

Optimization is well established in supply chain problem domains where it is often used to manage sourcing, manufacturing, distribution, and pricing. It might be used, for instance, to define which products to make on which machines in a factory to maximize the value of products produced given restricted access to the various machines needed to make the products. Scheduling is another common problem, where constraints include the need for workers with specific skills to be available at certain times while meeting requirements on working hours, shifts, and safety. Similarly, your airplane seat, rental car, and hotel room are all likely to be priced using optimization technology.

OPTIMIZATION MODELS CAN BE COMPLEX

Once again, the purpose of this section is to give an overview of how to use optimization in the context of Decision Services, not to define a complete methodology for doing so.

Define decision variables

The first step in building an optimization model is to define what you're trying to decide; that is, the output of the model. A decision variable can be either a true/false variable (such as modeling whether an activity is happening in a certain time slot or not), an integer (such as deciding the placement of an item in time or space), or a rational or linear variable (such as representing the required quantity of a raw material). The type of variables used in a model determines the type of the model and the algorithm used to solve it—linear programming, (mixed) integer programming, or constraint programming, for example. These variables will be part of the data being manipulated by the Decision Service.

Define objective

The second step in building an optimization model is to define its objective—what you wish to optimize. The objective is defined in terms of the decision variables and data, and calculates something that can either be maximized (or minimized) or defines a valid solution to a problem. The function defines what it is that you find valuable.

For instance, an optimization problem might be trying to fit an order on to the cheapest possible set of delivery trucks. The function would define the cost of using various delivery trucks so that the total cost of any given solution to the problem could be calculated. Sometimes the goal is simply to find a solution that does not violate any constraints, and in this case there is no objective defined.

Define constraints

The third and final element of the definition of an optimization problem is the set of constraints. This might define a limit on how many of something are available or might state that the value of one particular element of the solution must be greater than another value. In a scheduling problem, constraints might define which activities must be performed before another activity, or which resources can perform a particular activity. In an allocation problem, it might define how much of a particular product can go on a particular truck, which kinds of trucks can carry which products, or might limit which products can share a truck.

Constraints are typically divided into hard constraints and soft constraints. Hard constraints cannot be broken by a proposed solution. If no solution can be found that does not break a hard constraint, then the problem is overly constrained. Soft constraints can be broken, but a solution will be considered "better" the fewer such constraints it breaks. Sometimes soft constraints have a penalty value associated with them; this is used to reduce the objective value of a candidate solution if it breaks that constraint. For example, a scheduling problem might define "no one can be assigned to two shifts that overlap" as a hard constraint while "no one should be assigned to two shifts in a 20-hour period" might be a soft constraint with a penalty.

Constraints like those in Figure 6-5 often look a lot like the condition part of a business rule. Instead of defining the action to be taken when a set of conditions are true, a constraint simply states a set of conditions that must be true. Some optimization systems even share a condition evaluation engine with a business rules management system.

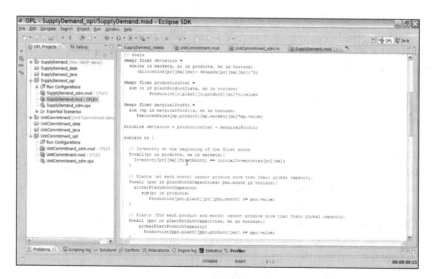

Figure 6-5 Defining constraints in an optimization model

BUILDING ON BUSINESS RULES

Optimization technology is often used when an approach focused on using business rules has reached a point of diminishing returns. When there are very large numbers of business rules or when those business rules must be constantly traded off against one another so that the minimum number are violated, a business rules-based Decision Service may not be effective or even practical. The rules developed up to that point are often a good basis for the definition of the constraints that an optimization system will need.

Some solutions also combine business rules and optimization more tightly than simply executing them sequentially in a Decision Service. A set of business rules can be defined where the actions of those rules configure an optimization problem. Different data will cause the business rules to take different actions and configure a slightly different optimization problem.

Solve

The final step is to solve the optimization problem using an engine known as a *solver*. The solver will use the data available in the Decision Service and then find the best possible solution to the objective. Typically, a variety of mathematical techniques can be used either singly or in combination. The solver will evaluate large numbers of potential solutions and use the degree to which the objective is met and the constraints violated to hone in on the best possible solution to the problem. If the problem has more than one solution that does not violate the constraints, the solver can be configured either to seek the best of the viable solutions or simply to return the first one that doesn't violate the defined constraints.

The output of the solver is a set of values for the decision variables defined in the model, and thus defines the objective value of the solution, as well as the feasibility and penalties of any soft constraints. These values might represent the actions that should be returned by the Decision Service or they might be input to further tasks in the decision flow.

OPTIMIZING WITH PREDICTIONS

One of the interesting areas for optimization is using predictive analytic models as inputs. For instance, optimization is often used to schedule pick-up or delivery routes. When scheduling pick-ups, one option is simply to use the pick-ups requested so far and re-optimize the remaining pick-ups during the day. As each new pick-up is called in, the schedule is revised. However, this could result in trucks being badly out of position if a sequence of pick-ups is requested in one part of town.

It is possible to use predictive analytics to address this. Data about previous days could be used to generate the likelihood that a pick-up will be called in today for each part of town. As pick-ups are actually called in, this information can be combined with information about the likelihood of additional pick-ups in the future to optimize the schedule based on what has already happened and what is likely to happen later.

Iterate as Needed

Decision Services are rarely complete when they are first deployed. Even when they are, the likelihood is that changing circumstances will cause regular and perhaps constant change to the decision-making approach used. An iterative development approach (in which the business rules in each rule set and the predictive analytic and optimization models used are developed incrementally) is much preferred over a waterfall approach.

Integrate Decision Services

Once built, Decision Services need to be integrated with the rest of the information technology environment of which they will be part. Data must be passed to the Decision Service so that it can process transactions, and data must be captured when it is returned from the Decision Service so that it can be acted upon. The Decision Service must be integrated with the business processes and event-based systems that need it. Many Decision Services do not handle 100% of transactions, so it is also worth considering how a Decision Service can be integrated with case management systems.

Data Integration

Decision Services vary in the extent to which they gather their own data once they have been invoked. Calls to Decision Services pass some data that will be used as the basis for the decision returned by the service. This is simple when the calling systems all have the information that the Decision Service requires. It becomes more complex for decisions that might require large amounts of data, or where the calling context varies a great deal. At one extreme are Decision Services that must be passed all the data they require. At the other extreme are Decision Services in which even long-running requests for data, say those involving a human, can be accommodated.

Four broad options for data in Decision Services exist:

1. Pass all the data available into a Decision Service and force it to either decide or to pass back some reason why it could not, so that the calling application can assemble any additional data required and try again.

The most "pure" kind of Decision Service, this approach is simple and fast. It can result in multiple attempts to get a decision more often than other options. It lends itself to remote operation because it needs no data access of its own. It can also result in calling applications investing time in collecting data that may or may not be relevant to the decision itself; this can be a problem when some data is only required occasionally.

BUSINESS PROCESSES CAN ASSEMBLE DATA

When a business process management system is going to be calling Decision Services, the assembly of data to pass to the Decision Service is rarely a problem. Business process management systems are well equipped when it comes to getting data from multiple systems, assembling it into a coherent package of data, and passing it to a service. This allows the Decision Service to be defined to expect a broad set of data.

2. Pass the data available to the Decision Service but allow it to make synchronous calls to external services and databases to gather the data it needs to complete the decision.

   The service must handle timeouts, and it must degrade gracefully if these additional data sources are not available. This approach is also fairly fast and simple. It allows costly or time-consuming requests for information to be deferred until and unless they are required. It does make the Decision Service dependent on other components, however.

3. Pass the data available to the Decision Service and allow it to gather the data it needs in any way.

   The Decision Service may need to be put "on ice" while waiting for data. The Decision Service can no longer be used in a real-time or interactive context, as it cannot be relied upon to make a decision in a reasonable time. It should be invoked asynchronously, gather the data it needs, and then transmit its result, typically as an event. This approach is better suited to event-based architectures.

4. Pass the data available to the Decision Service, and allow it to request additional data from a user interface.

   This might involve a customer (such as someone applying for insurance) or an employee (entering additional data required by a process). The decision continues to run until the data is provided through the user interface or the request for a decision is cancelled. These Decision Services usually require a definition of the decision and an additional set of business rules to handle the interaction, display the correct questions, and adapt the user interface to gather the required data.

Good Decision Service design requires a clear understanding of what is needed from a requirements perspective and plausible from an architectural and technical perspective. Option 1 is the most pure and most common, but can be limiting when large amounts of data are involved. Options 2—4 provide more flexibility but increase the challenges: The number of failure points increase, which can be crippling if not managed well. The complexity can rapidly increase because of maintenance, monitoring, and error handling needs, and more resources must be dedicated to manage the additional integration points in the infrastructure.

A HYBRID APPROACH CAN BE USEFUL

One of the most common hybrid approaches is to break a Decision Service into two parts. One determines what data is needed to make a decision in a particular case, while the other makes the business after the relevant data has been collected. For instance, the first might decide whether a motor vehicle report is needed to process a particular applicant for insurance, while the second uses that data as part of the underwriting decision.

Process Integration

Integrating a business process with a Decision Management System is generally very straightforward. The business process will generally collect all the information needed by the Decision Management System, accessing whatever range of systems are involved. This data is then passed as a package to the Decision Service using a standard service call for the environment—generally a web services invocation. The Decision Service runs and returns the result like any other service, and the process continues. Handling timeouts and other mechanical issues is built into the process design as it would be for any other service call.

Processes that use a Decision Management System often have worklists or case management steps to handle those transactions where the Decision Management System could not make a decision. As a result, it is common to see a branch immediately after the call to the Decision Service. This will contain one or more branches for those transactions where the decision was made, as well as one that routes the transaction to a worklist or a case management environment. Where the Decision Service was selecting a particular approach, such as one determining whether a claim should be fast tracked or referred for fraud investigation, each action will have its own branch and a set of process steps or a sub-process that is appropriate to that option.

Event Integration

Integrating a Decision Service with an event-based system is even simpler. The Decision Service is set up with a listener for the events that contain information about a transaction that must be processed by the Decision Service. When such an event is detected, the Decision Service or Decision Agent executes and makes a decision. Depending on the action, it then puts the relevant action event back on the event bus so that other systems can handle it.

The Decision Service can be passed only the event and the data associated with it, or it can be passed the entire collection of events whose correlation triggered the need for the decision in the first place. Sometimes the decision being made is an assessment of the need to trigger a new event. For instance, does the pattern of events warrant a fraud investigation? In this case, the whole sequence of events might be passed to a Decision Service that decides whether an "Investigate" event is called for.

Sometimes event and process integration are combined. A Decision Service may be triggered by an event and then kick off a business process to handle the decision action. Similarly, a Decision Service may be called from a business process and may result in additional events being generated that will be put onto an event bus in parallel with the rest of the process continuing to execute.

Case Management Integration

Case management systems are often integrated with Decision Management Systems. Many Decision Management Systems cannot make decisions in 100% of transactions, and often the remaining transactions are considered cases that must be managed through a manual decision-making process. This is generally only true for relatively high-value decisions. For instance, a Decision Management System that makes commercial underwriting decisions would likely put any application for insurance that it could not process into a case management system for an underwriter to review. Even if a Decision Management System can make a decision, it may still need to push that transaction into a case management environment. For instance, an organization may decide to manually review a certain randomly selected percentage of automated decisions. One of the most effective ways to do this is to push the information about the transaction and the decision made into a case management system. The simplest way to integrate a Decision Management System and a case management system is simply to hand off transactions that come back from the Decision Management System as undecided or as flagged for review. As far as the Decision Management System is concerned, that transaction is now dealt with and it will not see it again.

In the case of undecided transactions, however, the best practice is increasingly to consider the case management system as a supporter of the Decision Management System. When a Decision Management System cannot decide about a transaction, it is generally because there is some assessment or judgment called for that requires human intervention. Instead of simply giving up on the transaction at this point, the Decision Management System could put a much more specific request into the case management system. This request could identify the human intervention(s) needed, such as a visit to a commercial location to do an inspection, and request that the case management system manage them before returning to the Decision Management System and re-invoking it with the new data. This more focused approach to using the case management system avoids the situation where a transaction that was *almost* suitable for automated decisioning is processed completely manually. Instead the Decision Management System uses the case management system to gather additional data it needs so that it can, in the end, make a decision.

Best Practices for Decision Services Construction

Although the technical details of constructing Decision Services are outside the scope of this book, a number of best practices are worth noting.

Designing for Batch and Interactive

When integrating a Decision Service into a business process, the decision can be made before the transaction occurs—for example, pre-calculating the credit worthiness of known customers; interactively while the transaction occurs—for example, offering an up-sell offer to an anonymous web user; or after the transaction occurs—for example, deciding whether an insurance claim is likely fraudulent. The pre- and post- options could be managed as a batch process, with many items being processed through the decision as a batch to optimize the computing resources required. Often this is a design choice, but sometimes integrating the Decision Service to run during the transaction is required such as when some of inputs to the decision are only available after the transaction has started. The batch integration of Decision Services is often less complex.

An ideal design will allow a Decision Service to be designed once and deployed in a batch or interactive mode without recoding or changing the business rules, predictive analytic models, or optimization models. This can be important when a process that is initially deployed in batch needs to move to interactive because the business requires the decision to be made as the transaction occurs. For example, a fraud detection decision may move from a post-transaction batch process that occurs every 15 minutes to an online fraud detection decision to prevent fraud as it occurs.

The data available to the Decision Service is often different between a batch and interactive environment. In the interactive environment, some data may come from the transaction being processed—such as current browsing history or call center notes. These may also be combined with existing data sources such as customer history or product inventory. A separate data layer can be defined that is customized for these different environments without affecting the core Decision Service. Alternatively, two Decision Service entry points can be defined. These have different data inputs and are designed to handle batch or interactive decision-making. These can reuse the business rules and predictive analytic models involved to ensure that decisions are consistent between them. For example, a batch Decision Service might be used to determine the benefits for which a group of employees are eligible. This same decision-making might be available at an interactive kiosk for employees to see whether they would be eligible for various benefits in different what-if scenarios. The same logic is applied, but a separate data layer would be required for the batch situation.

When constraint-based optimization is involved in a decision, you are often choosing an optimal set of decisions from a large set of possible decisions. This tends to lend itself better to a batch process that can consider a large number of transactions and decisions about those trans-actions. Optimization can be used during interactive decisions, but often a simple ordering of decision values or other techniques can be used because the number of decisions being considered during a single transaction is often very small.

No Side Effects

One of the most important aspects of good Decision Service design is to avoid any "side effects." It is possible to use a BRMS to actually send emails, update databases, or approve transactions. This means that a Decision Service could also do these things. It is generally more effective, however, to have the Decision Service determine what should be done, and leave the calling application or process to actually take the action.

The reason for this is reuse. If the Decision Service takes the action itself, then it can only be called when that action is appropriate. For instance, a Decision Service that updates the price of an order based on the appropriate discount for a customer can be used when an order is placed but cannot be reused when a customer asks what the discount would be were she to place such an order. It also cannot be reused by a sales person who is trying to see how compelling the discount might be relative to a competitor.

In contrast, a Decision Service that simply returns the right answer and leaves it to the calling application to determine what to do with that answer is much more reusable. A Decision Service that calculates the discount a particular customer would earn on a particular order can be used by the process that places orders, as part of the sales person's environment, and in support of call center processes. Because the action is not taken by the Decision Service itself, there is much more flexibility in where the Decision Service is used.

Even if only one potential use of a Decision Service is apparent, building the Decision Service to recommend an action rather than taking it is a best practice.

Logging

Execution transparency is an important aspect of Decision Management Systems. All Decision Services should therefore have the ability to log how decisions were made—which rules fired, what data was used, what results were generated by analytic or optimization models. These logs can be written to some kind of long-term storage by the Decision Service directly, or the organization can have a standard design pattern for Decision Services that ensures this information is always returned by the Decision Service as part of its signature.

If a decision is regulated, it is worth storing these logs every time the decision is made. This will ensure that any decision made can be examined in retrospect to show that it was made in a compliant way—that the business rules executed when the decision was made were correct and appropriate. If the decision is not a regulated one, it may not be possible to justify the overhead of logging the execution of each decision, and the Decision Service will be set to log execution only sometimes. All Decision Services need the ability to log how decisions were made, however, as understanding how decisions were made will be important, at least to the continuous improvement process, if not to external regulators.

Organizations need to be able to tie the log data to the transactions, customers, and objects involved in the decision as well as to data that shows the downstream consequences of the decision. Generally, the input data contains a clear identifier for the transaction, and this can be stored with the log data. Failing that, the date and time of the decision along with identifiers such as customer ID can be stored to make it possible to reconstruct which decision is being examined when the log is reviewed.

Iterative Development

It is generally not helpful to try and get 100% of the Decision Service built in the first iteration. A more agile approach is preferred, where multiple iterations develop the functionality of the Decision Service. In general, two forms of iterative development are possible.

In the first, the number of transactions handled by the Decision Service gradually increases. This works well when the Decision Service makes a decision that would otherwise be made by a person but where the option for a manual decision still exists. The initial version of the Decision Service can thus handle relatively few transactions, leaving most for manual review. Reviewing the manual actions taken can define and shape the missing business rules. Candidate rules can be compared to the manual actions to see how close the rules are getting and to see whether the rules outperform the manual decision-making. Over time, the number of rules or their sophistication can be increased so that the Decision Service handles a larger percentage of transactions. This approach is used in underwriting, for instance, where the Decision Service gradually evolves to handle more products and more customer situations with fewer applications being referred to an underwriter with each of the iterations.

The second approach is more appropriate when an automated decision is required. For instance, a Decision Service that must return an appropriate ad to display on a webpage does not have the option of deferring that decision to a person—it must make some kind of decision. Such a Decision Service can still be evolved over time. It needs to have a reasonable default response, perhaps a standard and non-controversial ad that can be used whenever it cannot make a more appropriate response. Initially it might always make such a response, and over time, more rules and analytic models can be added to allow it to make a more targeted response in specific circumstances. Each of the iterations decreases the percentage of the times when the generic response is made.

Besides developing the initial Decision Service in an iterative approach, most Decision Services repay an investment in a decision analysis infrastructure for ongoing analysis and refinement after deployment.

7

Monitor and Improve Decisions

A typical IT project ends when a system is complete, installed, and running as expected. Future changes are considered maintenance work and require some kind of change order that feeds into a process for starting new IT projects to make the change. This is unacceptable for Decision Services.

First, because decision-making is more volatile than most other aspects of business being automated, change is likely to be greater and more rapid. Having to engage in a formal IT process for every change is likely to become burdensome, and failing to make needed changes will reduce the value of the Decision Service over time.

Second, it is often uncertain if a decision-making approach is an effective one. As a result it will be necessary to conduct experiments to see what approaches might be most effective, and these experiments will require changes to the Decision Service to implement their conclusions.

After a Decision Service is deployed, a new phase of Decision Analysis is entered, during which the decision must be monitored and systematically improved.

What Is Decision Analysis?

After a Decision Service has been deployed within an operational environment, there is a very real need to continuously update it. The most successful Decision Services are those that can be readily updated and modified by the line of business—the people who own the problem being addressed. You will need to be able to make changes to a Decision Service in response to external stimuli as well as continuously track its performance against your business goals. When and how you will need to refresh the business rules or predictive analytic models within a Decision Service depends upon four factors:

- Changes to the business goals
- New regulations or policies
- Changes to the underlying data patterns
- Overall decision performance

The first three are changes to which you must react, while the fourth requires an investment in proactive change. When any change occurs you must determine the appropriate response and then deploy your response to the change into your production environment.

Successful decision analysis requires an investment in monitoring decisions and in an environment that allows you to effectively assess the appropriate response. It requires a systematic approach for developing new decision-making approaches and an environment that allows these new approaches to be assessed for their potential business impact. After the appropriate response is designed and understood, it will need to be deployed, updating the Decision Service to the new approach.

DECISIONS SHOULD BE ANALYZED BEFORE DEPLOYMENT

This chapter is primarily concerned with the monitoring and improvement of decisions after a Decision Management System has been deployed. Many of these techniques and approaches should also be used prior to deploying the initial version of the Decision Management System. What-if analysis, simulation, and more are all useful for ensuring that the Decision Management System will behave as expected.

Monitor Decisions

The first step in decision analysis is monitoring deployed decision services, and the decisions that are being made by those services, so that you can determine whether a change is required. Monitoring decisions requires a focus on reacting to changes in business goals, in regulations and policies, and in the underlying data, as well as a focus on monitoring the performance of the decision service to see whether a proactive change is required.

Reactive Changes

The way you make a decision is determined by many things. The goals and key performance indicators or metrics of your business set a context that defines what a good or an effective decision looks like. Regulations and policies constrain how decisions are made. The data you have collected over time gives you insight into what works and what doesn't, which is reflected in your current decision-making approach. Any or all of these could change, and when they do, you need to react to these changes.

Changes to the Business Goals and Metrics

The way a Decision Service behaves is driven by your business goals. A decision's impact on those business goals determines whether it is a good decision or a bad decision. This is measured using the metrics and key performance indicators you have established for tracking the progress of your business against those goals. Part of the model you have of your decisions is their linkage to these metrics and business goals.

When business goals or key performance indicators change, the behavior of the Decision Services related to that goal must also change. For instance, the metric for customer retention success could change from a flat percentage—retain a specific percentage of all customers at the end of their contract—to one that involves retaining only those customers who are or could become profitable. Such a change will alter the way customer retention offer decisions are made, as well as other decisions that have an impact on customer retention.

It may also become apparent during operations that specific decisions should be linked to additional metrics and KPIs. For instance, a marketing manager might decide that a particular offer needs to be discontinued because the uptake for this offer has been so large that they are going to struggle to fulfill the requests—the offer was being accepted by around 500 people every day and was resulting in serious increases in wait times at the call center. The decision had been linked to the metrics for campaign effectiveness but not to the metrics for call center responsiveness. After the decision was being made in production, it became clear that this decision could have a negative impact on call center effectiveness.

With the decision now linked to two sets of metrics, the business objective changes from one of simply presenting a compelling offer to as many customers as possible to one that reflects the need for call center support. The marketing manager will need to change the Decision Service to deactivate this offer and replace it with one that requires less call center support. This level of agility is essential—waiting days for an IT change request will not allow the marketing manager to meet the changing business goal.

Identifying the need for this kind of reactive change requires that the decisions are linked to the metrics and key performance indicators of the business. This information needs to be up to date as metrics and business goals evolve. When business owners discuss changes to metrics and business goals, they can use this information to identify those decisions where a change might be required. In addition, when discussing the effectiveness of a decision service, they can review this information to see if it needs to be changed. Any change to the metrics linked to a decision should cause a reactive assessment of the decision making approach(es) currently being used for that decision.

New Regulations or Policies

Many decisions—and thus Decision Services—are dependent on regulations and policies to define how those decisions should be made. When these regulations or policies change, or when new regulations or policies are issued that affect how a decision is made, the Decision Service will need to be updated and business rule updates made based on best practices and changing policies and regulations. For instance, an eligibility service implements a government regulation that specifies certain circumstances in which an organization must approve requests for service from consumers. A court case related to the regulation clarifies how it should be interpreted, changing the organization's eligibility rules. The legal team needs to be able to make a change to the Decision Service to reflect this new interpretation quickly and accurately both to avoid fines and to minimize the amount of rework that would be required when people who were rejected under the old rules reapply.

This requires an understanding of links between source regulations and policies, types of know-how, and the decisions dependent on them. A process for ensuring that changes to the regulations and policies defined in the decision inventory are highlighted in a timely fashion will allow the identification of the decisions where the decision-making approach will need to be evaluated to ensure it will remain compliant.

SOME REGULATORY CHANGES ARE IMMEDIATE

Most regulation and policy changes are known about in advance. Most governments issue new regulations in advance of their effective date, and major company policies usually have an extended review process. This means that changes to decision-making approach can often be considered in advance with plenty of time to make the change. However, some changes are much more immediate, such as court rulings that interpret the meaning of a regulation or a policy change in response to a disaster or a problem at a competitor. These changes will need to be rapidly assessed and changes made almost instantly. You need to be prepared for both.

Changes to the Underlying Data

The most effective approach to a decision is often based on the analysis of historical data. Any Decision Service that uses predictive analytic models or rules derived from data mining is behaving the way it does because of the data that was analyzed. This data was analyzed at a point in time, however, and data recorded since then might reveal different patterns. Data changes mean that the result of this analysis can change also.

For instance, you may learn something new about the customer: You're a mobile telecommunications company and you begin sending customers at risk of leaving marketing offers to tempt them to stay. Some accept these offers and stay, some ignore them but stay anyway, and some ignore them and leave. After the offers start being made, you can see who accepts the offers and who does not—you start to collect data about offers accepted and offers ignored, as well as about the effectiveness of these offers. You now have new data that can be used to drive better decisions in the future. This new knowledge—who did and who did not respond to this particular type of campaign—should be used as input into the next round of modeling. The way in which future retention offers are selected may then be different.

You may also collect additional data: Obtaining access to new kinds of data is a common way to build better predictive analytic models. Many projects start with structured data within the organization, such as transactional data. Over time they move on to data from outside the organization, such as demographic data. They may also start considering unstructured data, such as information typed into call center notes during interactions with the customer, or high-volume data such as weblogs that show the items looked at in the online store. Even social and attitudinal data, such as that from surveys, can be included. Each time you gain access to new data there is an opportunity to rebuild and improve upon the predictive analytic models being used within the Decision Service.

Finally, people's behavior changes over time, and this is reflected in new data patterns. For instance, fraudsters are continuously looking for ways to defraud insurance companies. The pattern of data that shows something as fraudulent will therefore change as they try and outmaneuver your existing fraud detection approach. If you don't notice this, or if you cannot refresh your fraud Decision Service quickly, there may be a significant number of new instances of fraud that the Service does not automatically identify.

For example, there is a growing problem of staged car accidents where a well-organized criminal gang causes car accidents by purposefully braking hard in front of a distracted driver. They claim that they were not at fault and that they were rear-ended by the other driver. They make a claim for both car damage and expensive "injuries." You want your Decision Service to flag these new types of fraud as soon as you become aware of them.

Regular customer behavior also changes over time, with new trends and shifting markets and demographics being reflected in the data you collect about customer behavior. In all these cases, it will make sense to refresh predictive analytic models and business rules derived from this data as the data changes. The availability of new predictive analytic models will, in turn, cause new rules to be written.

Not all changes in data will require a change in decision making. Identifying those changes that merit a response requires an understanding of the data. You need to understand the data sources being used to make decisions as well as those being used to develop predictive analytic models. You also need an environment that monitors the data used to develop predictive analytic models to see whether its distribution has changed since the models were developed. This information and suitable analysis tools are available in most environments used to develop the predictive analytic models. A process is required for assessing new data sources to see whether they would change the models developed and for reviewing the changing characteristics of the data sources used.

ALWAYS MONITOR MODELS ONCE DEVELOPED

Some modeling teams take a "fire and forget" approach to developing predictive analytic models. They do data analysis as part of developing the initial model but fail to monitor the model once developed. There may be no central repository of models that can be used to see how each model was developed, or there may be no process for monitoring those data sources used to see whether the data characteristics are changing. This approach is unacceptable when developing predictive analytic models for use in Decision Services. Accurate definitions of how models were built and ongoing monitoring of those models to see whether a recalibration or a rebuild is appropriate is a necessity.

Proactive Changes

Many changes to decision-making approaches are driven by explicit change and are reactive. When deploying Decision Services, it is also important to be able to make proactive changes. Periodic analysis of the effectiveness of the decisions being made by a Decision Service can identify opportunities for proactive changes to improve decision-making effectiveness. You may not have implemented the most effective decision-making approach initially, but monitoring decision performance will allow you to eliminate responses that don't work or have bad outcomes, for instance. This is especially true when a Decision Service is handling a decision that has not been automated in the past. Ongoing assessments of Decision Services and updates to decision-making approach improve the performance of Decision Services either relative to its current behavior or relative to the likely behavior in the future if no change is made.

To effectively monitor and improve decisions, you need to capture data about decision effectiveness, create an environment to monitor the decisions being made, and link your business performance environment to this decision performance environment.

Capture Decision Effectiveness Data

Any good decision monitoring system will require data about the effectiveness of decisions to be collected. Three main kinds of data are involved—decision execution data, response data, and general business data.

- **Decision Service execution data:** As a Decision Service executes, it can record what decision was requested and what answer was returned through which interaction point. It can include a timestamp and a unique identifier, allowing it to be tied back to the subject of the decision—a specific customer or account, for example. A Decision Service can generate a wide range of additional execution information, including which individual rules fired, which predictive models were invoked and what the score was, any contextual data that was generated during the interaction, and more. All of this should ideally be logged for analysis purposes. You may even be required (for audit and compliance requirements) to retain the log data and the full set of data that was sent to the Decision Service to be able to precisely trace and audit any given decision. However, logging will usually add a processing overhead on the Decision Service that needs to be traded against the need for auditing and monitoring. Whether you have the complete or partial data for every decision or just some, execution data is critical for ongoing monitoring of Decision Services.

- **Decision Service response data:** When a Decision Service makes a decision and this decision is acted on, there will usually be some consequence for the recipient of the decision. For example, a customer being made a specific offer in real time may reject the offer, accept it, click on it for more information, defer it for another time, and so on. It should be possible to collect this data at the time the decision was returned to the recipient and be able to tie it back to the specific Decision Service execution data. Assessing the effectiveness of the decision-making approach will require this information. For instance, if a customer retention offer is presented to a customer and that customer is retained, it will be important to know if he accepted the offer, ignored it, or considered it but did not in the end accept it. Without this information, it will be impossible to understand exactly what impact the offer had.

- **Other enterprise data:** It will be likely that any useful monitoring system will need to incorporate information not directly generated by the Decision Service. Consider a Decision Service designed to make decisions about routing claims to a fraud investigator or not. Assessing the effectiveness of this decision will require a combination of data on which claims were referred by the Decision Service and which ones were later successfully identified to be fraudulent by the fraud investigators. Being able to tie outcomes like this back to each individual decision is vital for the ongoing improvement of the system. It provides the round-trip data required to refresh and improve any predictive models, and it gives insight into the performance of individual business rules.

Build Decision Monitoring Environment

The ongoing performance of a Decision Service will need to be monitored so that the business can track the success and effectiveness of the decisions involved. In addition, IT will want to monitor the performance characteristics of the Decision Service (response times, issues with timeouts, other failed requests, and so on). Monitoring will also help identify ways to make ongoing improvements on how decisions are being made. A suitable decision monitoring environment will need to be built that has access to data about decision performance, as well as links to the overall business performance management environment.

MONITOR EFFECTIVENESS AND APPROACH

Many of the drivers for change in a Decision Service can be monitored using an environment like this, but not all. In addition, it is essential that regulations and policies that affect the Decision Service are also monitored for changes that might require a change in decision-making approach.

A decision monitoring environment presents data that can be used to assess the performance and effectiveness of the Decision Service as well as data about how the decision was made. Various reporting and analysis tools are made available so that business owners can see what changes might make sense. Business intelligence solutions that provide dashboards and reports are ideal for building the basics of a decision monitoring environment. Business users and IT are typically very familiar with them, and they offer enough flexibility that users with different goals can be given custom views of the information that reflect what they are interested in.

Reporting facilities involve both predefined reports on the performance and effectiveness of a Decision Service, and ad-hoc query and reporting to allow the owner of a Decision Service to investigate its performance in new ways. All Decision Services should support reports on distribution of outcomes in a time period, response time, and the distribution of values in the input data. Specific Decision Services might also provide reports that are more specific to the particular decision being made. For instance, a report comparing the cost of retention offers accepted in a particular period with the predicted value of those customers who accepted offers during that period.

Although many Decision Services can be effectively monitored by regularly reviewing reports, it is likely to be more effective to set up monitoring and alerting facilities. Business users responsible for several Decision Services might find overall dashboards effective. A marketing manager, for instance, might want a dashboard that summarizes the performance of the cross-sell, up-sell, retention, and acquisition Decision Services. Alerts can also be defined based on performance of the Decision Service that is either out of acceptable bounds, different from recent results, or otherwise exceptional. As for reporting, some of this could be defined for a Decision Service independent of its purpose. Thus, an alert could be defined for any Decision Service if the distribution of results in the last 5 days was different from the last 30 in some statistically significant way. More usefully, each Decision Service has specific situations that are noteworthy, such as sudden changes in offer acceptance rates or hitting a particular target for fraud in a month.

REPORTING AND MONITORING BEST PRACTICES STILL APPLY

All of the best practices you have developed for building a reporting and monitoring environment apply to decision monitoring. The purpose of this environment is to enable business owners to make decisions about decisions— to make the tactical decisions about how to change the decision-making approaches for their operational decisions.

Link Performance Management and Decision Management

When conducting decision discovery, all top-level decisions were mapped to key performance indicators (KPIs) or metrics. This linkage helps ensure that all decisions are discovered and gives a basis for assessing Decision Service performance. If we know which decisions support which objectives and measures, we can make assumptions about the Decision Services that implement those decisions. If a Decision Service makes a decision that moves the associated metrics in a positive direction, it can be considered a "good decision." Our understanding of the metrics and objectives enables us to understand the difference between good decisions and bad decisions made by a Decision Service. This linkage allows us to track the effectiveness of decision making just like anything else in our performance management environment. We can track not only our financial performance but also our decision performance.

When developing the decision monitoring environment, give some thought to the way in which decision performance and business performance relate. An integrated approach to decision and business performance monitoring will make it easier to improve the decisions and so improve business results.

Determine the Appropriate Response

Monitoring a Decision Service and the regulatory environment in which it operates will identify the need for changes to the behavior of the Decision Service. Just because a change is needed does not automatically make it clear *what* change is needed. The specific drivers for change will need to be analyzed to see what change is required. The need for ongoing experimentation must also be assessed and a new approach or approaches designed.

The specific reasons why the behavior of a Decision Service must be changed can vary widely. A new regulation or policy may have been issued or an existing one updated. A court ruling or contract negotiation may have resulted in a new set of guidelines. Besides these external drivers, new data about customers and what they want may be available, or the behavior of customers may be shifting in response to market changes. Decision performance may also be an issue, either in terms of absolute performance or because a better approach has been proven.

Whatever the reason for the change, a number of elements must be analyzed to determine the appropriate change. Design time analysis, the internal structure, and specification of the Decision Service may show what needs to be changed. Alternatively, the root cause of decision performance issues may need to be determined. If multiple alternative approaches are being used in the Decision Service for either A/B testing or champion-challenger testing, the relative performance of these different approaches must be analyzed to see how to move forward most effectively.

Assess the Design Impact

The first step when deciding what change is going to be required is to conduct a design time impact analysis of the current Decision Service in the light of the change driver. At the heart of a Decision Service is a decision flow, an explicit model of the steps or tasks involved in making a decision. This is supported by a contract that specifies the input and output data of the Decision Service. Each task within this decision flow is described declaratively, either with a set of business rules—a rule set—or with a predictive analytic or optimization model. Because the Decision Service's behavior is driven by these explicitly modeled elements, it is possible to conduct detailed analysis and so design appropriate changes.

TECHNOLOGY FOR IMPACT ANALYSIS

Conducting impact analysis generally involves using functionality built into your BRMS or Decision Management platform. If you are using a service repository or a master data management environment, these too can provide functionality for impact analysis.

Design impact analysis involves finding the artifacts (regulations, data, policies) that are changing and then navigating through the design to see what other elements of the decision service might also have to change. For instance, if a regulation has changed, design impact analysis can be used to list the source rules that are linked to the regulation. For each of these source rules, the analysis would list the executable business rules that are linked to those source rules. In this way the scope of a potential regulatory change can be assessed in terms of the executable business rules that must be considered. Not all these executable business rules would need to change in most situations; the design impact analysis lists those with the potential to be affected by the change.

TRACEABILITY IS REALLY IMPORTANT

Change is inevitable, and Decision Management Systems are among the highest change systems in your portfolio. As a result, it is important that your tools support the kind of traceability needed for design impact analysis.

Although tool support is necessary, it is not, however, sufficient. You need to take traceability into consideration when designing Decision Management Systems and when implementing business rule repositories and business rules management environments. Build these systems with the need to trace the impact of change on your design in mind.

A similar approach can be used to see how information elements that change might affect the Decision Service. From an object or attribute it should be possible to list all the executable business rules or predictive analytic models that use a particular attribute in either their conditions or consequences. This can be essential when an attribute's allowed values change, or when some other element of the information model must be altered. Even when the change is a change to the distribution or range of values in an attribute, it will be important to evaluate each business rule and predictive analytic model that uses the attribute. Expected changes in the data values can be just as disruptive as changes to the structure of the data. For instance, a rule might be intended to identify which customers are top customers and the company might expect to have 10% of customers be in this group. If the distribution of values in the data changes, the same rule might start identifying significantly more than 10% of customers as "top" customers, and this could be very expensive and disruptive. When data elements change either structurally or in terms of the distribution of values, it is common for every affected rule to need to be changed.

IMPACT ANALYSIS IS RECURSIVE

Design impact analysis often needs to be recursive. For instance, when a change in data affects a predictive analytic model, it may be necessary to find all the business rules that refer to the model to see whether any of them must also change.

Assess Decision Effectiveness

The next step is to assess the overall performance of the Decision Service—is it making good decisions most of the time? This is true regardless of whether one approach is being used for all decisions, or if several approaches are being tried for comparison. If the overall perform-ance is unsatisfactory, some change must be made to the current decision approach.

THERE IS ALWAYS VALUE IN MONITORING DECISION EFFECTIVENESS

It might seem that for a completely regulated or policy-driven decision that there is no value to assessing the effectiveness of a decision. After all, there is no flexibility to the decision-making. In reality, most decision services have some flexibility—if not in how the decision is made, at least in which decisions are referred for manual review. A regulated decision may be assessed to see whether the rate of referral is acceptable, for instance.

Decision effectiveness is primarily assessed in terms of the impact of the decisions made on the business metrics and KPIs associated with the decision. If decisions are being made effectively, the decisions will be making a positive contribution to the overall KPIs and metrics. Decision effectiveness can also be assessed in terms of the number of decisions that cannot be made—that must be referred for manual review. Time and cost to make a decision might also be relevant, especially when outside data sources are involved. It may sometimes be possible to make an auto underwriting decision without paying for a report from the Department of Motor Vehicles. Considering the average cost of making a decision would then be part of the decision effectiveness measurement, even if this cost was not a KPI (although it is likely to be).

Decision effectiveness can be assessed both in terms of current performance and in terms of likely performance if the decision-making approach is not changed. When performance shows a slow but steady decline, for instance, it may not be a question of making a change to correct for a current problem but to prevent a future problem. Similarly, if it is clear that there is going to be a change in consumer behavior, after an election or natural disaster for instance, the effectiveness might be assessed in the light of that likely change.

When the current or likely future performance is unsatisfactory, some analysis of the root causes is called for. It may be that the performance of the Decision Service is unsatisfactory across the board. What is more likely is that it is unsatisfactory for particular subsets of the decisions being made. For instance, a cross-sell decision may not be driving as many additional sales as intended. It may be that this cross-sell decision is just underperforming. What is more likely is that the way cross-sell offers are being selected means that some segments of the customer base are getting poorly judged offers—perhaps high net worth individuals are getting inappropriate offers. Drilling down into the decision performance to find out exactly what is wrong is essential if systematic improvement is to be undertaken. Similarly, if large numbers of decisions are being referred for manual review, it may be that this is always because a particular set of information is missing or inaccurate.

The end result of this analysis is an identification both of the kind of change that is called for and the subset(s) of decisions for which this change is appropriate. Several different changes may be required for a particular decision, for different segments of customers for instance.

DECISION SERVICE PERFORMANCE MATTERS ALSO

The time it takes for a Decision Service to make a decision also matters. This performance should be monitored and tracked over time to ensure that the Decision Service performs adequately for the business need. If the Decision Service is supporting a customer interaction, for instance, the response time must reflect that. If the Decision Service must process every customer overnight in a batch, the expected growth in customers must not increase the size of the batch window beyond that available.

If the speed to decision for a Decision Service is not adequate or is trending to become inadequate, the design will need to be reviewed to see how performance can be improved, perhaps by rewriting business rules or re-evaluating predictive analytic models.

Compare Existing Approaches

If the current Decision Service has been implemented with multiple approaches, any assessment of decision performance should include an assessment of the alternative approaches currently deployed. The approaches should be compared both at the macro level—which results in the best overall results—and at the micro level—how the various approaches implemented work for different segments of the customers, partners, suppliers, or similar for which decisions are being made.

If the decision-making approaches have been implemented using an A/B testing mindset, then they should have been applied to the same number of transactions and the kinds of transactions should be similar between the two approaches. A simple comparison is therefore possible. If a champion-challenger approach has been used instead, the number of transactions and the kinds of transactions passed into each decision-making approach will have to be considered. For instance, a champion might handle 95% of all transactions, whereas a challenger only handles 5%. Although the number of decisions made with the challenger should be high enough that the distribution and average result can be compared directly, it is possible that the challenger will have too few transactions in certain categories. For instance, if there is a very low rate of fraudulent transactions, the number of fraudulent transactions handled by the challenger may be too small to be statistically significant.

As with the overall decision performance, the effectiveness of multiple approaches may not be consistently different. One approach may be more effective for a particular segment, whereas the other is more effective in general. Understanding the details of the relative performance is critical to designing an appropriate new approach.

Determine Whether Multiple New Approaches Are Required

When a decision is driven entirely by regulation or policy, there will generally only be a single decision-making approach to be implemented—all transactions will be handled using the same decision-making approach.

When a decision involves judgment or expertise represented as business rules, business rules derived from data, or predictive analytic models, then alternative approaches will be worth considering for the decision. Making decisions using multiple similar approaches allows different applications of judgment, different predictive analytic models, or different business rules based on those predictive analytic models to be compared in terms of their impact on actual transactions or customers.

> ## TAKE YOUR TIME ANALYZING DECISION-MAKING APPROACHES
>
> Alterative decision-making approaches in a Decision Service allow you to compare their effect on real transactions as they flow through your processes and systems. This is often the only way to really tell which approach works better or what the differences are in terms of outcomes. Design-time comparisons, as well as simulation, should also be considered for comparing decision-making approaches. An approach should not be considered for use in a deployed Decision Service unless analysis using historical data implies that it might work well.

A/B Testing

If the current decision-making approach has no particular significance and there is no reason to believe that one approach will be better than another going forward, an A/B testing approach can be applied. In this approach, several equally good approaches can be considered with the transactions distributed evenly between them. Marketing and other opportunity decisions often fall in this category, where there are few restrictions on how the decision can be made and no particular reason to believe that one approach is better than others.

The decision-making approaches implemented will generally all be variations on a theme. They may make one or more different assumptions about what will work or what a customer will find compelling. They might vary the messaging for an offer or the offer itself or apply different pricing and discount approaches. The resulting decisions are similar, but by running multiple approaches in parallel, you will be able to tell which is more effective in terms of its impact on business results.

Champion-Challenger Testing

When the current approach cannot lightly be changed or when there is a clear case that one approach will probably be best, A/B testing will be inappropriate. When the current approach has a long and successful history or when there are clear best practices for a decision-making approach, there will be strong pressure to use this approach for all decisions. After all, it is likely to be the best, so why wouldn't you want to treat all customers this way? If alternatives to such a strong decision-making approach seem worth considering, you should adopt a champion-challenger approach.

In this case most transactions are run through the established, or *champion*, approach. This ensures that, for instance, most customers continue to be treated using the established best practice. A small percentage of all transactions are not handled with this decision-making approach. Instead they are processed using one of potentially several *challenger* decision-making approaches. This approach creates data about the effectiveness of these alternatives while minimizing the number of decisions affected by the alternatives.

Sometimes the challengers have only small differences from the champion, and the purpose of conducting the experiment is to see whether a small change can make the current champion a little more effective. Sometimes, however, there is a sense that the current approach has been refined and tuned to a "local maximum." In these circumstances, any small change is going to be worse than the champion, so only more radical alternatives are worth considering. Sometimes a combination is appropriate—several incremental changes are tested as challengers, as well as one "out there" approach.

Because each challenger only handles a small number of transactions, this approach minimizes the risk of trying something radically different while still gathering the data necessary to see whether that radical approach is worth trying.

Using Optimization to Refine Decision-Making Approaches

Besides its use during decision-making, optimization technology can be used to analyze historical results to improve future decision-making. Two main scenarios exist—using optimization to prepare optimized actions for future decisions, and using optimization to improve the business rules in a decision.

After you have data about how a decision is being made, you can analyze how those decisions worked out in business terms. Using predictive analytic models, you can see what is likely to happen and what the behavior of customers is likely to be in response to specific actions. This information can be used in an optimization model to determine the optimal action to be taken in specific scenarios. For instance, an optimization model could determine that if a customer in a certain segment walks into a branch or contacts the call center, then the best action is to try and up-sell a specific credit product. The optimization model applied constraints such as the total amount of credit risk we are prepared to tolerate, managing the trade-offs of making this offer rather than another one, and considering the value of using our available pool of credit for this offer rather than for something else. These optimal actions then become input to the decision-making of a Decision Service.

TURNING OPTIMAL ACTIONS INTO BUSINESS RULES

Assigning optimal actions in this way works well for fixed sets of known customers. What it does not always do is suggest an optimal action for an unknown, new customer. One way to resolve this is to add the optimal action to the customer data set you have and then apply a decision tree-building algorithm to this data using a predictive analytic workbench. You can then mathematically build a decision tree that predicts who will get which action—a set of customer characteristics selects a branch in the tree that assigns a specific action to the customer.

Such a decision tree can then be deployed as discussed in Chapter 6, "Design and Implement Decision Services," for execution in a Decision Service. Now, instead of explicitly linking an action to a specific customer, the optimization links a set of customer characteristics to an action using the decision tree. This can be applied to existing customers or to new ones—even to anonymous web visitors. This approach also handles the situation where critical customer data changes between the execution of the optimization and the assignment of the action. For instance, if a customer deposits a bonus check and then calls the call center, her savings balance may be much higher than when the optimization was performed. The action assigned at the time may therefore be less accurate than the one that the decision tree assigns to people with higher balances.

In a Decision Service, policies and regulations often dictate eligibility at a fairly coarse-grained level. For example, a mortgage product might require a credit risk score of at least 800, whereas a gold loyalty card might require at least $3,000 of purchases in a year. Optimization could also be used to manage these thresholds at a more granular level. An optimization model could decide that the optimal score threshold for a particular customer segment, those existing customers with good history who live in the Northeast, should be 723, whereas it should be 745 for a similar customer living in the South. The optimization model considers all the constraints and trade-offs to maximize the value of your decision-making by setting appropriate thresholds and values in your business rules. This analysis can be repeated periodically using new data collected to keep the business rules in your decisions tuned.

In both scenarios, optimization technology works offline—outside the Decision Service—and allows you to do what-if analysis. You can define various risk/growth/profit scenarios, make an informed set of high-level decisions and then let the optimization work out the details. For instance, if you think you can take on another 2-3% in operational risk, you can use optimization to see what the impact of this would be. The optimization model will optimally allocate that additional risk, probably by allocating more credit to customers with lower scores, and will ensure you get the greatest return for your additional risk.

OPTIMIZATION IS NOT ALWAYS NEEDED

Optimization is not needed in every Decision Management System. In a significant minority of them, however, the use of optimization adds real value. Optimization can boost business performance by a few crucial percentage points, creating value that goes straight to the bottom line.

Develop New Decision-Making Approaches

After the appropriate response to a change in the environment or to current decision performance has been determined, it must be developed. New business rules, new predictive analytic models, and new optimization models must be designed and developed to implement the new decision-making approach(es) required.

Much of the design and development required is the same as the original steps in developing the decision-making approach for a new Decision Service, described in Chapter 6. Because there is an existing Decision Service, there are, however, a few differences. Business rules may be managed and changed using a business rules management environment specifically intended for ongoing changes. Predictive analytic models may need to be rebuilt from scratch, but they are more likely to need to be recalibrated and updated. If multiple decision-making approaches are in use already, these may form the basis for a new approach; if multiple approaches are going to be developed for deployment, these will need to be compared both to existing approaches and to each other before being finalized.

Build Rule Management Environment

By far the most common change that will be required as part of ongoing decision analysis will be a change to executable business rules. Business rules will have to be changed when regulations or policies change, as well as when the underlying data being used to make a decision changes. Any new decision-making approach for A/B or champion-challenger testing will involve new or at least modified business rules. Therefore, you should invest in creating a rule management environment designed for business experts.

The use of a BRMS makes the logic of a Decision Service much more accessible for non-technical business experts than traditional code-based approaches. The natural language-like approach of a typical BRMS, combined with a suitable executable object model and graphical business rules representations (such as decision trees and decision tables), make it possible for IT and business experts to collaborate effectively on the business rules. Whether the business experts code the rules themselves or rely on business analysts or IT professionals is less important than this ability to collaborate when defining the bulk of the business rules a Decision Service needs.

When a Decision Service has high volatility, however, and business rules changes must be made regularly, the situation is different. When the need to make a rapid business rules change is a common one, or when large numbers of business rules must be changed periodically, the value of having the business experts make the change themselves increases. The best way to support the decision analysis phase for these kinds of decision services will be to create a business-centric rules management environment.

A business-centric rules management environment has a number of characteristics:

- **Each business expert sees only the business rules for which he is responsible:** Multiple business experts might use the rule management environment, and they should be able to read those rules they have read permissions for and change those rules they have read/write permissions for. They should not have to navigate through a lot of other rules or rule repository structures to find them.

- **These business rules are presented in context:** Business users are making these changes in a business context—for instance, they are responding to new regulations or trying to improve the performance of the decision service. This context should be reflected in the rule management environment so that changing the rules feels like just part of running the business.

- **The business rules editing environment allows only those changes that make sense:** Some rules can only be changed in certain ways because of the underlying data—only certain values can be set as a consequence of a rule, for instance. Conditions and consequences that make no business or technical sense should not be allowed; if the overall decision service constrains the specific rules in question to behave within a range of allowed behavior, then this should also be enforced.

- **The business expert can rapidly see the impact of her proposed changes:** The rule management environment should be linked to the impact analysis tools and techniques described later.

- **No unnecessary technical information is presented**

With an environment like this, the business experts can take more direct control over the business rules changes that are required. This will reduce the time to make the changes and improve their accuracy by eliminating the impedance of a business/IT hand-off.

MANAGEMENT ENVIRONMENTS FOR THE REST OF THE SYSTEM

In theory, a similar argument could be made for building a business user-focused environment that allows management of predictive analytic and optimization models. In practice this has not yet become a mainstream proposition. Although both predictive analytic and optimization vendors are making it easier for less technical people to build models, the idea of a distinct management environment for ongoing evolution and maintenance has not gained much traction.

Updating Predictive Analytic Models as New Data Becomes Available

There are three main techniques used to keep a predictive analytic model that is deployed in a Decision Service up-to-date—self-learning, model refreshing, and champion-challenger.

Self-Learning

A self-learning predictive analytic model is automatically built and updated as new data is collected. This approach is good for situations where there are no analytic skills within an organization, when the situation changes rapidly (making manual assessment of model effectiveness impractical), and when models only need to be "good enough"—such as when delivering banner advertisements on a website. When model accuracy is critically important or when models must be explicable, such as in regulated industries like consumer credit, self-learning models are less appropriate. Self-learning approaches can also be useful for new situations where no historical data has yet been gathered. The initial recommendations made based on self-learning approaches are, by the very nature of this approach, somewhat random and therefore may not be appropriate. They will, however, rapidly improve as the model learns.

Model Refresh

When a predictive analytic model has been deployed into a decision service, it is based on the data available when it was developed. Over time the available data changes, and these changes need to be reflected in a refreshed model. Such a refresh takes the new data and uses it to tune or update the model to make more accurate predictions given the changing circumstances. This refresh should occur at regular intervals as new data is collected.

Predictive analytic models can be refreshed manually by the modeling team that originally created them. Such a refresh is quicker than the original construction but still requires some manual effort. Alternatively, an automatic model refresh process can be established. The effect is similar to self-learning models, although the deployed model was initially created by an analyst and usually starts from a position of strong performance. As new data is collected, the model is automatically rebuilt using this new data and then automatically deployed. The new model either offers improved accuracy or corrects for declining accuracy in the face of changing circumstances. This technique usually works best when the predictive model is an ensemble of multiple predictive analytic models where the final output being delivered by using voting techniques across all the models.

ALWAYS HAVE A PLAN TO REFRESH PREDICTIVE ANALYTIC MODELS

One of the worst mistakes an organization can make when adopting predictive analytic models is to have no process or plan for refreshing the models it is using. All models degrade over time, and some manual or automatic process is essential for any model that will remain in production beyond a single point in time.

Champion-Challenger

As noted previously, multiple decision-making approaches can be compared using a champion-challenger approach. When new data becomes available, it can often point to a potentially different predictive analytic model that might work more effectively. Using a challenger approach to deploy the new predictive analytic model to see whether it does, in fact, work better, is a very effective tool for evaluating new models in these circumstances. Many challenger strategies are different only because they include a new predictive analytic model.

Updating the predictive analytic models can be an automatic or manual process, depending upon the business requirements. This is the most complex way to update predictive analytic models but can deliver the best accuracy, as it allows a number of different types of modeling methods to be used as challengers.

Design New Approach

There are a number of possible ways to design new or changed decision-making approaches. If multiple approaches are already in use, it is possible that one of these approaches, or some combination of several, is the right approach to use going forward. Alternatively, a completely new approach may be called for, and this might involve also creating new challengers.

- **Promote challenger:** If you have been running multiple challenger approaches, it is possible that one of the challenger approaches will clearly outperform both the champion and all the other challengers. If you have such a challenger, and you are sure it outperforms in every segment, this can be "promoted" to become your new champion approach. Simply replace the existing champion's rule sets and predictive analytic models with the challenger's.

- **Select from A/B approaches:** If you have been doing A/B testing, it is similarly possible that one of the approaches will be clearly more effective than its peers. In general with A/B testing, you update the decision-making approach to use the most effective approach for all transactions for a period of time—the A/B test period will come to an end and a new standard approach will be implemented.

- **Synthesize a new approach:** Often you will find that a challenger will outperform the champion in some segments but not others, or that several challengers outperform the champion in different ways. You may find that several approaches in the A/B test have potential. In these circumstances you will synthesize a new approach by combining the effective elements of the various approaches into a new champion or standard approach.

- **Design a wholly new approach:** If your results have been poor, or if a major change to your environment has occurred, you may need to define a wholly new approach. In this situation, it will be important to conduct the maximum amount of design time analysis and simulation, as you will have little or no real effectiveness data on which to base your design.

■ **Build new challengers:** One last step is to create new challenger strategies. Regardless of whether the current champion outperformed your challengers or whether you had a successful challenger or challenger(s), you will likely retire the unsuccessful challengers. To continue experimenting, you will need to design new challengers with different characteristics.

EXPERIMENTAL DESIGN

Experimentation has many roles in Decision Management Systems. It can evaluate different approaches or fill in gaps in the data available for building predictive analytic models. It can be systematic, testing a particular hypothesis, or more random, taking actions on a random set of transactions that wouldn't normally get that action to gather new data, for instance. Indeed, there is a whole science of experimental design that is largely beyond the scope of this book. A summary of experimental design is included in Chapter 9, "Process Enablers."

Compare Alternatives

Before putting A/B or champion-challenger approaches into production, it is important that the approaches are compared and analyzed as extensively as possible. Static comparison of the decision-making approaches—comparing rule sets and predictive analytic models—is the first step to ensure you understand their differences. Historical or sample data (or both) should also be used to test the two approaches and compare their effectiveness. Only if the static comparison and simulation make it seem likely that the alternative approaches will be more effective should you deploy them into a running Decision Service as decision-making alternatives. This comparison should be conducted between new decision-making approaches being considered as well as between new and existing approaches.

One of the most effective techniques for comparing two decision-making approaches is swapset analysis. In swapset analysis, the decisions made for a set of transactions are compared for a pair of decision-making approaches. Each transaction or customer is processed using one of the decision-making approaches, and the outcome recorded. Each is then processed using the second decision-making approach. Each transaction in the test set now has two results that can be compared—the result of running that transaction through the first decision-making approach and the result of running it through the second decision-making approach. A swapset analysis is a report with two axes, the vertical showing the possible outcomes from the first decision-making approach, and the horizontal from the second. Each cell of this report contains a number—the number of transactions that had the outcome from the first approach corresponding to the cell's horizontal position, and the outcome from the second approach corresponding to the cell's vertical position.

In the example shown in Table 7-1, two different fraud detection approaches are being compared. Of the 10,000 test transactions, we can see that the first approach decided that 5,200 had the default response, 4,550 were fast tracked and 250 were referred for fraud investigation. When compared with the second approach, we can see that 230 of those that previously got the default response were referred for fraud in the second approach, whereas 45 of those referred for fraud under the first approach were not so referred with the second approach. Overall, the second approach showed an increased in fraud referrals from 250 to 435.

Table 7-1   A swapset analysis report

		Total	Approach 2		
			Standard	Fast Track	Fraud
Approach 1	Standard	5,200	4,970		230
	Fast Track	4,550		4,550	
	Fraud	250	45		205
	Total	10,000	5,015	4,550	435

This might be what was expected or it might not, and the swapset analysis gives both an easy-to-use overview of the difference between the two approaches and the ability to drill down into those transactions referred for fraud in the first approach, but not the second.

In addition, you should use the performance reporting tools developed to assess the effectiveness of approaches both at an overall level and in terms of specific subsets of transactions or customer segments.

Confirm the Impact Is as Expected

Before deploying any new decision-making approach, it is important to be sure that it will behave as expected. Although this may not be 100% possible—the responses of customers to new decision-making approaches cannot be completely modeled in advance, for instance—the most rigorous approach possible should be applied. The impact of a new decision-making approach should always be considered in terms of its *business* impact. The IT department will need to do testing to ensure stability, performance, connectivity, and so on. This is no different than it would be for any other change to a production application. Without an ability to do business impact analysis, however, the full value of decision analysis cannot be delivered.

This impact analysis can and should be performed at various stages throughout the creation of new decision-making approaches. Wherever possible, it should be led by the business users with support from the IT and analytics teams as necessary—it is business impact that must be assessed, after all. The analysis should:

- Verify that the authors of the new decision-making approach have entered the business rules and models accurately and that the results are as expected, or at least well understood.

- Make an assessment on the overall impact the new decision-making approach will have after it is deployed into business operations.

Four main approaches can be used to assess the business impact—testing, simulation, what-if analysis, and advanced simulation. In some cases, the decision-making approach can be assessed using tools within the design environment, but sometimes it must be available as a Decision Service outside the production environment.

Testing

In simple cases (for example, where a decision is based on a series of straightforward rules), it may be possible to validate that the decision-making approach will perform as expected simply by testing individual records (or a sample of individual records), and verifying that the Decision Service returns the expected answer (such as no gold customers get automatically referred for fraud investigation). This could involve scoring a sample of real (historical) data against the Decision Service, or it can sometimes be helpful to configure a data set that is specially generated to give a cross section of cases with known data permutations—true "test cases." This is especially useful when you want to test that certain rare, but important, situations will be correctly handled.

Simulation

Although useful for verification, individual record tests don't give any feel for what will happen over a period of time, or for a specific group of cases as a whole. For this, an aggregated rather than an individual-level analysis is required, usually referred to as simulation. For example, in Figure 7-1, it has become apparent that the Decision Service, if deployed, would result in the rules-based approach generating far more referrals than the model-based one.

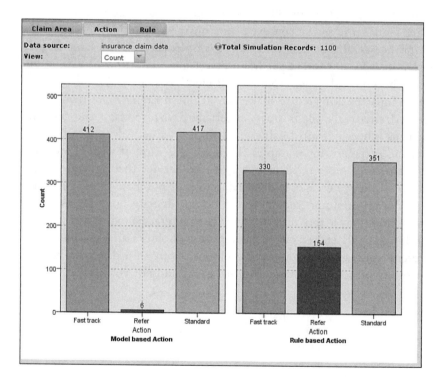

Figure 7-1   A simulation report

Although simulations can identify these kinds of unexpected outcomes, they don't necessarily identify whether the issue lies with user error (incorrect application of the business rules or models), or whether the result is actually an accurate representation of the Decision Service, and that the best scenario (that is, the most profitable) is really to refer this many claims. Testing may well help with the former situation, but the latter situation can be more difficult to deal with, perhaps requiring a more strategic decision to be made. Of course, there may be business reasons to make fewer referrals, and the Decision Service may need to be adjusted to force this to happen.

What-if Analysis

What-if analysis is really an extension of simulation, providing the same aggregate level information. In addition, it allows the user to compare the outcomes of the Decision Service when certain parameters are adjusted. The goal might be to refine the Decision Service so that it makes more sense in the context of the business situation, maybe at the cost of the overall business value. For example, the optimal solution may be to refer 10% of cases to the fraud investigation unit for investigation, but if the unit only has resources sufficient to assess 5%, the Decision Service must be adjusted to make sure it doesn't refer more than 5% of cases. Alternatively, the business expert may wish to assess and compare scenarios where certain business values are valued (available budget, costs and revenues, for example). Through this kind of what-if analysis, the user may be able to identify a Decision Service that generates more revenue without necessarily decreasing overall purchase rates, for example. Another common reason would be to identify how the Decision Service functions across different points of interaction such as the Web, mobile, and call center channels. Figure 7-2 shows an example where different approaches to processing claims result in a different balance between fraud referrals, standard processing, and fast tracking.

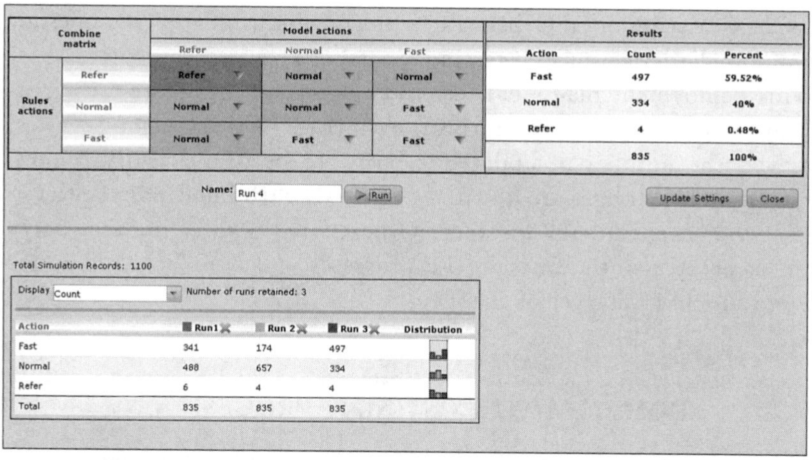

Figure 7-2 A what-if analysis report

Advanced Simulation

The importance of good sample data to simulate on cannot be under-estimated. Unfortunately, is it not always easy to obtain. Sometimes there will be no historical data available—perhaps this is a new Decision Service that hasn't been implemented before. In other cases, the situation being simulated could be so variable that no single sample of data will be sufficient. This is where advanced techniques such as Monte Carlo simulation can become useful.

These techniques can be used to generate the analysis based on less well-defined distributions of values in place of known data points that the user specifies based on his knowledge of the situation. As with a normal simulation analysis, the results will give an indication of the behavior of the Decision Service after it is deployed, but in addition, there will be some indication of how reliable the simulation result is.

Deploy the Change

After the new decision-making approaches have been developed and evaluated to ensure that the business outcome is as expected, they must be deployed. For most changes, this involves using the same approaches used originally to define the Decision Service. New executable business rules and new predictive analytic or optimization models are deployed to replace existing ones. Others are deployed alongside existing ones for champion-challenger or A/B testing.

This deployment may seem just like any other IT update for a production system. At some level, this is even true. With Decision Services, however, the number of updates is going to be dramatically higher. Some Decision Services are updated every day, with hundreds of pricing rules being changed, for instance. Others have regular updates every week or every month. Existing IT processes and approaches may not scale to support this pace of change.

COMPLEMENT EXISTING IT PROCESSES

It is generally not possible or desirable to change the IT processes concerned. Instead, develop a new set of processes specifically for deploying and managing changes to Decision Services. A business rule development lifecycle that coordinates with the existing software development lifecycle but is optimized for business rules will work better than force-fitting business rules into the existing approach. For instance, a change requiring only new business rules to be deployed should be simple and involve little IT coordination, whereas a change that involves both rules and new data requirements will require coordinated changes. Chapter 9 has a section on the typical changes to a software development lifecycle introduced by Decision Management Systems.

III

Enablers for Decision Management Systems

Part II walked through the key steps in building Decision Management Systems. It showed how to discover and model the decisions that should be implemented in Decision Management Systems. It walked through the design and implementation of Decision Services, the core of Decision Management Systems. And it discussed the importance of monitoring and systematically improving decisions over time and how to go about that.

As these chapters came together, it was apparent that there were some critical enablers for success in building Decision Management Systems. Rather than bulk up these chapters and make them less readable, these enablers have been grouped into the three following chapters of Part III:

- People Enablers
- Process Enablers
- Technology Enablers

These enablers can be thought of as tips and asides that were too long to be embedded as notes within the main body. Each enabler stands largely alone, and there is no particular reason they appear in the order they do within the chapters. You can dip in and out of these chapters as you like when and if the enablers they describe seem helpful in your journey to Decision Management Systems.

8

People Enablers

Decision Management Systems involve a lot of technology, but like all technologies they require people to use them. In particular, they require business people, IT people, and analytic people to work together to create what is sometimes called the "three-legged stool" of analytics. These three groups can and should be supported with a Decision Management Center of Excellence, a group of people committed to the success of Decision Management initiatives. Finally, the impact of Decision Management Systems on organizations and their customers is often great, creating a need for effective organizational change management.

The Three-Legged Stool

All information systems require effective collaboration between business people and IT departments to be successful. Decision Management Systems require collaboration between business people, IT departments, *and* analytic teams. Ensuring these three groups work together effectively creates the "three-legged stool" that provides stability for Decision Management Systems. A three-legged stool cannot be stable with only one or two legs and Decision Management Systems cannot be driven entirely by the business, by IT, or by analytic teams.

Decision Management Systems demand this kind of collaboration for several reasons:

- The decisions being handled by Decision Management Systems are *business* decisions. Even though each decision is small, their business impact is great because there are so many of them. Because they are business decisions, the definition of what makes a good decision or a bad decision is driven by the business. The actions that can be taken, the logic that should be followed, the policies, and regulations are all specified by and understood by the business.

- Decision Management Systems handle high-volume, low-latency decisions—decisions that must be taken often and taken quickly. This means automation; it means the decision-making must be deployed into a production or transactional environment. To make this work, IT must be part of the solution.

- Some Decision Management Systems implement decisions that are entirely constrained by policy and regulation. Many involve the use of analytics to predict risk, fraud, or opportunity. Some use optimization to manage trade-offs. Even when embedded predictive analytics or optimization are not required, the decisions made should be analyzed analytically, made by the numbers wherever possible, and continuously improved. This means analytics expertise is also going to be required.

These three groups don't have much of a history of collaborating, and many issues divide them in most organizations:

- IT departments and business users are often on different pages, with IT struggling to support changing business needs while business people get frustrated at their systems.

- Analytics people often focus on the accuracy of their model, not the business outcome. They produce models that they consider to be "best" because they have the best statistical measures—not because they produce the most profitable result.

- Analytics teams often build models that include data not available in the production environments that will use them, resulting in models that take six months or more to implement or that are simply too complex for

IT to use. In addition, IT often does not capture the data that analytic teams require to validate and improve their models.

■ IT departments design systems and specify enhancements without the kind of analytics skills that would let them see how analytics could improve the systems they are working on.

A lack of mutual understanding and an absence of collaboration may be typical in organizations but is unacceptable when building Decision Management Systems. To ensure a strong stable stool for a Decision Management System, you must begin a three-way conversation and start building collaboration skills. A focus on decision discovery and business results will improve alignment, but organizational issues must be recognized and addressed no matter what.

Start a Three-Way Conversation

Getting these three groups into a conversation and getting them thinking about collaborating is essential. The team has to participate in identifying the decisions that matter to their business and defining good and bad decisions. The IT team must be able to explain how the production systems that use those decisions work and be willing to discuss how they could bring the business people inside to define and manage the logic of these decisions. Analytic teams need to see the business need, talk to IT about the data available, and see what kinds of models they can build that will result in better business outcomes while still being deployable. If there are ways existing systems could be improved to get better analytic results (and so deliver better business results), then this too needs to be brought up. A simple awareness that these things are necessary, and that the three groups must work together, is the first step.

Build Collaboration Skills

The most important element of building collaboration skills for these groups is simply to expose them to each other and to create opportunities for them to talk and work together. Getting the whole team together for meetings and ensuring that the project's process or methodology reinforces this point of view is the foundation for collaboration.

Cross-training can be effective, too. This might take the form of overviews of the business, information technology, or analytic approaches. These overviews help the experts in one group get a basic understanding of the critical terms, technologies, and approaches of the other two groups. In general, everyone needs to understand the overall strategy—why this Decision Management System being built—as well as the basics of the approach and the supporting technology.

When new technology is introduced, such as a Business Rules Management System or Predictive Analytic Workbench, it may be possible to go further. Consider having everyone attend the first few days of such training to get an overview and some time using the software before having the experts drill into the details. Having business, IT, and analytic teams all attend training on how to develop business rules with a BRMS reinforces the mentality of a shared solution. In this case, the IT department will need some time to cover more technical aspects but it is very effective to have everyone sit in initially. Similarly, a graphical Predictive Analytic Workbench is remarkably approachable for business and IT users even if they are not going to be doing production-quality model development and refinement.

Finally, consider using brown-bag lunches or "lunch and learn" sessions to let experts in one group share their expertise with other groups. This builds a sense of the three groups as a team, spreads critical know-how among team members, and helps those presenting get a sense of the level of detail that is appropriate when dealing with others outside their own area of expertise.

Decision Discovery Is Critical

Experience with many Decision Management System projects is that decision discovery is the crucial phase for getting the three teams to work together. It is easy to think that this can be deferred until Decision Services are being built. In fact, earlier collaboration is better for several reasons:

- Decision discovery sets the context for all subsequent projects and activities. If the three groups begin collaborating early, this collaboration will carry forward into later stages. If decision discovery is carried out entirely by one group, the others will feel that the model created is being imposed and does not address their concerns. Begin as you mean to go on.

- Having the business and IT teams work together on the top levels of the decision hierarchy is critical, as this maps the Decision Management Systems into the business processes and existing systems that both organizations are familiar with. Building a shared sense of where the decisions fit also builds long-term cooperation.

- Analytics teams have a lot of experience thinking about how to use predictive analytic models to make decisions. Their engagement in the decision decomposition process will improve the model created and help them see the context for the modeling they will do later. Their ability to also say "we could probably predict X and Y, would that help?" is also very helpful at this stage, as it will guide the business and IT teams towards more analytic decision-making. They will also know what data will need to be available to build each predictive analytic model they suggest.

- Ensuring that the know-how identified in the model maps to the kinds of policies, regulations, expertise, and analytic insight available and that the information sources map to known or knowable data sources will keep the whole model grounded. This requires all three groups to be active participants.

Align Around Business Results

One of the most effective ways to get disparate groups to collaborate is to align their personal and organizational objectives. If an analytic modeler, for instance, is motivated to produce the most precise model possible, that will fuel a certain kind of behavior. If, instead, he is motivated to produce the model that has the most business impact as measured after the model is in production, he will behave differently. The new motivation will help ensure he focuses on making the model as easy as possible to deploy, whether or not the production environment has the data the model needs, and whether or not the model is actionable in a way that makes sense for the business.

As far as possible, ensure that everyone on the team is rewarded and measured based on the impact the Decision Management System has on business results as measured in production. Not the estimated results or intended results, but the actual results. Not IT-specific or model-specific measures, but business measures.

Resolve Organizational Issues

One of the ways you can strengthen the three-legged stool is by resolving organizational and reporting issues that push the groups apart. Start by identifying the reporting structure for all those involved in the project and ensuring that their managers understand the purpose and benefit of the Decision Management System. This can be used to identify the executive sponsorship that matters to each reporting structure. If the executive sponsor is someone that all three management structures care about, organizational issues will be suppressed in favor of overall success.

The locations of teams can also be an issue, with the three groups operating out of their own enclaves. Co-locating the team and providing a war room in which business, IT, and analytics people all work at least some of the time can make a big difference. This fosters a sense of togetherness and teamwork, while also making it easier to get answers to trade-off questions and what-if scenarios.

Finally, the workload of the three groups must be considered and managed by the sponsors of the project. It does no good to focus the analytics team on deployed results if they are immediately assigned to a new project as soon as their model is finished. Similarly, making sure the business team can make the business rule changes it wants may require some reassignment of workloads and responsibilities. It is essential to understand who assigns work to the team members involved and how issues can be resolved when they occur.

A Decision Management Center of Excellence

The concept of a Center of Excellence, or CoE, is not specific to Decision Management. Organizations can and should have a CoE for any strategic technology they are leveraging across the enterprise, whether it is BPM, analytics, business rule management, SOA, or Master Data Management. Whether you call them Centers of Excellence, Centers of Expertise, Competency Centers, or Communities of Practice, CoEs are a way to gather, harvest, formalize, and deploy best practices. They can help you maximize the likelihood of successful adoption of a new approach or technology while minimizing the costs involved in learning anything new.

Building Decision Management Systems uses a broad range of techniques, and the systems themselves often need to cut across organization silos to be effective. A central focal point to discuss and learn from Decision Management initiatives is particularly important as a result. Decision Management is a multi-domain field that requires the effective coordination of several historically distinct areas of expertise.

One kind of Decision Management CoE will not fit all companies and its needs. The shape of a CoE will also vary over time as Decision Management adoption progresses. An initial focus may be on providing early adopters with help getting their skills up to speed to ensure the rapid success of the first Decision Management Systems. A later goal may be on auditing numerous projects to ensure consistency and maximize the reuse of assets and best practices—not something worth pursuing when you only have two or three projects. Organizations should therefore establish a short and longer-term target profile for a Decision Management CoE.

There are many potential dimensions of a CoE that are worth considering. For each of the dimensions defined in Table 8-1, you should decide where, on a 1 to 5 scale, you want to start (your short-term objective) and where you want to be in the next 12 to 18 months (your longer term objective). This kind of profiling or assessment exercise produces a chart similar to Figure 8-1. It's a good idea if several stakeholders provide their own appreciation of each attribute to build a consensus. Indeed, such a profile basically defines the shape of the targeted CoE and greatly contributes to the refinement of the definition of its scope and mission statement.

Table 8-1 CoE Profile Attributes

Category	Dimension	Statement	Objectives				
			1	2	3	4	5
Business intent	Strategic vs. Tactical	The goal of the CoE is to:	Be strategic—leading & driving business adoption, including identifying new Decision Management Systems	Focus on managing a portfolio of business opportunities	Lead on both the business fit and IT implementation	Be very technical while paying attention to business relevance	Be purely tactical around product expertise
Role	Advise vs. Do	The CoE's most *prominent role* is to:	Advise		Train		Do
Role	Audit vs. Implement	The CoE's most *prominent role* is to:	Audit	Control	Oversee	Mentor	Implement
Role	Empower-ment	How much authority will the CoE have to set directions and apply implementation best practices?	Low		Medium		High

Table 8-1 CoE Profile Attributes

Category	Dimension	Statement	Objectives				
			1	2	3	4	5
Role	Best practice development	The CoE's most *prominent role* is to:	Identify best practices		Formalize and harvest the best practices of others		Create best practices from direct implementation involvement
Role	Best practice deployment	Will the CoE play a significant role in fostering reuse and application of best practices?	No		To some extent		Definitely
Role	Change agent	How much of a role will the CoE play in championing the new discipline and driving organizational change?	None	Some	Medium	Important	Key

continues

Table 8-1 CoE Profile Attributes

Category	Dimension	Statement	Objectives				
			1	2	3	4	5
Context	Experience	How many implementations have been completed and deployed?	0	1 to 2	3	4 to 5	More than 5
Context	IT adoption momentum	Is the *IT* organization welcoming the new technology and approaches?	No	With significant resistance or apprehension	Somewhat	Strongly	Very strongly
Context	Business adoption momentum	Are the *Lines Of Business* welcoming the new technology and approaches?	No (no LOB support)	With significant resistance or apprehension	Somewhat (varies by LOB)	Strongly (most LOBs are supportive)	Very strongly (all LOBs are supportive)

Table 8-1 CoE Profile Attributes

Category	Dimension	Statement	Objectives				
			1	2	3	4	5
Context	Analytic adoption momentum	Is the *Analytic* organization welcoming the new technology and approaches?	No	With significant resistance or apprehension	Somewhat	Strongly	Very strongly
Scope	Scale	The CoE will lead adoption across:	1 program	1 LOB	2 or more LOB	A division or a small enterprise	A large enterprise
Staffing	External vs. internal	The CoE will be staffed mostly:	Externally		Equally mixed		Internally
Staffing	Size	The CoE is expected to be:	Small (0.5-1 FTE)		Medium (4-6 FTE)		Large (10+ FTE)
Staffing	Formality	The CoE staffing will be:	Informal—a community of practice		Consultative and ad-hoc		Formal and well structured
Staffing	Funding	CoE funding will be:	Zero—a free-time activity		Partial cost recovery		Explicit and direct

continues

Table 8-1 CoE Profile Attributes

Category	Dimension	Statement	Objectives				
			1	2	3	4	5
Staffing	Skill depth	CoE resources will be:	Generalist and multi-purpose to maximize scalability & flexibility		Mix		Specialist with advanced product skills for delivery excellence
Orientation	Business vs. Technical focus	The CoE's orientation will be:	Business		Both		Technical
Orientation	Governance	The CoE be in charge of:	Business governance & strategy alignment		Both		Technical governance & technology alignment
Orientation	Business performance	Will the CoE be in charge of measuring business performance contributed by the technology?	No		To some extent		Yes

Table 8-1 CoE Profile Attributes

Category	Dimension	Statement	Objectives				
			1	2	3	4	5
Focus	Business modeling vs. architecture	The CoE will be in charge of:	Business architecture & modeling		Both		IT & SOA architecture
Focus	Discipline focus	The CoE's focus will be on:	A specific technology (such as BRMS)		Multiple products (such as BRMS and optimization)		Any Decision Management technology
Lifecycle	Implementation phase	The CoE's involvement will be through	Assess-ment	Launch	Implementation	Deployment	Evolution
Lifecycle	Methodology leadership	How much latitude will the CoE have to adapt existing methodologies?	None, will have to stick to company standard		Some		Significant—up to creating a custom process

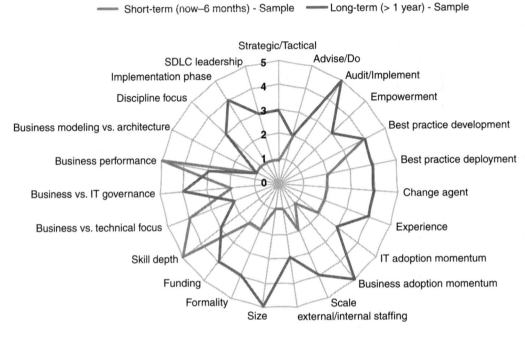

Figure 8-1 Short-and long-term CoE shapes

A few tips and best practices about the profiling assessment:

- Just as there is not a single CoE shape fitting all organizational needs, there isn't a perfect or optimal profile or shape, either. Profiles will vary depending on organization context, culture, and level of adoption maturity.

- There is no right or wrong objective value for each dimension; 5 is not necessarily better than 1 or 3.

- Having too many dimensions valued at 3 (half way) will often require more implementation work, as this corresponds to a dual objective. At least initially it is better to agree on which side of the scale you'd rather focus as an organization. The longer-term profile can be used to show areas of development and improvement.

RETURN ON INVESTMENT

The CoE is often the group responsible for leading and managing the return on investment, or ROI, for a Decision Management Systems project. Making sure the data is collected about the current state, ensuring that this data is not being "spun" to make people look good, tracking improvements due to the new system, and making sure that all this is honestly reported—at least internally—is an essential part of a CoE. Ensuring that an ROI evaluation is built into project guidelines and that CoE staff assigned to projects work on collecting this data will go a long way toward ensuring that ROI can be shown from these systems.

A Decision Management CoE needs to establish an organization, adequate staffing, processes, and missions corresponding to the three main differentiating characteristics of Decision Management Systems:

- More agile

    The best way to achieve business agility is to fully adopt the agile manifesto (http://agilemanifesto.org/) and an agile software development lifecycle. Many people use the agile paradigm as an excuse for looser project management and less documentation. By not applying the entire agile philosophy, they are missing the point and putting successful implementation at risk. Make sure that the CoE team is properly trained and experienced with the agile process. The CoE can set an example and enable others on this approach.

    The CoE team will need to have strong negotiation and influencing skills to facilitate organizational change and help project teams and stakeholders prioritize the implementation features that matter most, while taking into account the technical and operational capability of the organization.

- More adaptive

    One of the key roles for the CoE is to ensure that the Decision Management Systems being built are prepared for change. The CoE must remain up to date with technological advances as well as trends on the business side. This means that the CoE needs some members with strong business acumen, not only about the company's business but also about the overall industry and competitive environment. These members will help the CoE think several steps ahead of competitors and maximize the value delivered by the adaptability of Decision Management Systems.

The CoE should also formalize and streamline the feedback loop for Decision Management Systems. In particular, the team should ensure that end user suggestions about Decision Management Systems are taken into consideration and implemented in a timely fashion. Some members of the CoE will need to be "on the ground" and well connected with the user community to make this work.

■ More analytic

The CoE will need strong knowledge of and experience with analytic technology, tools, and techniques. The CoE will play a key role in ensuring that Decision Management Systems leverage the huge amount of data that typically resides in isolated systems or is duplicated across systems. This will require good data management skills and an organization-wide view of available data.

The CoE will also need to play a role across the whole observe-orient-decide-act loop (see Chapter 9, "Process Enablers"), helping the organization establish linkage between concepts that might otherwise not be connected because of organizational silos.

Decision Management Systems combine multiple techniques and technologies. They require collaboration between the lines of business, analytic teams, and IT. As a result, it is critical to select experienced members when establishing a CoE. Technical, business, and leadership skills will need to come from several members, as it is challenging if not impossible for one person to cover and master all these facets.

Organizational Change

It is generally a mistake to treat the development and implementation of a Decision Management System as a purely technical project. Decision Management Systems can cause significant organizational dislocation in a number of different areas:

■ Knowledge workers may move from transactional work (reviewing individual policies, for instance) to a role in which they manage policy and exceptions.

■ Supervisors may feel they are losing power because their approval is no longer required (because the system manages approvals).

- Front-line staff may feel more responsible without the comfort of referring things "up the line."
- Call center and branch staff may feel their options are being constrained by the system, and this may be true.
- Customers too may notice changes due to a Decision Management System, such as personalized pricing.
- Staff and customers may not initially trust the system's decisions.
- IT may not believe that the Decision Management System will remain stable and functional while its behavior is being modified by business users.

Any change from the implementation of Decision Management System must be managed to ensure that the adoption of the system proceeds smoothly. This requires an understanding of what makes change difficult, time to manage the change, a clear case for the change, and strong sponsorship.

What Makes Change Difficult

Any organizational change, such as the change introduced by a Decision Management System, can be difficult for people to accept. A change is hard to cope with if it seems to involve an increase in danger or risk ("I have to take more responsibility now because I can't refer things to someone else"), a decrease in opportunity ("these retention offers aren't going to work as well as the ones I used to use; there goes my bonus") or just more ambiguity ("What is the system going to do, anyway?"). Change represents a loss of control for those involved. Whether they liked the old approach or not, they felt in control because they understood what was happening. People don't handle a loss of control without an emotional shock, and that makes change hard.

One common mistake made is to assume that only a negatively perceived change will be resisted. In fact, positively perceived changes are resisted, too. Even if a new Decision Management System is widely regarded as a good idea, you will get resistance. Resistance is normal for both positively and negatively perceived change, and both kinds of change must be managed.

When a change is positively perceived, there is a common set of responses from those affected. Those involved will begin in a honeymoon period of uninformed optimism—they are not sure what the change is going to involve but it sounds great! As more details become clear, most will drop into what is known as "informed pessimism." Now they can see all the problems and difficulties—the extra training, the changes in procedures, the risk to their performance bonus, and more. Over time they will put these issues in perspective and their generally positive point of view will re-emerge as informed optimism—the platform for successful change.

A negatively perceived change has a lot more ups and downs. Many organizational change experts use the Kubler-Ross grief cycle as a metaphor. This cycle was an early attempt to categorize how people respond to traumatic events in their lives. It may not seem reasonable to you to consider changing the behavior of the call center application a traumatic event, but it may seem that way to those who spend all day, every day using the system. This cycle begins with immobilization and then *denial*—surely they won't make us use this stupid system? *Anger* at the change and an attempt to bargain with it commonly follow—we don't HAVE to use the offers it recommends, do we? *Depression* is common when *bargaining* fails to change anything, and then gradually people dig themselves out of this second trough and move towards *acceptance*.

You need to manage change even when it is perceived positively. It's definitely worth identifying which groups will have a positive and which a negative view of the change, as they will take a different path to acceptance.

Take Time to Manage Change

One of the things that is common to both positive and negative cycles is that they take time. Allowing time for organizational change—recognizing that it will take time to adopt a new Decision Management System—is sometimes hard to accept. There will be those who think it can just be mandated, and then everyone will be using it and we can move on. Having a coherent plan for managing the change over time will increase the odds that the benefits of the system will be achieved.

Some changes take longer to manage than others. Those changes that are against the current culture will take longer and be harder to make successful. An organization that stresses empowering its people will get less pushback from supervisors when automated approvals are built into the call center environment. An organization that has always valued customer retention no matter what will struggle with a system that tries to manage the cost of a retention offer against the long-term value of that customer. This alignment of change must be understood at both the individual and corporate level. A change may be well aligned with the overall organization's perspective but very counter to how specific groups or individuals may have worked in the past.

Making a Case for Change

As well as allowing time for the change to take root, it is essential that you create a driver for change. If the pain of change is exceeded by the pain of not changing, people will move more rapidly and more enthusiastically to the new state. All too often the pain of the current state is felt by the organization while the pain of the change is felt by individuals. To help individuals make the change, you need to expose them to the pain of not changing. This means bringing to their attention the unresolved issues, missed opportunities, or risks involved in the current approach. It means aligning goals and bonuses so that using the new system will be more profitable and less painful than sticking with the old approach. No change happens without a strong case being made at the organization level *and* at the individual level.

The Need for Sponsorship

Like any project, change management requires sponsorship. This is sometimes problematic for change management as the very people who would make good executive sponsors fall into the "if I tell them to change, that should be enough" school. Most change projects need sponsors to initiate the change and to sustain it. The initiating sponsor helps the organization see the value of the change and the Decision Management System that is going to cause the change. As the system is developed and the problem becomes one of getting individuals to use it, this sponsorship needs to be transformed into a sustaining one. This means developing a network of additional sponsors who can help make the change happen throughout the affected organizations.

MANAGING EXTERNAL CHANGE

Some Decision Management Systems affect customers or external partners extensively and this can cause them to have to go through a change cycle. This is harder to manage for organizations, as customers and partners are not employees. For partners, much of the preceeding advice does apply, although it may be harder to implement, as other organizations will need to be convinced. For customers, there are often limited ways to help them, but making sure the positive features of the change are promoted and that time is allowed for the customer base to change will both help.

9

Process Enablers

As with any new initiative, it is often helpful to develop new processes to support a focus on Decision Management Systems. A process for maintaining your decision inventory over time and a revised software development lifecycle are two such key processes. An understanding of the various patterns for adopting Decision Services can help in planning broader adoption. Developing a culture of experimentation and of fact-based decision-making can ease the acceptance of Decision Management Systems and help bring analytics to bear on them more broadly. Finally, an understanding of the Observe-Orient-Decide-Act- or OODA-loop can be informative.

Managing a Decision Inventory

One of the most important assets for building Decision Management Systems is an up-to-date, accurate, and managed decision inventory. You need an understanding of the decisions in your business, especially the repeatable decisions. A model of decisions and their dependencies, as well as their relationship with your performance management and business process environments, gives you a solid foundation for developing Decision Management Systems. Building out and managing such an inventory should be done business process-by-business process. Good decision inventories are built collaboratively by business, IT, and analytic groups. A decision inventory should be refactored as new information is gathered and kept synchronized with performance management changes. To maximize its value, it should also be linked to the implementation artifacts you develop as you build Decision Management Systems.

Business Process by Business Process

Some organizations like to create broad across-the-board initiatives to standardize any good idea. They try to ensure a single enterprise information model, create an organization-wide process repository, or manage a single service inventory. There is nothing inherently wrong with this mindset unless the objective is to create such an enterprise asset with a single project. It is extremely difficult to show the business value of an enterprise-wide standardization effort of this kind, and failure rates for these kinds of projects are high. Although an enterprise-wide decision inventory is worth having, it is not a best practice to try and create the whole thing in one project.

The best way to build a decision inventory is to populate it over time. The decisions that matter to the organization can be identified business process-by-business process. The decision discovery necessary is conducted in the context of a specific project, focused on improving the decisions within a single business process or a tightly coupled set of processes. After some experience has been gained in decision discovery, it is worth investing some effort in developing a framework to allow each process' decisions to be integrated coherently and managed over time. By waiting until some initial experience has been gained, it is more likely that a manageable approach and suitable internal processes can be defined. By doing it reasonably early, it should not be difficult to retrofit existing decision definitions into the new decision inventory.

CREATE A HIGH-LEVEL MAP

When first working on decision discovery, it is worth considering the different areas and business processes that will produce decisions to be captured. A wide but shallow view will help put each subsequent project into context and help keep the level of re-work to a minimum. Don't allow this effort to get out of hand, though, as getting into too much detail across the whole enterprise will bog you down badly.

Collaborate

Decision discovery, as already noted, requires collaboration across business, IT, and analytic teams—a Center of Excellence, or CoE. Maintaining the decision inventory should likewise be a shared responsibility. It should primarily be a business responsibility in most organizations, although well-established analytic groups could perhaps take overall ownership. Regardless of who is "on point," all three groups must be active participants. In addition, the various divisions and departments of the organization need to come together around the inventory. Decisions often involve multiple groups, with decision-making approaches defined by one organization, decisions made and delivered by a second, and having impact on many. Keeping all the various groups involved engaged in the decision inventory will improve its quality and make it easier to develop Decision Management Systems over time. Use coordinated review meetings and work with any CoE to make sure everyone stays engaged.

Refactor on Each Project

In an ideal world, each new project would reuse existing decision inventory content and add new content seamlessly. In the real world, the existing material won't always be right for every subsequent project. The assumptions made when the initial decision discovery was done, the level of detail that was needed, or the understanding of the business behind the model could all be wrong. When the time comes to reuse that material in a new project, it will require some work before it can be used. When decision discovery is being planned for areas that overlap with the current decision inventory, build in some time to both reuse and refactor the existing model of decisions. It is important not to write off the existing content and do it over, but it is unrealistic to believe that existing content can simply be picked up and immediately reused 100% of the time. After the decision definitions have been reused a couple of times, however, they are likely to be stable and highly reusable in subsequent projects as the friction of two or more different projects will take all the rough edges off.

Synchronize with Performance Management Changes

One of the most important aspects of a decision inventory is its set of links to the organization's performance management environment. The way in which specific decisions affect specific KPIs (key performance indicators) and metrics is important both for understanding good and bad decisions and for driving prioritization and design decisions in Decision Management System projects.

Because of this tight linkage, any change to objectives and measures should be considered to see what affect it has on the decisions that support them. These performance management changes may be made to drive organizational behavior, to reflect a new acquisition or business strategy, or simply to better motivate employees. Whatever the reason for a change, it may well impact the way decisions are made—at least it should. After you have a model of the decisions that support a particular area of the business, it should be used to ensure that the way people and systems are making decisions is as aligned as much as possible with the way the organization measures performance.

For instance, a company might be focused on growth, so it has been emphasizing customer retention KPIs as critical to its success. Retaining customers, at more or less any cost, has become the norm. A change to focus on profitability means that only those customers making a contribution to the bottom line should be retained. Decisions about customer retention offers, among others, will now have to be changed.

NOT ALL REPEATABLE DECISIONS ARE AUTOMATED

Although decisions in the decision inventory are likely to be overwhelmingly repeatable, they may not be 100% automated. It is not unusual, for instance, for most of the sub-decisions in a top-level decision to be automated, even though the top level is still a manual decision. Assessing the impact of a change in performance management approach should involve both looking at automated decision-making to see whether it should change *and* informing those performing manual decisions.

Link to Implementation

One aspect of a decision inventory is its ability to support impact analysis across projects—traceability. To provide this, the inventory needs to have links not only to the business process and business performance models of the organization but also to decision implementation. If the inventory contains information about what implements each decision in the decision inventory, then it is possible to tell when decision-making approaches change, as any change to one of the implementation components represents such a change. Similarly, the need to change a decision means that the decision inventory can be used to identify all the implementation components that should be considered. Linking decisions to the business rules, predictive analytic models, and optimization models that implement them should be part of the decision inventory.

Adapting the Software Development Lifecycle

Implementing a Decision Service takes decisions and typically deploys them as part of the business service layer in a Service-Oriented Architecture (SOA). When a Decision Service uses a business rule management system (BRMS) to support the implementation, the focus of the Software Development Lifecycle (SDLC) will be on rule harvesting, design, and implementation. As a service, it needs to support standard best practices around service specification, design, implementation, and governance. Therefore the SDLC should include all the tasks, work products, and guidance to support those new activities. But the technology used to support the implementation of the Decision Service provides a set of features to quickly implement decisions and business rules. It therefore makes sense to adapt the SDLC using an agile, incremental, and iterative approach, leveraging those agile products as early as possible in the development cycle.

Some years ago, IBM delivered the first open source methodology around business rules application, called Agile Business Rule Development (ABRD).[1] The ABRD methodology is an incremental and iterative software development process adapted to the software and business challenges of developing Decision Services. In contrast with a traditional SDLC, ABRD focuses on executable software over documentation, and on a strong involvement of business users as the main actors of the development process. The ABRD methodology groups activities into cycles, which build the Decision Service per iteration by growing its

---

[1] See the practices library in www.eclipse.org/epf.

scope over time. It is impossible to define up-front all the business rules supporting a decision; therefore, an agile and iterative approach is the best approach to make the project a success.

WATCH FOR PATTERNS

One possible downside of focusing quickly on executable business rules is that the team may miss patterns—natural variations on a theme. This can result in lots of explicitly coded business rules that obscure the fact that a repeatable pattern exists. For instance, there may be a series of business rules that check what type of customer someone is and then decide on an appropriate action. Teams should aim to identify these kinds of patterns early. They can then build templates or other infrastructure to make it easy to add new instances of the pattern as they are discovered. This will also allow less technical users to be able to add and change business rules within these patterns.

The changes start with requirements elicitation, as decisions and business rules are not pure specifications that must be documented at project inception. The business rules that support decisions are discovered, analyzed, and implemented from the very beginning. The project team enhances the scope over time by writing and testing newly discovered rules. Business users identify new rules and new ideas for existing rules. The SDLC must support this highly iterative approach.

This approach is a significant improvement over following a rigid plan that develops a contract between users and developers. The project team follows a loop of activities, grouping discovery workshops, analysis, prototyping, implementation, and testing tasks. Feedback is consolidated at the end of each loop. A loop may be completed every day at the beginning of the rule harvesting phase, but it should remain shorter than a week, even in later phases. Involving subject matter experts and business users in such a continuous feedback loop makes this SDLC unique.

Figure 9-1 illustrates the ABRD approach using the different phases of a traditional implementation (Discovery, Development, and Acceptance) and the underlying iterations. Each iteration may contain many loops.

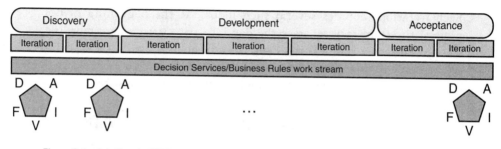

Figure 9-1 Iterations in ABRD

Iterations are time-boxed and usually last between two and four weeks. During the discovery phase the team is focused on working with subject matter experts to identify the logic behind decisions. It is a good practice to plan for short iterations to enforce continuous feedback at this stage—during development phase the iterations can be longer.

The project plan should organize project activities using different work streams or streams of tasks. Figure 9-1 shows only the business rules and Decision Service work streams, whereas in Figure 9-2, the other work streams are also represented. Work streams are helpful to develop a work breakdown structure, assign work to developers, and organize deliverables.

Discovery		Development			Acceptance	
Iteration	Iteration	Iteration	Iteration	Iteration	Iteration	Iteration
Decision Services/Business Rules work stream						
Data work stream						
Business Process work stream						
Integration work stream						
Architecture work stream						

Figure 9-2 Work streams in ABRD

For Decision Service implementations, the project team has to perform many tasks, including some that are recurring over time. The pentagon in Figure 9-1 represents a loop over five of those main tasks: (D)iscovery, (A)nalysis, (I)mplementation, (V)alidation, and (F)eedback.

Each iteration includes several such loops. At the beginning of the project, the team may separate the day into two parts, where morning meetings discover business rules and the afternoon is used for the analysis, implementation, and validation tasks. The next morning can be used to gather feedback on the current implementation using test results.

IMPLEMENT QUICKLY TO FIND AND ADDRESS GAPS

When the decision logic is supported by a BRMS, you can start implementation as soon as week two and leverage executable rules and tests to quickly identify and address the issues and gaps in the decisions. This represents a huge improvement over a traditional waterfall methodology, where there is a clear separation between documentation and implementation.

During the Discovery phase, the business analyst needs to identify the different decision points of the business application. Decision points represent anchor points in the business process or the use case model where decisions are made. Analysis of those decision points leads to the decomposition of those top-level decisions and creates a roadmap for the discovery, analysis, and implementation of the business rules supporting each sub-decision (see Chapter 5, "Discover and Model Decisions" for details). After this roadmap is defined, the team can perform the DAIVF tasks for each decomposed decision.

At the beginning of the project, one of the common challenges the team may face is that of finding the decisions. The team needs to know where they are, how they are enforced, and how to organize the work to discover and implement the supporting business rules. In the case of a business process-based approach (the most common), the search for decision points is done by searching for thinking and action verbs in task descriptions. The process context can be used to determine whether people are ultimately taking the decisions, or whether they can be automated by a Decision Management System. Even if the top-level decisions are not suitable for automation, decomposition may well identify sub-decisions that can be automated. A financial institution may decide that it wants loan decisions to be made by a loan officer, for instance. Within this decision there may be sub-decisions—such as a check for documentation completeness or basic eligibility—that can be automated. When the business rules behind a decision are numerous, change often, require a high degree of business domain knowledge to define, or interact in complex ways, the use of a BRMS to automate this decision is going to be worthwhile.

As noted previously, using a BRMS modifies the SDLC slightly, as it is possible to develop the data model for the rules and the rules themselves earlier than in a traditional implementation. Trying to document all the rules during inception and elaboration and then using the BRMS for implementation only after rule discovery is a bad practice and the SDLC should avoid this. A BRMS is designed to allow rapid definition of rule sets in parallel with discovering the rules.

During the analysis and implementation activities the team focuses on understanding the data model used. They build a glossary of business terms and link them to the conceptual, logical, and physical data models. As illustrated in Figure 9.2, the data work stream has to be considered and added to the SDLC. A Decision Service needs to have a rich data model that often has a different scope than the process variables, database, or user interface that calls it. This model is derived from the decision logic and the business rules description. It evolves over time. It begins as a business entity diagram that illustrates the major business entities and their relationships. Those business entities are mapped to concepts used as part of the rule description, and the model is enriched over time to conform to a conceptual data model. Analysis and design activities transform this model in a logical data model, from which any implementation specific physical data models are generated. As it is possible to use a BRMS early in the development cycle, the data model can be built incrementally. The BRMS has to have good support for refactoring with the vocabulary used for the business rules permanently synchronized with the underlying physical data model. This will ensure that rules are always using the current data model.

The other work streams illustrated in Figure 9.2 are business process, architecture, and integration. A project manager can also include more streams with related activities such as environment, project management, and so on. It is important to note that Decision Service implementation affects the data and integration work stream: For the data model, the architect has to take care of the unique needs of the physical data model. It will likely not be possible to use the same model for the business process, the user interface, the service design, and the database. This is covered in multi-tier application designs, where different models are used for user interface, database, and service tiers. Design patterns have been proposed to support these different views, including Data Transfer Object, Data Value Object, and Data Access Object.

Multiple Data Models and Business Process Management

In the business process approach, some practitioners have not adopted the use of multiple data-model views. They are still using the same model for UI, process variables, service design, and business rules. In reality, the data model used for a Decision Service includes more data elements than a business process should handle. The SDLC has to include activities to work on those different models. A Decision Service is materialized by an operation definition in a bigger service component. For example, a loan underwriting Decision Service is implemented within a loan software component. This component supports the implementation of a service offering a set of operations such as save loan, load loan, and underwrite loan. The operations are defined as part of the business services classification in the SOA. As such, the service design has to follow the standard best practices for service design and implementation. Service design considerations such as being loosely coupled, having coarse-grained operation and more, have to be analyzed by architects. Other metadata has to be gathered around service ownership, lifecycle, administration, deployment strategy, transaction support, failover, fault management, performance, and scalability, and so on. Simply exposing a rule set as a web service is not good SOA, and service design has to enforce reusability, not a peer-to-peer communication between products. Most current BPM integrations are focused only on plumbing and communication using web service for interoperability.

The final issue in the SDLC is that of coordinating a lifecycle that works for business rules development with one that works for other on going IT tasks. Although some projects will require changes entirely within the business rules components, some will require broader changes. When broader changes are required, the different lifecycles need to intersect so that the business rules components being developed can be deployed alongside components being developed that use more traditional tools. The intersection points are usually when new functional requirements are identified and when the various components are ready for deployment. When new functional requirements are identified, it is important to determine what changes are required for both the business rules and more traditional components. Two different approaches may well be taken at this point: one to develop the business rules, and one to develop the remaining components. The development of these different components can be managed separately, but after everything is ready, they will need to come back together for an integrated set of final tests and deployment.

Decision Service Integration Patterns

There are multiple scenarios—Decision Service integration patterns—for integrating Decision Services and business processes. Each pattern reflects specific business constraints and objectives. Each guides an effective business solution by developing a Decision Service and integrating it with either existing business processes, or with a new business process designed specifically to take advantage of the Decision Service.

The key business considerations in selecting a pattern are the urgency with which a need must be addressed, the timeline for implementing the business solution, and the effort needed to develop the solution. The effort involved includes the identification and development of a Decision Service and modifying an existing business process or designing a new process for the overall business solution. Patterns can be broadly classified into three groups: tactical, incremental, and strategic.

- Tactical patterns are used to address an immediate business problem that has little strategic value. These patterns are often one-off solutions that will have to be discarded or significantly modified as new business issues emerge and solution needs change. Tactical patterns involve little or no analysis of reuse or common problems—for example, an existing claims handling process that needs to avoid processing fraud payments by identifying "likely" frauds prior to payment processing. In this case, the existing business process is modified to insert a fraud detection Decision Service task. Based on the outcome of this decision, the process either continues with the existing process for payment or takes an augmented path for adjudicating the claim. Because this is a tactical solution there is no attempt to identify a common and consistent Decision Service for fraud identification across multiple processes.

- Strategic patterns focus on long-term strategic objectives and take a longer view. One such pattern involves evolving a Decision Service so it can be used in multiple processes. This would allow, for instance, a loan qualification Decision Service to be used for both marketing campaigns and actual loan application processing. Another strategic pattern involves refactoring and redesigning existing processes for consistent customer-centric interactions. Using Decision Services to continuously improve processes with root cause analysis and making business processes adaptive by embedding Decision Services are two other strategic patterns.

- Incremental patterns bridge the two ends of the spectrum. Incremental patterns can be applied in a localized way and can be evolved through later analysis. Typical patterns include externalizing and automating decisions embedded in existing processes or legacy applications and automating or assisting human decisions in the workflow to improve straight-through processing.

A Culture of Experimentation

Experimentation is an essential ingredient in Decision Management Systems and has been identified as a top technology-enabled business trend in *The McKinsey Quarterly* (Bughin, Chui, & Manyika, 2010), where the authors say:

> *What if you could analyze every transaction, capture insights from every customer interaction, and didn't have to wait for months to get data from the field?... many companies are taking data use to new levels, using IT to support rigorous, constant business experimentation that guides decisions and to test new products, business models, and innovations in customer experience.*

Experimentation is particularly important when considering operational or micro decisions—the transactional, customer-specific, small-scale decisions at the core of Decision Management Systems. Operational decisions and experimentation are tightly linked because:

- Strategic decisions are often those about picking between alternative approaches. Each approach can be an experiment, but it is the operational decisions that are being made differently in each experiment. For instance, the strategic choice might be to retain and develop customers rather than to acquire new ones. To experiment, you need to be able to vary both the customer retention and customer acquisitions you make every day. You cannot conduct the kind of experimentation being discussed in the article unless you have control of these micro decisions—that is, unless you have implemented a Decision Management System.

- Because operational decisions are repeated over and over, the value of experimentation is higher. If an experiment shows that one of two approaches works better, there will be more operational decisions to be made in the future, and you will be able to apply the approach that worked better to those decisions.

■ Predictive analytic models do not make definitive predictions—they turn uncertainty into a usable probability. Because the predictions are not completely definitive, you will have to make choices about how to use those predictions. Being able to experiment with different approaches will show you how to use the predictions to improve your results.

■ Many organizations don't have the data they need to define an effective decision-making approach or to build a predictive analytic model. Sometimes the only way to capture the data you need is to run experiments to see what happens in different circumstances. In particular, organizations need to run experiments to fill in gaps where certain actions are never taken with certain customers. If customers above a certain risk level are never accepted, there will be no data about the behavior of these kinds of customers unless an experiment is explicitly designed to capture it.

When you implement Decision Management Systems, you need to build in the capability for experimentation; this requires that both IT and business teams become more comfortable with experimentation. It also means that you need to develop a deep-seated awareness of the importance of control groups and a basic understanding of experimental design.

IT Experimentation

IT organizations have never really been able to build experimentation into a system. Legacy development approaches don't lend themselves to supporting experimentation and the rapid evolution that goes with it. In addition, most IT organizations work hard to find the "right" answer for any given problem, and then implement it. They want to work with their business partners and apply their own expertise to find the right answer so they can code it and hand it over to their business users. Yet experimentation is very important to many Decision Management Systems, so this history represents a challenge.

It can be difficult to persuade IT organizations that it is not always possible to know the right answer. Furthermore, the right approach, even if it could be determined now, is likely to cease being the right approach at some (unknown) point in the future. For a Decision Management System, this point may not be very far in the future either, as the pace of change is often very high in decision-making. It is a big change for IT to accept that the system should, therefore, constantly challenge the approach believed to be the best one to see when it begins to fail.

Decision Management Systems that are not 100% based on regulations and fixed policy must allow for multiple approaches to be tried. What's worse is that most of the alternatives tried will, in fact, underperform the default. The IT organization must accept that building this capability into the system anyway has long-term value for a Decision Management System. There is no particular trick to this other than to build on the collaboration that is so important for Decision Management Systems to help them understand how Decision Management Systems are different from their past experience.

Business Experimentation

Many business people also don't like experimentation when it comes to customer treatment decisions. They are unhappy with the idea that some customers will be "tortured" with an experimental approach that is likely to be worse than the default. They want to treat every customer the best they can and often have a hard time letting go of this approach. They too may resist experimentation.

From a business perspective, experimentation is a way to balance the short-term with the long-term. Experimenting with an alternative approach means risking treating some customers sub-optimally in the short-term to build understanding about customer responses for the long-term. Unless an organization experiments with how it treats its customers, it will not learn about their likely responses to alternative approaches, and it will be locked into a short-term, "what works now" mindset.

Experimentation is going to be more and more important. Companies that can use their data to push the envelope, to get better and better, will outperform those that stick to the tried and true. Making test-and-learn part of your normal approach to business will be important, although not easy.

The Importance of Control Groups

A control group is a group of customers (or partners or suppliers) who are put aside when a new approach is attempted. The control group continues to be treated following the old approach, while the remainder of the population is treated according to the new approach. When first implementing a Decision Management Systems, this means using the old approach to decision-making on some customers while treating others using the Decision Management System. For instance, a new customer retention Decision Management System might be used to calculating retention offers for most customers, while a small number are still getting the default offer of the month. Over time, as new approaches are tried using the experimentation capabilities built into a Decision Management System, a control group is formed by ensuring that the old approach continues to be used on some transactions even if most are now processed using one of the new approaches.

Control groups are critical to effective analytic decision-making. Gary Loveman, the current CEO and president of Harrah's Entertainment and an ex-Harvard Business School professor, is famous for his analytic approach to running the company and for the success of this approach. In particular, he has established a culture of experimentation and analytic decision-making. Loveman is often quoted as saying there are three ways to get fired at Harrah's: steal from the company, harass customers or other members of staff, or institute a program without a control group. This is a perhaps extreme point of view, but the importance of control groups should not be underestimated.

Building or buying Decision Management Systems, like any investment an organization makes, must show a return. It must be possible to show the positive results of the system in terms of reduced cost, increased revenue, or improved profit margins. Because Decision Management Systems typically enhance rather than replace existing systems, the focus is generally on how they can improve the effectiveness of the organization, as well as the more common focus on efficiency found when calculating the value of systems. To establish the increased effectiveness of the system, you need a baseline; that's what a control group gives you.

In preceeding the customer retention example, if we identify a control group and use our previous approach for them, we have a basis for comparison. We can route some percentage of customers who are calling to cancel to call center representatives who don't have the new system. This is the control group. After a while, we will have data that shows who was retained in the control group and who was retained in the group processed with the new system. Any improvement from the system will be clear and unambiguous. In contrast, with no control group, we would be comparing results now with results from before the system was implemented. Any difference might be explained by the system but might also be explained by changes in the way competitors price their plans, by new advertising campaigns, or by other factors outside the system. Proving the new system is effective would therefore be much harder.

Experimental Design

Experimentation and control groups are important in Decision Management Systems. It is not enough, however, just to run experiments. You need to design these experiments so that the data you collect will allow you to compare results and learn from the experiments. This requires effective experimental design. The classic work on experimental design is Ronald Fisher's book *The Design of Experiments*, first published in 1935 (Fisher, 1971). In it, he outlines the key elements of experimental design. All of these are worth keeping in mind as you design your experiments:

- **Comparison:** It must be possible to compare the results of your different experiments. You need a control group, so you can compare each experiment to the control group. You also need to make sure that the different experiments are similar enough to be compared. For instance, running two experiments with different customer retention offers will not result in useful data if the average value of offers in one experiment is twice as high as the value in the other. Think about the elements of an experiment that will allow the results to be compared effectively and used to convince someone that the comparison is valid.

- **Randomization:** Which approach gets used should be determined randomly, as noted in the "Build Test and Learn Infrastructure" section in Chapter 6, "Design and Implement Decision Services." Be careful this is not undermined by elements outside the system. For instance, you might experiment with a new approach by having 3 of your 30 call center representatives use the new approach and the others the old one. If the assignment of calls to the representatives is geographic or by product type, you may not get a random assignment.

One of the most powerful features of Decision Management Systems when it comes to experimentation is the sheer number of transactions involved. Because you are handling thousands or tens of thousands of decisions, you have plenty of transactions that can be randomly assigned to experiments to create statistically significant result sets.

Again, be careful with external factors. If you are handling self-selecting customers, such as those who responded to a survey, you may need to consider how this group relates to the whole population when assessing randomness.

■ **Replication:**   Any experiment must be repeatable to be valid. This is not generally an issue with Decision Management Systems, as they are inherently repeatable—the same business rules are being applied to every transaction in an experimental group. The number of transactions involved also helps, as the transactions in an experimental group can be broken up into days, weeks, or months for comparison.

■ **Blocking:**   Some elements of a person or transaction may be significant to an experiment. For instance, we may expect a different response to the same retention offers for customers who have never renewed (this is their first year) and those who have renewed before (second or subsequent year). Blocking is the use of this information to divide possible transactions or customers into blocks before randomizing them into an experiment. Rather than randomizing all customers calling in to cancel their service into our experiments, we might first divide them up into first-year customers and others before randomly assigning some of each category to an experiment.

■ **Orthogonality:**   In any experiment, there are only a certain number of independent, or orthogonal elements that can be considered. If two things are related—such as the length of time someone has been a customer and the total value of their business to date—then these need to be considered together in experiments. Understanding the orthogonality of your experiments will help determine what can and cannot be reasonably compared between them.

■ **Factorial experiments:**   Sometimes there are a number of factors you wish to consider. You could test each one sequentially by designing an experiment to test the various options for the first factor, gathering results, then moving on to the second factor. Factorial experiments take multiple factors and combine them into the minimum number of experiments. For example, if you want to experiment with the value of a retention offer and the length of renewal contract necessary to get the offer, you have two factors to consider. If you decide there are three levels of value (high, medium, and low) and two renewal periods (one year and two year), then a factorial experiment would consider every possible combination plus a control group—seven experiments, as shown in Table 9-1.

Table 9-1 Factorial Experiment

Experiment	Value	Renewal
1 (control group)	-	-
2	Low	1 year
3	Low	2 year
4	Medium	1 year
5	Medium	2 year
6	High	1 year
7	High	2 year

Moving to Fact-Based Decisioning

Creating a culture of fact-based decision making is critical to long-term success with Decision Management Systems. If an organization believes that making decisions "with your gut" is the best way to work, it will tend to resist Decision Management Systems no matter what. Over time you need to create a fact-based culture. To quote Gary Loveman again:

> *"I am purely empirical. I am not attached to any romantic notion of how the business should be run."*

Fact-based decision-making requires a focus on the decision-making approach as well as the results. It requires a broader statistical awareness and a policy of presenting data and decisions as a set. It does not dismiss the value of experts but complements it, and builds on a data strategy foundation.

Decision-Making Approach, Not Just Results

Tom Davenport, author of *Competing on Analytics* and *Analytics at Work*, once asked a rhetorical question: Suppose you had two executives, and each had to make one decision that really mattered to your business results. One had a really thorough and coherent approach to making the decision that involved analyzing data, considering options, and carefully thinking through consequences. The other liked to go with her gut—essentially to guess which option to pick. Which one would you rather promote and employ? It seems pretty obvious. But what if the first executive was unlucky, and his choice did not pan out, while the second one did get lucky and was successful. Which one would your performance assessment and reward process actually promote and reward? The answer for most organizations is that the guesser would do well, and the better decision-maker would do poorly.

To become an organization that values fact-based decisions, you have to value the decision-making approach, not just results. Ideally, this reaches from top to bottom with executives being evaluated this way as well as managers, supervisors, and front-line staff. This kind of culture will make the adoption of Decision Management Systems easier and will be strengthened by those same systems. It also creates the environment necessary for experimentation to flourish, as it establishes the value of improving decision-making approaches—not just making good decisions right now.

Statistical Awareness

Most people don't have a good sense of statistical concepts. They don't understand what "statistically significant" means, and they don't have the skills or experience to look at what's happening to see whether there are material trends that should be considered. They are also poor at differentiating between correlation and causation. Organizations that are attempting to become fact-based need to worry at least as much about this broad problem as they do about recruiting those with deep mathematical and statistical skills. The latter are important for building predictive analytic and optimization models, but the broader base of statistical awareness is critical if those models are to be adopted and effectively used.

One of the biggest issues in this regard is the tendency of people to take personal experience, stories from friends and colleagues, and dramatic examples to heart, even when they are not statistically significant. In law, there is even an expression for this—"hard cases make bad law." In other words, the more dramatic and unpleasant a case is, the less likely it is to be a good basis for making a new law. This problem comes up with designing Decision Management Systems also, when specific remembered examples of unhappy customers are given greater weight that the overall pattern of outcomes.

The inability of many to differentiate between correlation and causation is also problematic. People are good at spotting patterns but can easily mistake a simple correlation (customers who have this product are the most profitable) for causation (customers who buy this product *become* more profitable). The correlation can be useful as a shorthand way to tell, more or less, profitable customers apart. If there is no causation, however, the selling of this product to new customers may not make them more profitable. It might be more true, for instance, that the organization tends to only offer this product to those who are already profitable because it is an expensive product that is good at generating loyalty. Selling this to new customers may make them loyal but unprofitable.

Present Data with Decisions Together

Many systems just present data, expecting the user of the system to make the right decisions using that data. Others might present only the decision, with no supporting or explanatory data. In general, a fact-based decisioning culture is best served when the two are presented together.

This means building decision support systems that are explicit about the decisions they are supporting so that data is presented in that context. It means identifying which actions might be recommended or unavailable, even if the decision cannot be automated completely using a Decision Management System. It means prioritizing predictive analytic models that are explicable, and ensuring that the reasons models make predictions are presented as part of the decision itself. Combining data and decisions will make it clearer why a decision is being recommended and improve the ability of those consuming data to make the right decision.

To support this approach, organizations need to invest some time and energy in managing data lineage and ensuring transparency in data transformations. Presenting summary data without any explanation of where it came from, or using model results that rely on data that is not well understood, can undermine the best intentions. Predictive analytic models can be considered new data elements in this context, and their lineage and explicability can be part of the data presentation.

Role of Experts

In his book *Blink* (Gladwell, 2005), Malcolm Gladwell describes the way in which a group of experts rapidly identified an ancient Greek kouros statue purchased by the Getty Museum as a fake. Their reaction to the statue turned out to be more accurate than the initial set of scientific tests. Essentially, their know-how and years of experience let them perform a kind of complex pattern matching—taking a pattern they had in their head about real kouros statues and matching it to the actual example in front of them. Thousands of hours of experience trying, failing, learning, and trying again had developed their ability to make accurate snap judgments.

At first sight, this would seem to contradict a focus on fact-based decisioning. After all, if these experts can make snap judgments this good, then perhaps "gut" decisions are going to be more effective. But there are several reasons to doubt this. Most obviously, there is a limited supply of experts. Even if your most experienced customer service representative makes great judgments, they are not typical of your call center. Embedding their judgment and experience in a Decision Management System helps everyone else make better decisions. More than that, though, a focus on fact-based decisioning can also help exploit the power of experts.

The judgment of experts is often mysterious—the experts have no idea why they make the decisions they make. This reliance on the unconscious makes it hard to explain decisions; this can be a real problem both in terms of sharing what works and in terms of explaining decisions to regulators, or in legal cases. Decision Management Systems can help by exposing and making transparent decisions so that the knowledge can be taught and shared. Snap judgments are also prone to corruption and bias. An emotional investment in a particular decision can seriously undermine judgment, and bias exists and distorts judgment in many areas. Data-based approaches can show where bias is undermining the quality of decisions. Data-oriented systems can also improve the quality of feedback given to experts and so increase the value of experience in building judgment.

Predictive analytic models are particularly useful also in supporting expert judgment. Human judgment tends to work best where there is just a little bit of data. For instance, insisting on doctors asking just a few pertinent questions (four, in fact) when someone is admitted to an emergency room for a suspected heart attack improves their decision-making dramatically. Many decision-making failures can be traced to too much information. Using predictive analytic models to simplify large volumes of data into a probability clarifies and focuses decision-making on the information that matters. A Decision Management

System can create an environment where the allowed options and most relevant data are presented to focus experience and expertise effectively.

To get the best decisions from your decision-makers, you must build tools to nurture and protect those decision-makers.

Have an Information Strategy

Last but by no means least, you need to build this approach to data-driven decision making on a coherent information strategy. Understanding the information you have, use, and accumulate is critical, as is having a plan to bring that information together so it can be integrated and consumed. A multi-step approach, where an information platform is developed incrementally, and using specific projects to build an increasingly sophisticated environment, is key. Organizations should resist the temptation to build a whole information strategy and platform first and *then* think about analytics and Decision Management Systems. Building specific solutions, expanding the platform, and implementing an information strategy should happen in parallel.

The OODA Loop

The OODA loop (Observe, Orient, Decide, Act) was developed by US Army Colonel John Boyd and originally applied to combat operations. Boyd's insight was that decision-making involves a repeating cycle of observation, orientation, decision, and action. He argued that an individual or organization could gain advantage in combat by processing this sequence faster than their opponent. This would allow you to get "inside" their decision loop.

The OODA loop has subsequently been applied in non-military circumstances, and with its focus on decision-making, it has much to offer an organization that is developing Decision Management Systems. The OODA loop helps organizations manage the ongoing decision analysis process in the context of Decision Management Systems. It also helps clarify the relationship between strategic and (particularly) tactical decisions and the operational decisions at the heart of most Decision Management Systems.

Observe

The need to measure and understand the performance of Decision Management Systems has been noted repeatedly. Unless the decisions made by Decision Management Systems and their outcomes can be observed effectively, it will be impossible to systematically improve results over time. The Observe part of the OODA loop can and should, therefore, be applied to the decisions in Decision Management Systems.

But the OODA loop also links strategic and tactical thinking with operational decision-making. Observing the results of large numbers of operational decisions in the context of strategic and tactical imperatives is more useful than simply observing the results themselves. Operational decision-making approaches are designed to ensure those day-to-day decisions are made in alignment with the strategy and tactics the organization has chosen to adopt. Observing both the detailed results and the overall behavior of the organization is essential.

Orient

Any observations must be interpreted before they can be used. As Boyd himself once said,

"The second O, orientation—as the repository of our genetic heritage, cultural tradition, and previous experiences—is the most important part of the O-O-D-A loop since it shapes the way we observe, the way we decide, the way we act."

As noted previously, the cultural norms and expectations of the individuals and organizations evaluating data observed in the first part of the loop will play a crucial role in the use of that information.

Besides these more unconscious elements, the Orient part of the loop allows the context of the ongoing strategy and tactics of the organization to be applied. In addition, the links between decisions and performance management objectives and key performance indicators also shapes what happens next. Performance is observed not only in terms of measures but also in terms of the decision-making that resulted in the actions that drove those results.

It can be helpful to think of the Observe-Orient part of the loop resulting in new strategic and tactical objectives. They represent the control part of the loop.

Decide

When applying the OODA loop to Decision Management Systems, the Decide part can be mapped to the determination of appropriate decision-making approaches. As a result of the first three parts of a cycle, we may decide to change the way we are making decisions in one or more of our Decision Management Systems.

Act

Actually running the Decision Management System and determining which action to take in each situation is the Act part of the OODA loop. These actions are what will affect customers, partners, and suppliers. The Decision Management System and its users perform this element of the OODA loop. Decision Management Systems are instrumented and produce data about the decisions made, the actions, taken, the results of those actions, and the choices that drove the decision. All this information feeds back into the Observe step, and the loop continues.

10

Technology Enablers

There are a wide range of technologies that enable the development of Decision Management Systems. The core technologies are the business rules management, predictive analytic, and optimization systems that can be used to build Decision Management Systems. Pre-configured Decision Management Systems are also increasingly available, offering pre-packaged systems for particular decision areas such as insurance claims, loan approval, or marketing offers selection. Database and data warehouse technologies, especially those that offer in-database analytics, have a role, as does a service-oriented architecture that supports both a process- and event-centric development approach.

Business Rules Management Systems

A Business Rules Management System (BRMS) is a complete set of software components for the creation, testing, management, deployment, and ongoing maintenance of business rules in a production operational environment. A BRMS contains elements targeted at developers and other IT staff as well as elements intended for less technical users. These BRMS features give business users and business analysts the ability to make routine changes and updates to the business rules that drive Decision Services, while freeing IT resources to concentrate on higher value-added projects and initiatives.

A BRMS provides capabilities that support:

- The development and testing of business rules
- Linking of business rules to data sources
- Identifying business rule conflicts and quality issues
- Measuring and reporting decision and business rule effectiveness
- Deployment of business rules to Decision Services in different computing environments
- Ongoing business user rule maintenance after business rules are deployed
- Integration with other applications and services

The business rules managed by a BRMS are typically represented as near-natural language structured statements or using the visual metaphors described in Chapter 6, "Design and Implement Decision Services." Business rules are based on a vocabulary that uses business terms to represent the underlying objects and attributes that are going to be manipulated by the business rules. Additional management properties and related objects such as patterns, functions, and decision flows are typically also managed by the BRMS.

Business rules can be executed by a BRMS in several different ways:

- **Sequentially,** with each rule being evaluated in turn to see whether its defined action should be taken. Every rule is evaluated, and the business rules execute in the order defined for them.

- **Inferentially,** with a run-time engine using an algorithm such as the Rete algorithm[1] to determine which business rules need to be evaluated and in which order. Such an algorithm also determines whether a business rule needs to be re-evaluated because data has been changed by another business rule.

- **Designed,** with each rule being evaluated in an order determined algorithmically at design time. The BRMS outputs code or execution information after analyzing the business rules to see what the most effective execution order is going to be.

---

[1] Charles Forgy, "On the Efficient Implementation of Production Systems." Ph.D. thesis, Carnegie-Mellon University, 1979.

All three approaches have their pros and cons, and many BRMS support more than one, some allowing individual rule sets to be executed in different ways. Besides an ability to execute the business rules, a BRMS requires the elements shown in Figure 10-1:

- Business Rules Repository

  An enterprise-class repository that stores all the business rules and other artifacts necessary to define a Decision Service. The repository should support version control and maintain audit trails of any change made.

- Design tools

  Design tools aimed at technical users that allow them to integrate business rules with the rest of the environment. This includes setting up data sources for the business rules to access, defining the data passed in and out of a Decision Service, and specifying additional integration parameters.

- Rule Management Interfaces

  Tools aimed at less technical users that allow the creation and management of business rules. The users of these interfaces may be technical users familiar with the underlying technical environment, but they may also be business users and business analysts who are creating and managing business rules only for their own area of the organization.

- Validation and Verification tools

  The completeness and correctness of business rules can and should be verified and validated by a BRMS. These tools should be accessible to both business and IT users.

- Testing tools

  Both business and IT users need to be able to test business rules to confirm the outcomes are as expected. A BRMS should allow a complete set of unit and system tests to be maintained to test both standard cases and boundary conditions.

- Business Simulation tools

  Both business and IT users need to be able to simulate the impact of proposed changes in business terms. A BRMS should allow non-technical users to see what impact a change would have on business metrics before they make it. IT users will make use of this functionality, but it must be focused on *business* impact, not technical execution.

■ Deployment tools

Decision Services may be deployed on a variety of technical platforms and the business rules created must be deployable on the platforms required.

■ A high-performance Business Rules Engine

A Business Rule Engine determines which rules need to be executed in what order. Some BRMS generate code in place of using a business rules engine.

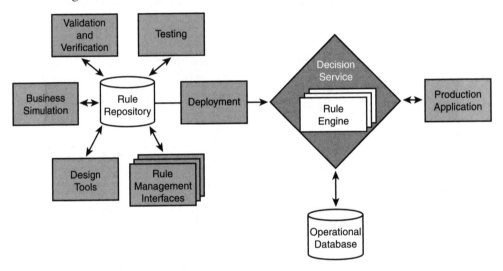

Figure 10-1   Components of a Business Rules Management System

Predictive Analytics Workbenches

A predictive analytics workbench, or data mining workbench, is a set of software components designed to enable the analysis of a set of data sources to determine the mathematical relationships within that data and to produce a predictive analytic model that embodies those relationships.

A predictive analytics workbench is most commonly targeted at an analyst—someone with a working knowledge of predictive analytics, a reasonable understanding of the data that is available within the organization to be analyzed, and a good understanding of the business needs. They are usually found within a centralized analytics team or within a line of business working as a marketing analyst or fraud analyst, for example.

Predictive analytics workbenches provide a set of capabilities that enable the user to perform the following tasks:

- Connect to data
- Prepare the data for modeling
- Visualize the data
- Build predictive and statistical models
- Test predictive analytic models against hold-out data
- Assess business impact of models
- Deploy models into production
- Manage deployed models

THE ITERATIVE PROCESS OF BUILDING AND TESTING A MODEL

The process of building a predictive analytic model is usually iterative. The analyst will hold back a random sample of the data on which to test the performance of the model—and will continue to rebuild models until the model performance is deemed to be acceptable. Performance is typically measured in the context of accuracy of the predictions being made. The speed with which the model will run against large data sets may also be a factor. The iterative process is likely to involve obtaining new sources of data, or a larger sample of data, if the model performance does not meet the business goals.

A predictive analytics workbench supports many different modeling techniques, the most common of which are as follows:

- Rule induction
- Decision trees
- Linear regression
- Logistic regression
- Clustering
- K-means
- Affinity analysis

- Nearest neighbor
- Neural networks
- Genetic algorithms

These techniques can be used to build four main classes of models:

- **Predictive analytic models:**   These look for patterns or trends in the data and provide a predicted outcome. The output could be binary (Will Churn / Won't Churn), numeric (Churn likelihood is 80%), or one of multiple results (of the 20 campaigns we have running today, this customer is likely to respond to the Churn Campaign).

- **Clustering models:**   These group similar sets of data together and provide ways of looking at the profiles of each of the clusters. Cluster models are often used to gain a broad understanding of a customer base; for example, "I have 5 different groups of customer types and the most profitable is made up of women between the age of 18 and 25 who have been customers for more than 6 months." Cluster models can also be used to segment the data prior to building predictive analytic models on each of the individual segments for finer-grained predictions.

- **Association models:**   These look for situations in the data where one or more events have already occurred and there is a strong possibility of another event occurring; for example, "if a customer purchases a razor and after-shave, then that customer will purchase shaving cream with 80% confidence." This is commonly used in analyzing customer basket data and when delivering recommendation engines behind online shopping sites.

- **Statistical models:**   In the context of a workbench, these are often used to validate hypotheses; for example, "I think that young men who have been a customer for more than 24 months are a high churn risk—what is the probability that this is a reliable finding, or just due to random variation?"

CHOOSING WHICH MODELING TECHNIQUE TO USE

For each of the categories of model types within a workbench, there could be more than 20 different algorithms available to the analyst to use. Picking the right algorithm can be tricky—there is no guarantee that any one algorithm will work best in any particular situation. Often an analyst will start with a brute force approach—building a number of different models using different algorithms. As soon as a good candidate is found, the model can be further refined by tweaking the model-building parameters.

Automation can help reduce the difficulty of model building—especially for new analysts; automated modeling often builds a whole range of different models and keeps the top three or five models that performed the best. During scoring, the output is determined by using a combination of the top models or selecting the model result that has the highest accuracy, profit, or ROI.

Another factor that can be important in deciding which types of models are used is understandability of the model output. A number of predictive analytic modeling algorithms generate output that is human-readable in the form of rules or decision trees. For some applications, it is essential that the models being can be understood (such as to maintain compliance in retail banking). Other algorithms produce output that is more mathematical or statistical in nature and less easily understood and explained.

A predictive analytics workbench allows a user to create, validate, manage, and deploy predictive analytic models. A predictive analytics workbench consists of the components shown in Figure 10-2:

- **Model repository:** A place where models and the specification of the tasks required to produce them can be stored, revised, and managed. Not all predictive analytic workbenches have such a repository, and some still store models as script files.

- **Data management tools:** Building predictive analytic models requires access to multiple data sources of various formats; a predictive analytics workbench must be able to connect to and use this data.

DATA CLEAN-UP IS IMPORTANT

A significant part of the time spent on building predictive analytic models is actually spent in data management. Cleaning up data, removing items with irregularities that would skew results, extrapolating values to fill in missing variables, and much more all use up valuable modeling time. Good data capture, effective IT/analytic collaboration, and experimental design can all help reduce these problems.

- **Design tools for a modeler:** Modelers need to be able to define how data will be integrated, cleaned, and enhanced, as well as the way in which it will be fed through modeling algorithms and the results analyzed and used.
- **Modeling algorithms:** Predictive analytic workbenches have a wide array of modeling algorithms that can be applied to data to produce models.

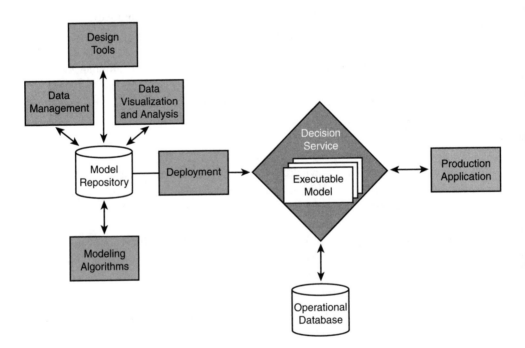

Figure 10-2 Components of a predictive analytics workbench

- **Data visualization and analysis tools:** Modelers must be able to understand the data available, analyzing distribution and other characteristics. They must also be able to analyze the results of a set of models in terms of their predictive power and validity.

- **Deployment tools:** Models are not valuable unless they can be deployed in some way, and predictive analytic workbenches need to be able to deploy models as code, as SQL, as business rules, or to a database using an in-database analytics engine (see the section "In-Database Analytics," later in this chapter).

Optimization Systems

As each operational decision made in a Decision Management System contributes to the performance of your business, each decision should be done in support of and in alignment with your broader business strategy. Each decision can be seen as an instantiation of your strategy, and collectively they determine your operational costs, business risk, customer loyalty, and financial return.

Although the term "optimization" is used generally to describe the notion of improving decisions through analysis and tuning, there is one technology that provides a very rigorous and analytical approach. Also known as "operations research" and "management science," *mathematical optimization* is applied to a specific problem by modeling the business objectives and constraints, instantiating the model with the actual data, and solving for the mathematically (near-) optimal decisions.

Mathematical optimization is a very powerful technique to apply to improve the quality of your operational decisions. It is model- and data-driven, and by managing how you use shared and limited resources across decisions, it allows you to align your operational decisions with the objectives of your overall strategy. In contrast to a predictive analytic model, an optimization model is not something that is generated. It is something that you write to represent the business problem at hand and use to "solve" the model to arrive at a set of actions.

Mathematical optimization can be applied operationally to a single transaction. It can be used to find feasible configurations of complex products or services, for instance, or to maximize the fit of a product or service to customer's requirements. It can also be used tactically to optimize across a set of related micro-decisions that share a limited resource, incur a cost that needs to be used where most beneficial, or impose a risk that needs to be contained globally. Optimization can also be used to tune the thresholds or parameters of business rules in an existing Decision Service.

An optimization system has a number of components:

- **A solver:** A piece of software that uses a variety of mathematical approaches to finalize an optimal or best solution to a defined problem. Such problems generally involve an objective function that defines an outcome to be maximized (revenue, for instance), as well as a series of constraints on the variables used in this function. These constraints can be hard or soft. Hard constraints cannot be broken, while the solver will attempt to minimize the number of soft constraints being broken.

- **Modeling language:** A language designed to allow the effective speci-fication of the problem that is going to be submitted to the solver or optimization engine. Such a language supports the definition of variables and their allowed ranges, the specification of constraints in various ways, and the definition of the objective function.

- **Design tools:** A workbench for an optimization modeller to craft, test, and tune optimization models. Often includes a set of tools to allow the model to be visualized so that relationships between elements can be explored and understood, as well as tools to visualize results and perform-ance, and to compare various approaches to optimization.

- **Interactive user interface:** Supports business analysts in the creation of scenarios and the adjustment of model parameters. Allows the compar-ison of solutions and their business results.

Pre-Configured Decision Management Systems

Organizations that invest in the Decision Management approach usu-ally do so based on the need to solve a specific business problem. This solution focus has a number of benefits. Organizations understand the business problem to be solved and can quantify it. They are also able to put measurements in place to validate that the problem has been addressed. This moves the focus away from the technology and makes it easier for organizations to justify the investment in Decision Management.

Pre-configured Decision Management Systems are targeted at this audience—providing a more "out-of-the-box" implementation of a Decision Management solution. This often includes the ability to deliver the solution through Software as a Service (SaaS), or is delivered as an add-on to existing applications (such as Campaign Management Applications). The solutions are usually made up from a combination of business rules, predictive analytics, and/or optimization that has been wrapped up in a single application, allowing the decision management user to work in a single, simplified, user interface.

Here are some examples of the applications that can be addressed through pre-configured Decision Management Systems:

- Targeted direct marketing
- Next best offer
- Inbound and outbound marketing
- Retail assortment planning/merchandising
- Optimizing customer service
- Credit risk
- Insurance fraud
- Healthcare fraud
- Human capital management
- Debt collection
- Price optimization

There are both pros and cons of using a pre-configured Decision Service versus creating a solution based on the separate pillars of a BRMS, predictive analytics workbench, and optimization system.

Pros of a Pre-Configured Solution

- **Simplicity:** The focus of the application is solving a single business problem. The business rules are usually limited in scope, complexity, and number. The number of predictive analytic models is typically small, and there is very limited ability to control how the predictive analytic models are built. The optimization method is usually fixed and has a user interface (not code). The application provides the user with a simple focused solution.

- **One integrated user interface:** A single interface exists with which the user can interact to create, configure, deploy, and maintain the Decision Service.
- **Lower IT requirements:** If the solution is being deployed in-house, then it is the only application that is being installed and managed.
- **Software as a Service option:** Providing data can be easily transferred to/from the cloud-based application; the management overhead of these solutions is low when purchased as Software as a Service, and these implementations have even less IT overhead.
- **Implementation focus:** The pre-configured solution addresses a single business problem—the organization (business, IT, and analysts) can rally around addressing that problem.
- **Easier to deploy updates:** Reduced complexity of the solution usually makes it easier for the user to update the deployed application with new rules, predictive analytic models, or new constraints for an optimization model.
- **Content:** Solutions can be delivered with pre-build reports, pre-defined rules, and predictive analytic models, reducing the time taken to deploy the solution.

Cons of a Pre-Configured Solution

- **Less flexibility:** As soon as you try applying the pre-configured solution to an application for which it was not intended, problems usually start to occur. These solutions make simplifying assumptions that may not be reasonable in new situations, as they are built to solve one problem and solve it well.
- **Few options outside marketing or fraud:** For marketing and fraud problems, there is a good chance that a pre-configured application exists. For other applications, there is more limited availability.
- **Poor integration with existing predictive analytics/business rules initiatives:** Most pre-configured solutions are closed, and cannot easily be integrated with existing business rules or predictive analytic models. Decisions will now be defined in multiple systems, increasing the complexity of managing your decision inventory.

- **Limited cross-silo learning:**   A pre-configured solution may solve one problem very well, but it is unlikely to give your organization the sense of the potential for Decision Management Systems more generally. Even more than with a custom solution, there is a danger that the approach will be pigeonholed as a marketing or fraud solution with no validity in other areas of the business.

Data Infrastructure

Data is critically important to Decision Management Systems. It is the basis for predictive analytic models that are embedded in Decision Management Systems, as well as for the analysis of decision effectiveness. Decision Management Systems must be integrated with data infrastructure so that the data needed for a decision can be effectively passed to the system and recommended actions and associated information returned. Information about how decisions were made must be stored, so it can be accessed and analyzed later.

Five particular aspects of data infrastructure are important for Decision Management Systems. **Operational databases** must be integrated with Decision Management Systems. **Data warehouses** contain information on performance and often represent the only cross-silo information store available for analysis. **Analytic data marts** are increasingly common for solution-centric analysis. Finally, **in-database analytics** and **big data platforms** are increasingly playing a role in many organizations.

Operational Databases

Operational databases contain both the raw operational data often used for building predictive analytic models and the transactional information for use at decision time. Generally, operational databases will support the transactional element of their role effectively. Decision Management Systems need very similar access to transactional data that other systems need. They need to be able to quickly access live data for the transaction being processed and they need to be able to write data back—both action data and supporting information such as decision execution logs and reason codes. Neither of these is out of the ordinary, and most organizations' operational databases will support them well.

The use of operational databases to support the creation of predictive analytic models is more problematic. Building predictive analytic models requires history and transactional detail over time. For instance, building a model to predict customer retention requires access to information about when customers cancel or renew their subscription, as well as information about their behavior in the period leading up to a cancelation or renewal. The detailed history of this customer behavior is not always available in a data warehouse or analytical data mart, so the models will be built with information extracted directly from operational databases.

Operational databases are often not designed for this kind of analytic work for a number of reasons:

- **Data is overwritten:**   When new data is written back to the database, it simply overwrites existing data. This can create what is known as "a leak from the future," as it will not be possible to recreate the data as it was at a particular point in time. For instance, a field that records total value of orders placed to date by a customer is updated after each order. As a result, it is not possible to use it when building a predictive analytic model, as its value at a point in time cannot be determined.

- **Not all records are available:**   If records are removed from the database under certain circumstances, the data may suffer from what is known as "survivor bias." If all customers who fail to renew within 12 months of canceling are removed from the database, then it may look like everyone who canceled renewed in the subsequent 12 months. Everyone who did not was removed, and the survivors therefore are no longer representative.

- **Outliers are eliminated:**   Many organizations have programs to clean and manage data to prevent bad data from getting into systems. These programs can be very effective, but they can also cause problems if they are too aggressive about removing outliers. Particularly when predicting fraud, it is the outlier values that are often most important, yet these can all too easily look like "bad data."

- **Change logs are not kept:**   Few operational databases keep an easily accessible log of changes made to the database by systems. The number and types of changes made to data can be very important in predictive analytic models. For instance, in warranty claims, one of the best predictors of fraud is the number of attempts it took to get the address right for a service call. Most operational databases will only record the address once it is correct, however, and this means crucial data is lost.

Data Warehouses

Most organizations have either an enterprise data warehouse or a set of more localized data warehouses to complement their operational databases. Data warehouses typically contain data from multiple organizational silos. This data is often more integrated, better understood, and cleansed more thoroughly.

Data warehouses are often not used to develop predictive analytic models, despite the fact that these models often require data from multiple operational databases. Partly this is because data warehouses can suffer from the same problems noted previously—cleansing the data for the data warehouse can eliminate critical outlier data, and the data warehouse may not store enough history to avoid leaks from the future. Despite this, data warehouses can be very useful for the construction of predictive analytic models, if built correctly:

- Data warehouses are often not as space-constrained as operational databases and are more likely to be used for historical analysis. As such, there is less pressure to delete unused records, and less likelihood of survivor bias problems in the data.

- Similarly, the ability to store more data makes it more practical to store a new version of a record every time it is updated in one of the source systems. If this is done, the data warehouse will not suffer from future leaks.

- Many data warehouses are built to produce reports and analysis at a summary level. If only summary data is stored, they will be of little value for building predictive analytic models. The warehouse will be useful if transactional data is stored as well as the roll-up and summary data, and if cleansing and integration of data is handled at a transactional level.

If a data warehouse is built correctly and with sufficient detail, it is a great source for building predictive analytic models, not least because it is the source for the ongoing reporting and analysis that business user see and use every day.

BEST PRACTICES IN DECISION-CENTRIC DATA

One of the best practices for successful Decision Management Systems relates to the management of data across your data infrastructure. Experience suggests that widespread adoption of Decision Management Systems and predictive analytic models requires that the data your business users see in their reporting and analysis tools, the data in your predictive analytic models, and the data in your operational systems need to be kept highly synchronized. This synchronization is required at two levels.

First, the data elements used must be available in all three environments. If a piece of information is being used in a predictive analytic model ("Number of times a customer has been late making a payment in the last 12 months"), this should also be available to business users in their reporting and analysis environment, as well as available in the operational environment so that it can be used in a Decision Service.

Second, the data business users see when they run reports should be the same as the data they see when evaluating models. If a predictive analytic model divides customers into various buckets, the total number of customers should match the reporting environment.

The first form of synchronization is important for deployment and adoption of predictive analytic models. The second is essential for building trust and understanding between analytic and business teams.

Analytic Data Marts

Some organizations have developed analytic data marts. Data is extracted from operational databases or from an enterprise data warehouse and organized to focus on a particular solution area. Owned by a single business unit or business area, analytic data marts allow a particular group of users more control and flexibility when it comes to the data they need.

Reporting, spreadsheet access, and Online Analytical Processing (OLAP) needs often drive the creation of analytic data marts. They can and should also be used to support predictive analytic model creation. Applying the same criteria as noted for operational databases and data warehouses can ensure that the data has the characteristics needed to build a predictive analytic model. Because an analytic data mart is focused on a particular business problem, it is probable that all the data needed to build a predictive analytic model to support decisions in that business domain will be present in the mart. Similarly, all the data needed for performance analysis for a Decision Management System may well be included in an analytic data mart for the business area.

In-Database Analytics

A number of database vendors, including IBM, Netezza (now IBM), Microsoft, Sybase, Teradata, and Oracle provide predictive analytic modeling that is built directly into the database. The benefit of in-database analytics is that models can be built/scored without the need to extract any data from the database. This has a positive impact on performance by limiting the amount of data movement, and allowing the execution to take place on the—often larger—database hardware rather than the analytic server hardware. Analytics within the database can be highly scalable if they can take advantage of the parallelism of the database infrastructure and by analyzing the data in place inside of the database.

Just because a predictive analytic model runs within a database doesn't mean it will perform better than a predictive analytic model running external to database—it depends on the implementation of the algorithm whether it takes advantage of the parallel/distributed infrastructure of the database. In-database analytics can involve in-database creation of predictive analytic models, in-database execution of predictive analytic models, or both.

In a standard analytic environment, an analyst extracts an analytic dataset from the database or data warehouse—integrating multiple sources, flattening the structure, and cleaning things up—before creating potentially large numbers of variables from the data. These variables often collapse behavior over time into a variable—taking payment records and creating a variable "Number of times payment was late in the last 12 months," for instance. This enhanced analytic data set (original data plus calculated variables) is then run through multiple modeling algorithms and either the best algorithm is selected, or an ensemble of the models is built.

In-database predictive analytic model creation involves running some part of this process on the database server—either the data integration and variable creation process alone or the whole process. Not only does this use the server processing capacity, it also eliminates the need to extract and move the data. By accessing the data directly from the same server, performance can be significantly improved, especially in the integration and variable creation pieces (less so in the modeling piece).

Integration, cleansing, and variable creation can also be easily shared across multiple models, reducing the management and calculation overhead for multiple models. Predictive analytic model building is embedded within a relational database, usually as a set of stored procedures. If these routines do not take advantage of the parallel/distributed architecture of the database, they will offer little advantage over running analytics outside of the database environment.

In-database analytics can also take a predictive analytic model (whether or not the model was produced in-database) and execute it in the database. This pushes this execution onto the database server and lets you score the records in the database or warehouse by running them through the algorithm and storing the result. More interestingly, it can also mean being able to treat the model as though it is an attribute and calculate it live when the attribute is requested. So for instance, the segment to which a customer belongs can be treated by calling applications as though it is a stored a data element, even though it is calculated in real time from a model when it is needed. In this approach, the data is not persisted, and the in-database engine acts like a layer on top of the stored data, enhancing it with the model results.

Predictive analytic model scoring is embedded within a relational database, usually as an extension to the SQL language. Because business analysts do not usually want to spend their day writing SQL, some workbenches support the use of the database algorithms. In this case, the workbench becomes the interface for the analyst to generate SQL automatically (without actually having to write SQL).

The other in-database technique that is gaining acceptance is the creation of SQL User Defined Functions—or UDF—that allows vendors to create code that can be executed by the database. Today, this is being used to enable the vendor's predictive analytic models that have been built within the workbench to be scored directly within the database. These functions can be called by an application as part of their transaction as one way to integrate a Decision Service. These scoring functions can also be called during batch decision processes to efficiently process a large number of decisions at once. A well-designed system can process millions to billions of decisions within a small batch window.

When deploying predictive analytic models to a database for in-database scoring, some systems will require the model to be re-coded, or a database administrator to deploy the model. This limits the agility of a Decision Service to pick up new versions of a predictive analytic model to be used in the Decision Service. In some scenarios (such as fraud detection, online product up-sell, and so on), the time between when new patterns are discovered in model building and the time to deploy those models can result in significant revenue or opportunity losses.

If you have in-database analytics, it is worthwhile to rethink the balance of pushing models into the database for execution and exporting them to a BRMS using PMML. The former will work well for something like a regression model or neural network and for models where it is "all or nothing" and the business users are comfortable with the idea of a model as a "black box." When you need to interact with the model (to see which association rules to use, for instance) or when the visibility of the model is critical to the business, a BRMS is proven to be a very effective way to deploy the models. Exposing the models as readable, manageable business rules makes it easier to gain acceptance and to integrate the model results with the rest of the business rules involved in a business decision. Regardless, building the model in-database is still worthwhile.

Big Data Platforms

The topic of big data and big data analytics is hot in the industry because new hardware systems and software are making it affordable to collect and analyze much larger volumes of data than previously possible. *Big data* is defined as many terabytes or petabytes of data.

Often this data is not as highly structured as data that is typically stored in relational databases, and the term *semi-structured* data is often used. Semi-structured data is typical of log data from applications, data from sensors or devices, or data from network traffic or operations. The data has discrete data values, but the format may vary across files, or even within records in the same file, and the format may evolve over time. Big data also includes the ever increasing volumes of unstructured data such as text documents, audio, and video.

Organizations are being driven to retain this type of information for long periods of time, which is driving a need for new storage approaches. They are also finding value in analyzing this wealth of data to make better decisions, and each type of data requires different analysis techniques for deriving value.

A big data solution starts with a system that can efficiently handle the volume and type of data to be stored and analyzed. Apache Hadoop is one of the most prominent platforms for big data; it can affordably scale to many petabytes of storage using Hadoop Distributed File System (HDFS), and it provides an infrastructure for analyzing this efficiently called Hadoop Map/Reduce. There is an ecosystem of projects around Hadoop that add capabilities to query, restructure, and analyze data using the infrastructure of HDFS and Map/Reduce.

To efficiently process such large quantities of data, big data systems combine data storage and processing on the same piece of hardware, which reduces the amount of data that needs to be moved in order to be analyzed. The data in big data systems is divided and distributed to the various machines in the cluster so that analysis can be performed in parallel on the different divisions of the data. To run in this type of distributed system, traditional analytics need to be redesigned to run in parallel and within the big data infrastructure.

Many Decision Management Systems make decisions about customers, and it is often helpful if these decisions are made based on a true 360-degree view of a customer. A big data platform can ensure that website logs, call detail records, social media, call center and customer service emails, and more all feed into these decisions. The non-traditional data managed by the big data platform can be analyzed, perhaps to derive customer sentiment, and this analysis can be fed into the existing data infrastructure for use in a predictive analytic model, for instance. The flexibility of big data platforms also has a role to play here. It is often not clear if a particular data source will add enough value to a decision to justify the cost of integrating or purchasing it. Using a big data platform initially can make it easier to use a new data source to improve a predictive analytic model, for example, and see whether the improvement justifies the cost.

MORE DATA IS USUALLY GOOD BUT NOT ALWAYS

Most data miners and builders of predictive analytic models will say that more data is (almost always) better. Although this is generally true, there are circumstances where more data is not helpful. Too much data can cause analysis paralysis and over-engineered rules that consider too many outliers rather than focusing on the core issues that drive success. It can also cause performance problems if lots of data elements must be made available at decision time. Finally, it can become an end in itself rather than a means for better decisions.

Additionally, given the volumes and velocity of big data, it is unlikely that people will be able to be plugged into the solution after it is up and running. Their role will be to do the analysis, make the judgments, and set up a system to handle the transactions as they flow through. When you are talking about decisions that involve real-time, streaming data in huge volumes, you are talking about building systems to handle these decisions. Not visualizations or dashboards—but systems that handle things like multi-channel customer treatment decisions, detecting life-threatening situations in time to intervene, managing risk in real time, and so on. Decision Management Systems thus represent a powerful tool for making the most of big data platforms.

ANALYTIC CAPABILITIES FOR THESE PLATFORMS ARE NOT MATURE

The analytic capabilities in these new big data systems are evolving quickly, but users will find that tools in the big data space have not yet reached the ease of use and deep capabilities of traditional analytic tools.

A Service-Oriented Platform

Decision Management Systems can be built and deployed in any architectural framework. Many successful Decision Management Systems are used to extend and modernize legacy applications, with the core Decision Service deployed to a mainframe environment. Some Decision Management Systems are deployed to kiosks or are embedded into machinery or control equipment. Most are deployed using a service oriented architecture (SOA) and are integrated with Business Process Management Systems, Event Processing Systems, or both.

SOA

Using a SOA means breaking up systems functionality into a series of coherent services that cooperate to deliver the total functionality required. Each element has a well defined set of interfaces that allow other services to rely on it. These interfaces also hide the details of the implementation, allowing services to be built in different languages or following different design approaches, yet still collaborate. The services are said to be "loosely coupled" because they do not need to know much if anything about the innards of other services—they can rely on the defined interfaces and standard protocols for accessing them.

The core of a Decision Management System is conceptually a Decision Service—a service that answers decision-making questions for other services. Decision Services do not need to be deployed as a formal service. They can also be deployed as a mainframe program module or an embedded software component. The use of a SOA is a perfect fit for Decision Services, as it allows Decision Services to be deployed as loosely coupled, coherent, well-behaved services that mesh easily with other services. They follow all the guiding principles of any service and implement a single decision or a closely related set of decisions.

The use of an SOA platform is no different for a Decision Service than it is for any other service. The definitions of the Decision Service and its interfaces should be kept in a service repository like any other service. SOA platform technologies should be used to keep track of the use of Decision Services by other services, to version the interfaces for the Decision Service and to do impact analysis before making changes.

VERSIONING DECISION SERVICES

From a SOA perspective, it is important to manage versions of a Decision Service appropriately. The business rules within some Decision Services change often. These changes represent tweaks to business policy or to regulatory interpretation rather than a fundamental change to the behavior of the Decision Service. When the *intent* of the new business rules is the same as the intent of the old business rules, then the Decision Service should not be versioned as far as other services are concerned. Essentially, the versioning happens within the Decision Service.

Obviously, if the interfaces to the Decision Service must change or its behavior changes in some material way, it should be versioned like any other service. Differentiating between changes that are internal to the Decision Service but do not change its behavior at a business level and those changes that do is essential. For instance, changing the pricing rules may happen every day. Each new set of rules is a new version of the pricing decision but not a new version of the Service. If the pricing is made customer-specific, however, then the Decision Service has clearly moved to a new version.

BPMS

A Business Process Management System (BPMS) allows the definition and execution of all the necessary tasks to execute a business process and so fulfill a business need. These tasks may involve data entry, integration of multiple systems, human tasks such as inspections or reviews, as well as automated tasks. Many business processes include tasks best implemented using Decision Management Systems—automated decision-making tasks. In addition, Decision Management Systems can be used to determine which transactions need review or need to be routed to which users.

Business Process Management Systems are made up from software components that aid in the following:

- Defining and managing the tasks in a business process
- Integrating multiple systems into a single process flow
- Executing both human and system tasks to achieve a business outcome
- Monitoring and reporting on process execution

Define and Manage Tasks

Business processes are often long running sequences of tasks that cut across organizational boundaries. These sequences of tasks must be defined, managed, and successfully coordinated to ensure a business outcome. The order-to-cash process, for instance, handles all the tasks between receiving an order and getting paid for it. A strong BPMS will support a wide range of tasks and will provide a collaborative environment for business and IT teams to jointly define the tasks, the interconnections of those tasks, and the sequence. Some of these tasks will be decision-making tasks; those that are automated will be represented by Decision Management Systems.

Integrate Multiple Systems

Many business processes cut across organizational silos and require functionality and data embedded in multiple existing systems. A BPMS will allow data to be brought into the process from multiple systems and written back out to them in a well-defined way. It will also allow the invocation of functionality in existing systems, both as services in a SOA and otherwise. This integration must be defined and managed along with the necessary data transformations to move data between them. BPMS are built on a service-oriented foundation, making the integration of services and of service-enabled applications straightforward. This includes the integration of the necessary Decision Services.

Execute Tasks

A process engine handles the execution of automated tasks and the coordination of human tasks. It handles timeouts when systems or people respond too slowly, puts transactions that need review on worklists, parcels out work to available resources, and much more. When these tasks are represented by Decision Management Systems, they are invoked appropriately.

Monitor and Report

Finally, a BPMS provides accurate information on the execution of business processes. Status information is presented to allow supervision of specific running processes, and performance information shows how well or poorly the process behaves overall. This monitoring information is integrated with information about the performance of the Decision Management Systems that support the process.

Event Processing Systems

An Event Processing System allows the correlation of events from any source over any time frame so that an appropriate action can be taken. As shown in Figure 10-3, many different event sources create a "cloud" of events that the Event Processing System evaluates and correlates so that action can be taken in response. Often, Event Processing Systems are used in conjunction with Decision Management Systems, with the Event Processing System determining what question to ask and the Decision Management System providing the appropriate answer.

Event Processing Systems are made up of software components that aid in the following:

- Capturing live data from various sources
- Enriching this live data with information from within the business
- Seeking correlations and evaluations of conditions on enriched live data in real time

■ Triggering action on detected patterns through a variety of external connectors that provide simplified access to execution components

■ Tools to allow business users easily handle constant change to the environment by adding and modifying existing pattern and action logic expediently and reliably.

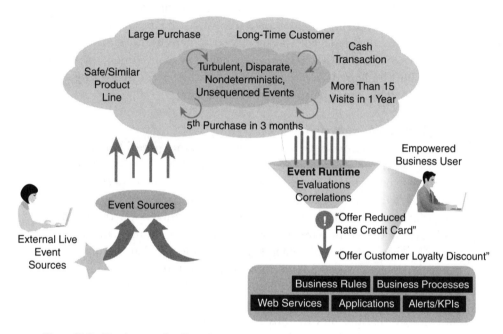

Figure 10-3   The elements of an Event Processing System

Live Data Capture

A distinguishing feature of Event Processing Systems is their ability to work with data in motion, in addition to data that has already come to rest in a database or other secondary storage. Data is acted on directly as it comes through messages, buses, or data streams by keeping it in an in-memory cache. A superior Event Processing System will provide many native connectors to directly access many forms of live data to ease the integration into existing IT infrastructure.

Enrich Live Data

Captured live data forms the basis for understanding the constantly changing environment. However, the components that enable the enrichment of this data provide the value-added discrimination that a business can bring to interpret the changing conditions. Additional information from a user's profile in conjunction with live data can lead to new intelligence that can bring out added opportunities or mitigate risk. This enrichment can include adding existing predictive analytic models to the live data. For instance, a customer churn prediction may be added to live data about customer behavior. Enrichment may also involve building predictive analytic models using the streaming data possibly in conjunction with non-streaming data.

Evaluation and Correlation

Making connections between various data points in real time is a critical feature in an event management system. A variety of engines are possible—from those that specialize in correlating vast data streams but in narrow windows of time, to those that can match a wide variety of data inputs across longer time periods. Depending upon the primary application, the right kind of event correlation engine can be used. Common characteristics of a good engine include one that is scalable and can handle large throughputs of incoming data in real time.

Typically, instantaneous correlations are possible by large in-memory caches that classify and collect various bits of relevant information that come in. Evaluations on this subset of organized data are constantly performed to correlate them to the desired patterns using a variety of algorithms. A similar syntax to that used in business rules is often used to define these evaluations and correlations.

Trigger Action

After a pattern is detected, the Event Processing System acts by triggering a defined output channel. A good Event Processing System will have numerous native connectors to activate common action components. Simple actions can typically be acted on by the Event Processing System itself, but more complex responses are best delegated to the appropriate sub-system within the business infrastructure. For example, after a condition is detected, if there are complex conditions that must be evaluated to decide upon the best course of action, triggering a response in a Decision Management System may be ideal. In other examples where a business process must be activated in response to a condition, a Business Process Management System can be triggered. In some cases, the action may just be to update a dashboard showing a business KPI to keep a human apprised of the occurrence.

Tools

Business user tooling that helps with the authoring and maintenance of the event patterns and action triggers is an essential aspect of an Event Processing System in a business setting. Business user tooling should include pattern development tools, pattern-testing tools with simulated data, and a strong versioning and audit system to control changes made to the system. Ideally, these sets of tools should be provided through visual graphical user interfaces that require no programming knowledge to fit within the profile of an empowered business user.

Epilogue

As I hope this book has shown, Decision Management Systems are an exciting class of information systems. Organizations have been building Decision Management Systems for long enough to prove how well they work. Decision Management Systems have helped many organizations reach new levels of business performance—delivering always-on, customer-centric systems that maximize operational effectiveness. These organizations could not operate at the level they do without these systems.

Yet many organizations have few Decision Management Systems in use today. Their systems remain hard to change and manage, with business people and IT teams on opposite sides of an ongoing argument. Analytics are kept separate from operational systems, limiting the ability of the analytic team to apply their insights in day-to-day activities. And these systems don't learn, so they continue to behave the way they have always behaved even as markets, consumers, and competitors change around them.

The opportunity for these organizations is clear. They can develop agile, analytic, and adaptive Decision Management Systems and change their organizations for the better. Furthermore, they don't need to wait for technology to come out of a research lab somewhere or adopt "bleed-ing edge" systems. The technology they need—business rules manage-ment systems, predictive analytic workbenches, and optimization systems—is proven, mature, and robust.

Decision Management Systems are a powerful tool for enhancing existing business processes and legacy systems. Often requiring only minor changes to existing infrastructure, Decision Management Systems add value to what you already have. Bringing together business, IT, and analytic professionals around a common purpose, Decision Management Systems will change how your organizations see their information sys-tems. Focusing on the four principles of Decision Management Systems—keeping the decision in mind; being transparent and agile, becoming predictive rather than reactive; and committing to test, learn, and continuously improve—is the key.

Building Decision Management Systems is a well understood and defined process that has just three steps:

- First, you must discover and model the decisions that you will embed in new Decision Management Systems. The repeatable operational and tac-tical decisions that drive day-to-day behavior are the decisions that mat-ter here. Understanding, describing, and modeling these decisions is the foundation for Decision Management Systems.

- Next, you can design and implement these decisions, typically as service-oriented components or Decision Services. Easy to integrate, manage, and change, Decision Services are a new class of service. Each Decision Service brings together the right combination of business rules, predictive analytic models, and optimization technology to deliver accurate, repeat-able decisions.

- Finally, you create the processes and infrastructure to continually monitor and improve the way your decisions are made. Responding to changing circumstances, challenging existing approaches to find better ones, and experimenting with new data all help ensure that your decisions are always as effective as possible.

Adopting this approach, making Decision Management Systems part of your organization is an ongoing process. Because there are always more decisions to find and automate, you must keep looking for new opportu-nities. Changing business conditions, new opportunities and evolving attitudes to automation all mean that your decision inventory will grow.

Because decisions keep changing, your existing inventory must be monitored and improved constantly. This is not a one-time effort but a permanent change in how you think about information systems.

One final piece of advice: Don't wait to begin developing Decision Management Systems. Your organization *can* benefit from Decision Management Systems today. Many Decision Management Systems can be developed and integrated quickly into your existing systems and processes. They can make the systems you have, and the people you have, smarter, and they can do so now.

Bibliography

Any bibliography for Decision Management Systems must include the only other book explicitly about Decision Management. In addition, books are listed on each of the core technologies—business rules, predictive analytics, and optimization. A selection of business and IT books relevant to the topic follows. *Smart (Enough) Systems* is the only published book on Decision Management. However in 2012, Wiley is expecting to publish a new book by Alan Fish, tentatively called *Knowledge Automation: How to Implement Decision Management in Business Processes*, that will cover Decision Management and decision dependency modeling particularly.

Books on Decision Management

Taylor, James, and Neil Raden. *Smart (Enough) Systems: How to Deliver Competitive Advantage by Automating Hidden Decisions*. New York, NY: Prentice Hall, 2007.

Books on Business Rules

Business rules have been written about for many years. Some of these books, such as those by Barbara von Halle and Ron Ross, discuss business rules as a general concept. The more recent books are more focused on the specific use of Business Rule Management Systems. The book by Boyer and Mili covers Agile Business Rules Development (ABRD) in more detail.

Bali, Michal. *Drools JBoss Rules 5.0*. Birmingham: Packt Publishing Ltd, 2009.

Boyer, Jerome, and Hafedh Mili. *Agile Business Rule Development: Process, Architecture, and JRules Examples*. Heidelberg: Springer, 2011.

Browne, Paul. *JBoss Drools Business Rules*. Birmingham: Packt Publishing Ltd, 2009.

Ross, Ronald G. *Principles of the Business Rule Approach*. New York, NY: Addison-Wesley, 2003.

Ross, Ronald G. *Business Rule Concepts*. Business Rule Solutions Inc., 3rd Edition, 2009.

von Halle, Barbara. *Business Rules Applied: Building Better Systems Using the Business Rules Approach*. Wiley, 2001.

von Halle, Barbara, and Larry Goldberg. *The Business Rule Revolution: Running Business the Right Way*. Silicon Valley, CA: Happy About, 2006.

von Halle, Barbara, and Larry Goldberg. *The Decision Model: A Business Logic Framework Linking Business and Technology*. Boca Raton, FL: Auerbach Publications, Taylor & Francis Group, 2010.

Zeigler, Carsten, and Thomas Albrecht. *BRFplus: Business Rule Management for ABAP Applications*. Boston, MA: Galileo Press Inc., 2011.

Books on Predictive Analytics

Data mining and predictive analytics are the topic of many very academic and technical books. This list focuses on more accessible books that introduce the topic and discuss it in some detail without requiring a PhD in mathematics.

Berry, Michael, and Gordon Linoff. *Data Mining Techniques: For Marketing Sales, and Customer Relationship Management*, 3rd Edition. Indianapolis, IN: Wiley Publishing, Inc., 2011.

Davenport, Tom, Jeanne Harris, and Robert Morison. *Analytics at Work: Smarter Decisions, Better Results*. Boston MA: Harvard Business Press, 2010.

Fisher, Ronald A. *The Design of Experiments*, 9th Edition. Macmillan, 1971.

Fung, Kaiser. *Numbers Rule Your World: The Hidden Influence of Probability and Statistics on Everything You Do*. New York, NY: McGraw Hill, 2010.

Nisbet, Robert, John Elder, and Gary Miner. *Handbook of Statistical Analysis and Data Mining Applications*. Burlington, MA: Elsevier, 2009.

Tan, Pang-Nin, Michael Steinbach, and Vipin Kumar. *Introduction to Data Mining*. Boston, MA: Pearson Education, Inc., 2006.

Books on Optimization

Optimization is the hardest of the three technologies to find books for. There are some solid references, however, and these are listed, as is one great new book.

Rossi, Francesca, van Beek, Peter, and Walsh, Toby (editors). *Handbook of Constraint Programming (Foundations of Artificial Intelligence)*. Elsevier Science, 2006.

Sashihara, Steve. *The Optimization Edge: Reinventing Decision Making to Maximize All Your Company's Assets*. McGraw-Hill, 2011.

Williams, H.P. *Model Building in Mathematical Programming*, 4th Edition. Wiley, 1999.

Business Books

Many books written for a more general business audience are relevant to those considering using or developing Decision Management Systems. These books focus on the value of data-driven decision-making and on how you can improve day-to-day operations.

Ayres, Ian. *Super Crunchers: Why Thinking-by-Numbers Is the New Way to Be Smart*. New York, NY: Bantam Books, 2007.

Bossidy, Larry, and Ram Charan. *Execution: The Discipline of Getting Things Done.* New York, NY: Crown Business, 2002.

Davenport, Tom, and Jeanne Harris. *Competing on Analytics: The New Science of Winning.* Harvard Business School Press, 2007.

Gladwell, Malcom. *Blink: The Power of Thinking Without Thinking.* New York, NY: Little, Brown and Company, 2005.

Iyengar, Sheena. *The Art of Choosing.* New York, NY: Twelve, Hachette Book Group, 2010.

Kaplan, Robert, and David Norton. *Strategy Maps: Converting Intangible Assets into Tangible Outcomes.* Boston, MA: Harvard Business School Press, 2004.

Osinga, Frans P.B. *Science Strategy and War: The Strategic Theory of John Boyd.* Abingdon: Routledge, 2007.

Pfeffer, Jeffrey, and Robert Sutton. *Hard Facts, Dangerous Half-Truths, and Total Nonsense: Profiting from Evidence-Based Management.* Boston, MA: Harvard Business School Publishing, 2006.

Pfeffer, Jeffrey, and Robert Sutton. *The Knowing-Doing Gap: How Smart Companies Turn Knowledge into Action.* Boston, MA: Harvard Business School Publishing, 2000.

Information Technology Books

A couple of more general purpose IT books may be useful also to put some of the discussions in this book in context.

Bonnet, Pierre and Jean-Michel Detavernier, Dominique Vauquier, Jérôme Boyer, Erik Steinholtz. *Sustainable IT Architecture: The Progressive Way of Overhauling Information Systems with SOA.* Hoboken, NJ: John Wiley & Sons, 2009.

Erl, Thomas. *SOA Design Patterns.* Prentice Hall, 2009.

Larman, Craig. *Agile & Iterative Development: A Manager's Guide.* Boston, MA: Pearson Education, Inc., 2006.

Case Studies

The case studies in the book are reproduced with permission from the following documents:

Aéroports de Paris reduces congestion at airports (WSC14104-USEN-01) © Copyright IBM Corporation 2009.

Benecard builds a smarter claims process with WebSphere ILOG JRules (WSC14242-USEN-01) © Copyright IBM Corporation 2010.

Bharti Airtel grows at a stunning pace by keeping its focus on the customer (ODC03064-USEN-00) © Copyright IBM Corporation 2008.

Carrefour strengthens customer loyalty and its brand with a new promotions strategy (ODC03121-USEN-00) © Copyright IBM Corporation 2009.

Curbing crime with predictive analytics: Richmond Police Department employs IBM® SPSS® modeler software to proactively deploy resources (YTC03038USEN-01) © Copyright IBM Corporation 2010.

Fighting financial money laundering: Bancolombia strengthens anti-money-laundering capabilities with Predictive Analytics (YTC03092USEN-01) © Copyright IBM Corporation 2010.

HealthNow builds a smarter member enrollment process with Websphere® Process Server and ILOG® JRules (WSC14257-USEN-00) © Copyright IBM Corporation 2011.

Smarter insurance: Infinity P&C improves customer service and combats fraud with IBM® SPSS® predictive analytics (YTC03160USEN-00) © Copyright IBM Corporation 2010.

KPN transforms its approach to direct marketing (YTC03174-NLEN-00) © Copyright IBM Corporation 2011.

New York State saves $889 million by optimizing audit case selection (IMC14523-USEN-00) © Copyright IBM Corporation 2010.

Intelligence-based medicine: Sequoia Hospital mines patient data with predictive analytics to improve health outcomes (YTC03204-USEN-00) © Copyright IBM Corporation 2011.

Beauty care retailer achieves four times more business agility and 20% lift (WSC14258-USEN-00) © Copyright IBM Corporation 2011.

Transforming telecom retention with analytics—Bharti Airtel © Copyright Decision Management Solutions 2010.

Index

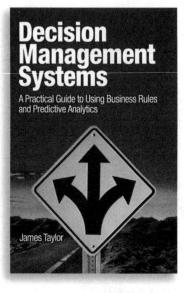

Decision Management Systems

A Practical Guide to Using Business Rules and Predictive Analytics

James Taylor

FREE Online Edition

Your purchase of *Decision Management Systems* includes access to a free online edition for 45 days through the Safari Books Online subscription service. Nearly every IBM Press book is available online through Safari Books Online, along with more than 5,000 other technical books and videos from publishers such as Addison-Wesley Professional, Cisco Press, Exam Cram, O'Reilly, Prentice Hall, Que, and Sams.

SAFARI BOOKS ONLINE allows you to search for a specific answer, cut and paste code, download chapters, and stay current with emerging technologies.

Activate your FREE Online Edition at
www.informit.com/safarifree

> **STEP 1:** Enter the coupon code: UIYAYYG.

> **STEP 2:** New Safari users, complete the brief registration form. Safari subscribers, just log in.

If you have difficulty registering on Safari or accessing the online edition, please e-mail customer-service@safaribooksonline.com

Safari
Books Online